Forgotten

Forgotten

AN ABUSIVE CHILDREN'S HOME
A CHILDHOOD DESTROYED

LES CUMMINGS
With Jeff Hudson

PAN BOOKS

First published 2008 by Pan Books
an imprint of Pan Macmillan Ltd
Pan Macmillan, 20 New Wharf Road, London N1 9RR
Basingstoke and Oxford
Associated companies throughout the world
www.panmacmillan.com

ISBN 978-0-330-46687-5

A CIP catalogue record for this book is available from
the British Library.

Typeset by SetSystems Ltd, Saffron Walden, Essex
Printed and bound in the UK by CPI Mackays, Chatham ME5 8TD

Visit **www.panmacmillan.com** to read more about all our books
and to buy them. You will also find features, author interviews and
news of any author events, and you can sign up for e-newsletters
so that you're always first to hear about our new releases.

'In the little world in which children have their existence, whosoever brings them up, there is nothing so finely perceived and so finely felt, as injustice.'

Charles Dickens

Author's Note

Some of the names used in this book have been changed to protect the privacy of those children who may not want to disclose details of their past. But the stories themselves are, unfortunately, all too true and are accurately and faithfully retold.

To my loving daughter Cilla
and grandchildren Brett, Hallie and Macy

In memory of my dear son Russell (1968–95)

I dedicate this book in honour of all victims who could not tell their stories. Mine is only one voice among many thousands of victims. I say to all victims: you do not stand alone. Hold your head high in the sound knowledge that you are all heroes because you have walked down the long road of abuse as children and have won. Be strong and always fight for what is right – and be assured your day of justice is right.

Acknowledgements

I thank all those who helped me in my quest for justice, especially my daughter, Cilla, whom I love so very dearly, for her never-ending support.

Also Jeff Hudson for his patience and understanding; Will Brown, Senior Researcher, for his tireless efforts and exciting, innovative ideas; and Malcolm Prior of the BBC for putting a massive arrow into my bow in my fight for justice.

Finally to my loyal agent Robert Smith who believed in me and supported the truth.

Contents

PROLOGUE: *One of the Forgotten*

They say an Englishman's home is his castle. You're taught that as kids, whatever problems you have in the world, once you close your front door you're safe. The bad men of your nightmares can't get you once you're inside.

But what if the bad men are inside the house as well? What if you're a child forced to live with them? What if you shout and scream and they don't stop hurting you? What if you tell your teachers and they don't believe you? What if doctors ignore your bruises? What if you run to a policeman for help and he sends you back to the home of your abusers?

What if you feel like you could vanish off the face of the Earth and no one would care?

That was my life until I was eighteen. I was one of the forgotten. Forgotten by my family and forgotten by society. Nearly forty years later, though, I thought I was safe. I had built a new life in San Diego, America, 5,000 miles from the abusers of my past. I had a beautiful wife, a lovely home and a wonderful family back home in Portsmouth. My career was going from strength to strength and I had successfully managed to bury the torments of my past.

And then I saw his face and I knew my life would never be the same again.

Thursday, 1 July 1999. I'll remember that day until I draw my last breath. I was sitting in my home in San Diego, half working, half surfing the Internet for word of the old country. The World Wide Web is a wonderful thing. Even though I lived on another continent, I could still read online the daily news from my local Portsmouth paper. I don't know why I did it. I can't say the place holds good memories for me. But it was just about all I had to cling to from my past.

The newspaper was full of stories about people I didn't know in places I only vaguely remembered but I was addicted to each issue. It was like a soap opera for me. Would the police catch the men who robbed the post office yesterday? Would the football team sign any decent players that summer? Would permission for the new ring road get the green light?

As usual I wasn't giving my full attention as I flicked through various headlines. I think I looked more out of habit than real interest. But something caught my eye that made me stop. In among the stories about 'have a go heroes' and supermarket openings was a name that sent chills down my spine.

But it couldn't be him, could it?

A local man called Peter Baker had built a replica of Disney World in the back garden of his terraced house. It had cost all his savings and taken him years to complete.

There were pictures and more details if I clicked on the link.

I clicked.

And then my world fell apart.

It was the unmistakable face of Peter Baker – *my Peter Baker* – from my childhood. He was one of my tormentors. His mother was worse. His father was the worst of all. But he had played his part in terrorizing my younger years.

I grew up in a children's home run by Portsmouth Council where physical assault was a way of life. I was sent to live with the Bakers when I was seven years old. I couldn't believe my luck. I was going to become part of a family. My life was about to get better at last.

I was wrong.

At the hands of the Bakers I was tortured, starved and sexually abused for two and a half years before being sent back to the children's home. I was fostered again a few years later – by another paedophile. Every time I ran away I was sent back. No one listened to my complaints. Not doctors, not teachers, not policemen.

That was my childhood. But at the age of eighteen, when I became an adult, I walked away from the care of Portsmouth Council and I never looked back. Until then. Until that day when Peter Baker's face appeared on my screen.

A shiver ran through my body. How had this been allowed to happen? How had this man managed to invade my home? I was 5,000 miles away but there was his face – forty years older but unmistakably him. I started to cry. I wasn't even safe in my own home. He and his family had helped ruin my childhood. Now they were going to destroy my new life as well by bringing it all crashing back.

I began to panic. Every second I sat there my heart pounded harder and faster. My clothes suddenly felt too tight and damp as I started to sweat. I was aware of hearing my own breath as I gulped for air. It felt as though the world was closing in on me just like it did when I was seven and I was locked in a cupboard under the stairs for days at a time. I didn't know what to do. I was scared. I was in tears. And there was Peter Baker's stupid, ugly face staring at me still.

I couldn't help it – I lashed out and watched as the computer monitor crashed to the floor. I don't remember hearing it hit the floor or smash into pieces. I was too numb. I stared at the mess of shattered hardware. The face had gone from the screen but it was still in my mind. Four decades of denial and running from my past came flooding out of me and I cried like I had never cried before.

I stayed in that chair for what seemed like hours, sobbing, shouting at the memories the computer had awakened. I wanted to curl into a ball, close my eyes and hide for ever. But eventually something happened to me. I wiped my eyes and thought about the man I had become. I was stronger now than when I first knew the Bakers. They had terrorized me when I was young, when I was small and when I was alone. But that was going to change.

I realized then that I had two choices. I could let the image of Peter Baker's face ruin the life I had created for myself in San Diego. Or I could stand up. On that day in July I made a decision that would change the rest of my life. I decided to stop running.

I had never told anyone my story: that was about to change. I was going to return to England and seek justice from the people who had put me in harm's way. The City of Portsmouth had been entrusted to look after me. They had abused that trust and they needed to pay.

I would not be forgotten any longer.

ONE: *What Will Happen to My Children?*

My biggest fear as a child was being noticed. From the day I arrived at the Children's Cottage Homes in Portsmouth as a two-year-old, I learned that the trick was to not be seen. Blending in with everyone else became a necessary survival tactic. If I looked and acted like the other boys around me, I found it was possible to disappear off the staff's radar. It was almost like being invisible. But one word said too loudly, or if I moved left when everyone else turned right, and all that could change in an instant. The worst crime you could commit was to stand out. If you gave the staff any reason to notice you they probably thought you'd done something wrong.

And there was only one result after that.

There was never a good time to stand out, but the worst was during the inspection which took place every day after breakfast. All of the children from the eight cottages would line up outside the Superintendent's building and he would walk up and down, searching for an untied shoelace, unwashed hands or an inappropriate facial expression. Minor transgressions were dealt with there and then, usually by the back of a hand across the face. More serious crimes were punished by a cane in his office later in the day. It was an intimidating ritual which became more of an ordeal the longer you lived there. I never got used to it in twelve years. Every day, in good weather and bad, 100 boys and girls would line up along the pathway that ran around the building, all thinking the same thing: 'Please don't notice me. Please walk past. Please!'

There was only one day a year when being singled out didn't mean you were in trouble. Anyone with a birthday that day would be asked to step forward and receive a bar of chocolate. It wasn't a bar by today's standards – just about four squares, really – but it was often the only chocolate anyone had from one year to the next.

I remember lining up on my eleventh birthday. The previous couple of years had been wet but 17 March 1955 was a dry day and quite warm. And, of course, it was St Patrick's Day, which was another reason for a lad with Irish roots to be happy.

For the first time that year I wasn't scared as I took my place in the line.

It wasn't long before the Superintendent, Mr Otterbourne, asked if anyone had a birthday.

I raised my hand and said, 'Me, sir. Leslie Cummings.'

He asked me to step forward. As I did so, I saw him check his records.

'You say today is your birthday.'

'Yes, sir,' I said.

'You're a liar. Your birthday was yesterday.'

'But I always—'

I never finished that sentence. Mr Otterbourne swung his open hand into the side of my head and I was knocked clean off my feet. I landed on my back on the grass verge next to the building, on the other side of the path. I knew I had been punched in the head but every bone in my body felt broken. I felt nauseous, I couldn't breathe. Slowly I raised my hands to my head and half expected to find it split in two. But there was no blood. Not this time.

I remember being so confused. 'I can't see.' That was my first thought because the world seemed to be spinning when I opened my eyes. A few seconds later, 'I think I'm deaf.'

But I wasn't deaf. I could hear a thunderous buzzing noise, like a large chainsaw. Then I realized the noise was inside my head. Mr Otterbourne's hand had landed clean on my left ear. For all I knew he'd destroyed my hearing for ever. I began to panic. The more I concentrated on trying to hear, the louder the buzzing got. And that's when I was sick.

Not one person came to help me. No one even dared look. I was a liar and this is what happened to boys who lied. Even though I had received my chocolate on 17 March every year that I could remember. Even though it was the Home that had told me my date of birth in the first place.

I would like to say I had never known pain like it. I wish I could say that. But I had felt pain like it. And worse. And always from the hands of the people I was told were looking after me. As I struggled to get to my feet I remember feeling angry with myself. What had I been thinking? I had let my guard down because I had been looking forward to the chocolate and that was my mistake. 'They always get you when you least expect it,' I thought.

Mr Otterbourne had caught me out this time and I was in shock. But I wasn't surprised at being hit. The vomiting was a physical reaction but I don't think I even cried. When you've been hit as often as I had, you run out of tears. Looking back, I think that was the Home's biggest crime. It trained us to believe that violence like that was 'normal'. We were raised to accept that a casual punch in the stomach was just a natural part of life. Like doing chores, having baths or walking to school in the rain – just one of those things that adults make you do because they 'know best'.

As I returned to my place in the inspection line I realized I was swaying. The buzzing in my ear seemed to be affecting my balance. I knew that if I didn't get a grip on my coordination I could expect another wallop but at least I would be ready this time. With my head still buzzing I made a promise to myself. 'They won't catch me out like that again.'

The irony of that day in 1955 is that Mr Otterbourne was right. I discovered my birth certificate years later and it proved conclusively that I was born on 16 March and not 17 March as I had been told for so many years. The incident was typical of so much of my life. I took all my information from the staff at the Home. If they told me it was time for breakfast, then it was time for breakfast. If they said it was Christmas Day, then as far as I was concerned it was Christmas Day. And the same with my birthday. It didn't matter to me then one way or the other whether it was the 16th or 17th, although I quite liked the Irish connection. Apart from a few squares of chocolate I had never had a single birthday present in my life.

I was the third child, and the third son, of Jean Cummings. She wasn't married and I didn't learn the name of my father until many years later. I didn't even know if it was the same man who had fathered my brothers, Robert and Richard, in 1941 and 1942 respectively. By the time we were old enough to ask, my mother wasn't around to give an answer.

I was born in Ophir Road in the North End district of Portsmouth on 16 March 1944. The city itself is renowned for its historic naval roots and with World War II still raging it would remain a military centre for years to come. Compared to the rest of the country we probably had more men around the area, but not the man who mattered to us. Home was a rented room in a family house. A single woman with three children under four could not have been the easiest lodger, but it got worse for the owner. We were evicted when my mother began stealing money from the landlady.

Rationing was still in force, and would remain for six years after the war's end, and there was very little money around anywhere. Even so, we seemed to have less than most.

My mother's only income was from the 'Naval Allotment' scheme. This was introduced to ensure sailors' families were catered for financially and worked by automatically wiring a percentage of a serviceman's salary to his wife in order to prevent it being spent in a pub the moment the ship pulled into port. She never told us the name of the sailor who was supporting us but every so often he deserted his ship – and then Mum would be asked to return her payments book.

After the lodging house we were given beds in a part of St Mary's Hospital. By the 1940s the 'poorhouses' or 'workhouses' of Charles Dickens's time were supposed to have been closed but – despite Dickens being one of Portsmouth's sons – to all intents and purposes that's where we were. The hospital was set up to give shelter to the homeless. A lot of kids were separated from their parents in there but we lived as a family.

Mum moved a lot. She could never pay the rent wherever she stayed and she stretched each room out for as long as she could. 'Oh, the money'll be in next week,' she'd promise her landlady. Or, 'I'm expecting a payment any day now. I'll sort you out then.' She earned a bit of a reputation eventually and sometimes she called herself 'O'Brien' to new landladies. But it always ended the same way. If she wasn't thrown out we would disappear in the night before the police could be called.

Sometimes she wasn't quick enough, though. My second-eldest brother, Richard, was born in a remand centre in Petersfield so she was obviously arrested for something to have been sent there. One of my later siblings was born in Holloway Prison in north London. Mum went on to have eight children and I don't think it was by choice. It seems she only needed to look at a man to get pregnant.

She came over from Dublin as a teenager, but she had obviously kissed the Blarney Stone before she left. She could charm anyone. Everyone who met her liked her. That's how she got away with so much. She had that way about her that meant men and women liked her. She presented herself well, always fashionably dressed, and slim, about 5 feet 4 inches, with long, mousy-coloured hair, although it was often hidden under a hat. By the time I came along she was still only twenty-five years old. I think she tried to hide the lilt of her accent when she was in England, because it was seen as lower class back then. She was always interested in trying to better herself. She was a very aspirational woman – and that was the problem.

To some extent I think she was a victim of her environment. Her partner was away and although she received a payment while he was in the Navy, she never had a profession. Her only trade was living off her wits – and her quick hands. She was always popping out to go 'shopping'. If she didn't think she'd be long, then Robert, as the eldest, would be instructed to look after my brother and me. Sometimes she managed to persuade the landlady to keep an eye on us or, if she thought she might be longer, a friend might suddenly appear to take charge. When my mother returned she usually had an item or two of clothes in her bag. We were too young to question how she afforded them although she always hid her purchases from our landlady. She needed to avoid the accusation: 'If you can afford new hats and dresses then you can afford to pay my rent.'

The truth was, of course, that she wasn't paying for her shopping. In July 1945, when I was just four months old, she was caught stealing a pair of shoes from Marks and Spencer. I don't know if she intended to keep them for herself or try to sell them. She was fined 40 shillings – the equivalent of about £190 today – and allowed to pay in weekly instalments of 5 shillings. I don't know how she found the money, but at least she was spared any time in prison.

A year later she was caught again. By then my sister Janet had been born, bringing us to a family of five dodging around the boarding houses and tenement buildings of south Hampshire. This time Mum was accused, along with a friend called Anne Colwell, of stealing a camel-hair coat worth £13 10s from the tailors Creed & Lawrence in Kingston Road. They both pleaded 'not guilty' and again escaped punishment.

A few months later, however, her luck – and ours – ran out.

The man who was supporting us through his Navy payments had a track record of jumping ship whenever the opportunity presented itself. Considering my mother had had four children since the start of the war, if he was also the father of any of us, he was obviously taking any chance he could to get back to his lover. By law, since he was no longer actively serving during his abscondments, he was not entitled to a salary. But because she still had the payments book and the Allotments were paid separately, my mother had continued to draw her allowance. What else was she supposed to do?

She never told us anything about this. We were living in a room in Seymour Street, Buckland at the time when my mother suddenly announced that her friend would be coming to look after us for the afternoon. She kissed us all goodbye, then left as though she were nipping out to the shops as usual.

We didn't see her again for six months.

She had been arrested a few months earlier for obtaining money by false pretences and told to appear for trial in November. She was charged with stealing £44 of Navy Allotment to which she was not entitled. She pleaded guilty, saying, 'I did it to keep my kiddies.' Even though she was pregnant with her fifth child, the magistrates had no hesitation in sentencing her to six months' imprisonment.

After her earlier experiences in court, I don't think for one moment that my mother expected this verdict. As the sentence was delivered she broke down and cried out, 'What will happen to my children?'

The magistrate consulted his notes and replied, 'The police will arrange for their care, Mrs Cummings.' Then, nodding towards the court's sergeant-at-arms, he said, 'Take her away.'

I don't know whether my mother would have done

things differently at home if she'd thought she might not be returning that night. Maybe she might have hugged us more warmly or even cried. Or perhaps she would have arranged for someone to look after us on a more long-term basis. As it was, the first thing we knew about it was when the doorbell rang. The landlady called up the stairs. The tone of her voice announced that it wasn't good news. When the two policemen appeared at the door of our room this was confirmed.

And that was that. We were scooped up and taken downstairs where a large police car was parked in the street with the engine running. We were all so scared. We didn't have a clue what was happening to us. I didn't know where we were going and I was too young to ask. Robert, as the eldest, was old enough but he didn't dare say a word. In those days you only spoke to policemen when you were asked to. But what if he had found the courage to speak to the constables? Would they have been honest with him? Would they have told him the truth?

Would they have said, 'You're going to Hell'?

TWO: *I'm Never Going to Leave You Again*

I can't decide who that day was the toughest on. I was not yet one and a half, my sister was a year younger while my brothers were five and three. They had known my mother longest, they were more used to having her around. And because they were older they were more familiar with the pattern of daily life. Robert had even started going to school occasionally. Chaotically as she lived her life, my mother had routines which helped her cope with such a large young family, so my brothers sensed something was wrong. Not just different – but actually wrong.

As a sixteen-month-old toddler I was quite small for my age and, like all my family, I could have done with a few more pounds on me. I had taken my first steps a couple of months earlier and I could say a handful of words. One of those, of course, was 'Mama'. At such a young age my mother was my entire life. I depended on her for everything, just as Janet did. In the police car as we were taken away from Seymour Street, that's the only word I said. 'Mama? Mama? Mama?' Over and over again.

I didn't stop even when we arrived at our destination.

My brothers recall that was the only word I would say for days in between bouts of sustained crying. Whenever someone came into the room I said the same thing.

'Mama?'

If someone looked at me or tried to feed me, it was the same.

'Mama?'

I obviously expected her to appear and pick me up and couldn't understand why she didn't. I didn't recognize the faces of the people around me and I couldn't understand their words. All I knew is I wanted my mummy. Why wouldn't she come and pick me up?

Robert and Richard were not told much more than I was. They understood the words 'Your mother has been bad so you're going to live here for a while' but they didn't appreciate the significance of their meaning. Not for a long time.

We were taken in the police car to a place called Cosham, which is a suburb in the northern part of Portsmouth. Until the 1920s it had been a separate village, even being mentioned in the Domesday Book, but by the end of the war it had become quite a busy area. The journey seemed to take for ever but it cannot have been more than twenty minutes. That's how long it took to reach the Children's Cottage Homes.

This was an institution set up by Portsmouth Council as part of a wider Home Office initiative to take care of the destitute and the disadvantaged. It had mixed responsibilities: part orphanage, part refuge and part borstal. Some of the children were in there because they were said to be too 'unruly' to stay at home. I later learned that this was often a code word used to describe a child who had been a victim of paedophilia or physical assault from one of his family members. In those days it was more acceptable to remove the child from risk than to tackle the problem parent. If a father was abusing his son or daughter but still bringing home a wage for his family, that was taken into account.

Other kids had been in trouble with the police, so they were taken away from their parents as a kind of punishment. One boy I met had been caught stealing cakes from a baker's shop. He was actually sentenced by magistrates to spend time in the Homes. His parents were allowed to visit on a Saturday. During the week he stayed with the rest of us.

And then there were children like us. Our only crime was being homeless. We hadn't been abused by anybody and we weren't there as punishment. But it felt like it. Our mother was in prison, we didn't know who our father was, and as far as we were concerned we didn't have another living relative. We had no one. We were orphans in the eyes of the state and so they stepped in.

Sixty-two years later, I really wish they hadn't. All my problems began the day I first set eyes on the Children's Cottage Homes. I just didn't know it yet.

The Homes were organized like a small prison compound. There were five two-storey, orange-brick buildings, and various outhouses, including a lodge, Scout hut, fire station and fuel sheds. One of the main buildings housed the assembly hall, the clothing store and the seamstress's quarters. The other four were divided into two 'cottages' each, all named either East or West 1–4. In between East 3 and West 3 the Superintendent had his office, and on the floor above that his living area. There was a sick bay, like a small hospital ward, in one of the other cottages but this was usually used as the Deputy Superintendent's living space.

A large driveway swept down to the cottages from the main entrance. On the day we arrived, the police car was stopped at the gate then directed towards a building marked East 3. I don't know whether police cars were the usual method for arriving at the Homes but the dozens of enquiring faces pressed against one of the windows of the building as we were helped out of the car suggested not. Janet and I were passed to two women while our brothers were told to follow them inside the building.

While the Superintendent and his deputy maintained overall control of the Homes, the day-to-day running of each individual cottage was the responsibility of 'house-parents' – usually a housemother and housefather, or a housemother and an assistant called an 'Aunt'. We had all been given over to the custody of an old woman called Mrs Ingram. 'I'm your housemother,' she said. Her voice was firm but kind and her round face, beneath her grey hair tied into a bun, looked friendly. I was fascinated by the dark-rimmed glasses perched on the end of her nose. The other lady was introduced as 'Aunt Ross'. In contrast to Mrs Ingram's open face, this woman had sharp, scrawny features. Her nose was beak-like and there was a permanent scowl on her forehead. She appeared to have a layer of fluffy hair on her cheeks and especially on her top lip.

I have my brothers' memories to thank for all these early events but the recollection of that woman's face is my own.

Once the policemen had left we boys were stripped of our own clothes and given new ones, all roughly the same colour – grey jumper, grey shorts, white shirt – and all very much secondhand. We arrived without any possessions – I don't know what happened to the few toys and books we owned – although I had brought a dirty sheet I liked to sleep with. I don't remember what happened to that sheet. It was in the police car but no one remembers seeing me with it after we arrived.

Boys and girls lived in separate cottages so Janet was quickly taken away. The rest of us were taken upstairs and shown our beds.

The cottage had two dormitories, long, dark rooms with bare, grey walls and each containing eight beds. We were told that, because of the war, the Homes were very overcrowded. 'It will be two boys to every bed,' Mrs Ingram said. Richard was told to share with a smaller lad; Robert and I were put in the same bed. It was his duty to stop me, as a baby, falling out and injuring myself. The dark wooden floorboards that ran the length of the dormitories were cold and hard.

The beds themselves were heavy and made of metal. I

think they were old hospital beds, but lowered for children. Once I saw one of the gardeners, Mr Stanley, come in to fix a problem with one of them. I was fascinated by how the metal tubes fitted together. At the time I had never seen a jigsaw, but it was like that.

There was a chair next to each bed to keep our clothes on but no wardrobes or chests of drawers because none of the boys had anything to put in them. We all had the clothes on our backs and a pair of pyjamas. That was it.

Next, Mrs Ingram took us downstairs to a large room she called the 'playroom'. The first thing my brothers noticed was the absence of toys. At one end was a shelf of books. These had all been donated so they were very tatty. The children fell silent as soon as we entered the room. Richard thought they were intrigued by us. We soon learned that wasn't the reason. Anyone caught talking when Aunt Ross entered the room would have been severely punished.

So much had happened to us in such a short space of time that only now could we finally stop to think. But what about? My brothers had no idea what was happening to us. We weren't used to all these rules. We weren't used to being split up or having so much space – or to how cold everything seemed. When you're used to living in a cramped room and sharing one bed, you get accustomed to the warmth, to the cuddles.

We were so scared. What was happening to us?

By this time it was nearly seven o'clock and time for supper. All the boys filed into a downstairs hall and queued up to be handed a plate from the kitchen. I was put into a high chair and fed by one of the staff. And then it was time for bed.

And that was it. We had started the day as a family of five in a room on Seymour Road. By night-time my sister was in another building and my mother was who knew where. As the lights went out I said the only thing I could think of.

'Mama?'

The next morning my first words were the same. 'Mama? Mama?'

I know I started crying when she didn't come. My brothers did as well. I was too young to appreciate that she wouldn't be there that day or the next or for many more after that. When you're a toddler you have no understanding of time. Even though Robert and Richard were older, they were just as confused as I was. We hadn't been told our mother was being sent away for six months. The police didn't tell us and Mrs Ingram hadn't either. But even if we had known, it would have meant nothing. All we knew was that she wasn't there when we woke up. And that had never happened to us before.

I don't remember much of that time first-hand. My brothers and other friends from that period have filled in a lot of the gaps. But the one thing everyone is agreed on is this: I hated being there. I spent entire days calling for my mother, then sobbing because she hadn't come. I would cry first thing in the morning and again last thing at night. Always the same reason, always the same desperate plea.

I can only imagine how ecstatic I must have felt when Mrs Ingram pulled us aside after breakfast one day. 'You've got a visitor,' she said calmly. We were taken next door to the Superintendent's office. Waiting there was the unmistakable figure of Jean Cummings. Our mother was back.

It didn't take long to get our things together. About an hour later we were all marching up the long drive towards the gate and freedom. I wanted so much to hold my mother's hand but she was busy carrying Janet. I remember tugging on her coat as we walked. I was almost having to run to keep up but it didn't matter. We were all together. And we were going home.

I don't know how she managed it, but Mum had taken another room in a house in Buckland. I also don't know if she'd warned the landlady that her room for one was about to become a room for five. Actually it was a room for six. Mum had been pregnant when we'd last seen her. Waiting for us with a friend at her room was a little baby boy. My brother Philip, born in April 1946. We were an even bigger, happier family than we'd been before.

I think we all did a lot of crying and screaming and hugging that day and for days afterwards. I still kept saying her name over and over again, just like I had done for the last six months, but there was no question in my voice this time. She really was there. I could see her and smell her and kiss her. And the best thing of all was the fact that

Mum was as excited as we all were. As we curled up together in the room's one double bed, she kept squeezing us and saying, 'I'm so sorry for leaving you. I'm never going to leave you again.'

And we all believed her.

Our room was very cramped with all six of us sharing one bed and a small sofa. We all took turns being next to Mum but obviously most of her time was taken up looking after Janet and Philip. For meals we all traipsed or were carried downstairs to the landlady's kitchen where she served up basic food. Sometimes Mum was allowed to cook but I don't think she liked it. If Portsmouth hadn't been so damaged by bombs falling, I wonder now whether the landladies would have been so accommodating. I think they must have felt sorry for her.

We stayed at that same address for several months, which was quite a long time for the Cummings family. Then one day the landlady called up to say we had a visitor.

I don't know who my mother was expecting but it wasn't the person who clambered up the stairs and stood in the doorway of our small, untidy room. He was quite old and tidily dressed.

'How are you, Jean?' the man asked.

'Dad?' she said quietly.

We had never met any of our grandparents before. We didn't even know they existed. But this was our grandad. He was the first relative any of us had ever set eyes upon.

If only he'd been around earlier. We could have stayed with him instead of being sent to the Children's Cottage Homes.

It turned out that that had been his plan as well.

'You're a hard girl to track down,' he said as he sat down to cuddle as many of us as he could. I don't know how long he had been searching for Mum or how he had done it, but he had managed to find us. Somehow, even in Dublin, he had heard of his daughter's brush with the law – and he wanted to help out.

'Come back and live with your mum and me,' he said. 'You know we've got room for you all.'

I think he could see that Mum wasn't at all keen on that idea. He tried again.

'At least let us take care of the children,' he said. 'Look at you, you can barely afford to feed yourself. Let us take these kids off your hands for a while, just till you get yourself on your feet.'

Grandad stayed all afternoon and played with all of us. It was nice having a man around. It also felt good to have someone who was real 'family' after so long spent calling strangers 'Aunt' this or 'Uncle' that.

He kissed us all before he left and hugged Mum at the door. They had obviously come to an agreement.

'You know it makes sense,' he said. 'You can visit them whenever you want. And it'll just be till you sort yourself out.'

Mum nodded. 'See you tomorrow,' she said, and closed the door behind him. That night we moved out of Buckland and we never saw our grandfather again. Mum never mentioned it either. She refused. She just kept saying, 'I'm not leaving you again.'

Despite falling foul of the Navy Allotment before, Mum was allowed to pick up her payments once more, as long as her partner in the Navy remained with his ship. We soon noticed, however, that her 'shopping' trips began again. Sometimes a friend would look after us for an hour or two, sometimes we'd tag along with Mum and sit in a park while she disappeared for a short while. Or sometimes Robert was given responsibility again, just as before. He might have been only six, but there was another small baby to care for. Mum obviously trusted him and Richard a lot.

I remember being happy at this time. I was nearly three years old and I was as happy as I had ever been in my life. The memories I had of our time at the Children's Cottages and that feeling of always being scared seemed like unpleasant nightmares. I spent a lot of time checking with my mother that we wouldn't be going back there.

'Please don't send me to the nasty house,' I remember saying. 'Please don't make me go back.'

And she always said the same thing. 'You're not going back. We're all staying together.'

My recollection of why I dreaded the Cottages so much is vague. The main reason was almost certainly the fact that I was separated from my mother. But I'm sure there was something more to it. Everything about the Homes filled me with fear. Even if Mum had been allowed to come with us, even if we'd been invited to live as one big happy family, the idea of going back would have terrified me. What had happened to me there? To this day I can't quite remember – but the sensation of apprehension whenever I thought of the place as a child has stayed with me. As much as I hated it, the Cottages came into my thoughts a lot – especially at night. I would often wake screaming, out of breath. My mother would comfort me as best she could and ask what was wrong and I could never explain exactly. All I could manage was, 'I don't want to go back.' The nightmares were always the same, always the Homes terrifying me. The tall, grey walls, the constant fear – and the absence of my mother's warm cuddles.

As each day passed, so my memory faded. Whatever it was that had scarred me while I was there would soon be lost to me.

At least, that is what I thought. Before I knew it, I was presented with the opportunity to refresh my memory.

In the past, Mum's special 'shopping' expeditions had been largely successful. The worst she had experienced were a couple of fines and a slap on the wrist. In May 1947, however, her past misdemeanours came back to haunt her. Two months earlier she had been arrested for breaking into Blundell's clothes store. She hadn't managed to actually steal anything, but intent to commit a crime was enough to see her brought before a magistrate on 20 May. A guilty verdict was handed down without hesitation.

Considering she hadn't actually stolen anything, Mum fully expected to be handed a fine and told to go. But the presiding magistrate took a firmer line. He said that with her colourful track record, 'I have no choice but to commit you to a custodial sentence.'

For the second time in as many years, my mother was incarcerated. For the second time we were deserted with neither warning nor contingency plans.

And for the second time the police were despatched to take us to the Children's Cottage Homes.

The happiest days of my life were over.

THREE: *She's Not Coming Back*

I remember it was summer. I remember looking out of the police car window and seeing people enjoying themselves. They all seemed so happy. Adults were smiling, children were laughing. The mood was light. It was such a contrast to the atmosphere inside the cramped car.

Including the two police officers, seven of us were squeezed in, with us Cummings children on the back seat. My brothers held Philip and Janet, who both cried for the entire journey.

I kept my face pressed against the car window and stared out. My stomach was churning, but I knew it wasn't from excitement. Why was everyone out there so happy? Didn't they know what was happening to us? Didn't they care?

Looking back, the weather was probably responsible for a lot of the good mood. But there was another factor. Two years earlier, the war had been in its sixth year and the very real fear of a foreign invasion on British soil had yet to retreat. Now, after so long living in the shadow of air raids and suffering sons and husbands lost on battlefields overseas, the people of Portsmouth were enjoying a taste of freedom. They had no idea that inside the passing police car we were suffering the second enforced incarceration of our short lives.

I know from speaking to survivors of the war that one of the greatest frustrations was the lack of information. Propaganda was at its height and nobody knew what to believe. Media outlets were censored, news that arrived in cinemas was sometimes a fortnight old, radio broadcasts were limited for fear of enemy ears hearing sensitive information. The man in the street relied on scraps of news from friends and whispers from men returning from the front.

That was just how it felt in the police car that day. We weren't told where we were going. We weren't told why we were being sent there. We were just expected to get on with it.

It had started the moment the men had appeared in our doorway. Memories of their last visit flooded my mind. They were the ones who took us to that place, I realized. 'You're not taking us back, are you?' I asked quietly. No one answered. One of the policemen just said, 'Pack your things. You're coming with us.'

I saw them speak to Mum's friend. She looked sad – and angry.

We were all scared now. 'Where's our mummy?' one of my brothers asked.

'I'm sorry, darling, she's not coming home tonight,' the friend said, tears in her eyes. We were already sobbing hard ourselves.

She helped us pack and went downstairs with us. My head began to spin with anxiety. Mummy had said she would be home. Why would she lie? Where was she?

I was inconsolable. So was Janet. So was Richard. So was Robert. Only Philip, less than a year old, was too small to realize what was going on.

Being stripped of our mother again was too much to bear. It had come out of nowhere. The last few months had been wonderful. The best of my life. We had been a normal family. We didn't have much room to play in and our toys were few. But we had one another. That had meant everything to me. I couldn't believe it was all going wrong again. Not after her promises last time.

'Where are we going?' one of my brothers asked.

Again, no reply from the policemen. Mum's friend just shook her head sadly. I prayed it wouldn't be the same destination as before. I couldn't really remember the details – I still can't – but I knew I hadn't been happy there. Every time I had thought about it I cried. All those nights of waking my entire family with my nightmares were caused by that place: the Children's Cottage Homes.

'Please don't take us back there,' I said, but more to myself than anyone else. My head was flooding with half-formed recollections, pictures of places, reminders of emotions.

From the moment we were led downstairs and out to the car my fears grew stronger. Moving house with my mother had always meant catching the bus. Cars fascinated me as a little boy – but I only had bad experiences of travelling in them. The moment I saw the shiny black police car waiting for us I prepared mentally for the worst.

As the journey progressed I felt the butterflies in my stomach grow stronger. Still nobody had said anything about our destination. I decided to try again.

'Are we going back to that place?' I asked the officer who wasn't driving.

'Yes.'

'I don't like it there. I don't want to go back.'

Nothing.

'When can we see our mummy again?'

Again – nothing. Eventually he spoke. 'You'll be told everything you need to know when you get there. Now, enough talking.'

The ride continued in silence, apart from Janet and Philip's crying. At the Cottage Homes we were given the usual cursory introduction and we boys were once again placed in the care of Mrs Ingram in Cottage East 3. She remembered some of us from the previous year and smiled as we all filed past, Philip in Robert's arms. Janet was removed to a girls' dormitory. Bad as it was for everyone to be ripped away from our mother again, at least Robert, Richard, Philip and I had one another. My poor sister was on her own.

At the first chance I got, I asked Mrs Ingram the same question the policeman refused to answer.

'When can we see our mummy again?'

'Don't you be worrying about that now,' she said firmly. 'All in good time.'

I don't know if she knew and wasn't telling or she genuinely had no idea. I decided I would ask again later.

I had so many questions but we were thrown into the routine of the Cottage immediately. We were shown our beds and told to change into our play clothes. Once again everything had seen better days and had obviously been repaired many times. Even though each item was freshly laundered, there was the underlying smell of something unpleasant from my jumper. Whatever had originally caused it had obviously been there a while. As soon as we were changed Mrs Ingram's voice called into the room.

'Come on, you boys. Suppertime.'

A shiver ran through me. I vividly remember the feeling as memories of my first stay at the Cottage came rushing back. I'd hated mealtimes then. In the months since we'd left I'd forgotten this fact but it was suddenly as fresh as ever – and I couldn't remember why.

I was soon reminded.

I was ordered to queue with everyone else at the door to the kitchen. Mrs Ingram stood in the doorway and handed everyone a plate. The dining room had six round tables. I took my meal and struggled silently to a seat next to my brothers. The whole room was silent. Nobody was talking. That was the rule.

The food at the Cottage was not enjoyable. That night we had bread and dripping. For dessert we had baked apple pudding. Mine tasted stale. I was about to comment to Robert. I'm glad I didn't.

There was the crash of metal on stone from behind me.

I span round and saw a boy holding the side of his head. Aunt Ross was looming over him.

I will never forget the look of that woman for as long as I live. Her hair was in a bun, tied up inside a pale-blue hair net, and like all the female staff she wore a light house-coat over her clothes. Her angular, faintly hairy face was as unsmiling as ever. Her eyes were like a vulture's, scour-ing the area for bones to pick.

I knew instantly what had happened. The boy had committed some offence in the eyes of Aunt Ross and she had delivered her brand of punishment.

'Are you expecting me to pick your knife up, boy?' Mrs Ingram's assistant barked.

Cowering and with his eyes red, the boy ducked under the table and retrieved his knife. Without checking to see if it was dirty he quickly began to eat. Aunt Ross glared at him and walked away to hunt for new prey. As soon as she moved, all eyes returned to their own plates. Nobody wanted to catch her attention. They all knew – and I knew – what the consequences would be.

I realized that was the reason I had been intimidated by the idea of mealtimes. I had witnessed that scene so many times before. You could never relax when Aunt Ross was around. You could never just sit and enjoy your food – whether it was cooked well or not – when she was patrol-ling the room. If you said anything at all and Aunt Ross was moving near you, you could expect to feel the full force of her hand against your head.

The scenario was so clear to me from my first stay at

the Cottage. But, I wondered, had I ever been the boy on the receiving end? I was a baby when I'd first been brought there. All I knew is that some memory of mealtimes had made me fear them. And looking at this woman again now, she was almost certainly the reason.

The apprehension I had felt on the way there had grown steadily worse since the moment we'd entered the building. The butterflies in my stomach now felt like a sack of cats fighting inside me. I could barely face each spoonful of my pudding but I knew that I would be hungry in the night if I didn't eat now.

My memories of our first stay in the Children's Cottage Homes are hazy and helped a lot by the recollections of others. I recall much more from our second visit even though I was still so young. Once again, I'm grateful to my brothers and friends for filling in the gaps. Some things, however, are as fresh in my mind today as then.

I remember feeling scared as I tried to sleep that night and it took me ages to get off. Every sniffle from me or my brothers was amplified and seemed to echo round the large room. I desperately tried not to cry because I didn't want to wake the boys who were used to it, the ones who had no trouble sleeping. But it was hard. The longer I lay there, the more eerie the wind rasping through the trees outside sounded. The worst part was the occasional sound of footsteps thundering through the upper floor. It was probably just one of the staff going to bed – but what if it wasn't? My imagination ran riot.

I remember wrapping my sheet tightly over my shoulders for protection. We all had our own beds this time and so I didn't even have company. I only had a vague sense of what was frightening me but it must have been powerful.

All I knew for certain is that when I woke the next morning, I had wet my bed.

Now I really was scared. I could hear Mrs Ingram calling the other boys to get up and get down to the bathroom for a wash before breakfast. She spotted me crying on my bed and came over. I didn't have to explain what had happened.

'You,' she ordered an older boy near me, 'take him to the bathroom and help him wash these things.'

The boy, who was about eight, looked unhappy at the chore but he didn't say a word. He scooped up the sheets from my bed and threw them at me so hard that I fell backwards. The bundle was bigger than I was and of course it was damp, but I managed to get my balance and carry it to the bathroom. 'Do this to me again and you'll know all about it,' the boy muttered under his breath as we walked in. I felt a stab of shame. I'd only been there a day and I'd made an enemy.

It was a large, cold room that had several toilets and four large baths standing on the slippery stone flooring. The whole room smelled of stale urine. I was relieved to see two other boys washing their sheets at one of the baths. At least I wasn't the only one who had wet his bed. And from the odour in the air, many had done it before me. My mood darkened when I noticed that Aunt Ross was the monitoring adult in the room and not Mrs Ingram.

The older boy picked up my sheets and threw them into the bath. Then he told me to take my soiled pyjamas off. These went directly into a laundry bin. Once a week a lorry came to take away the Cottages' laundry and deliver fresh supplies. But sheets were obviously in such short supply that they had to be washed there and then.

Damp as the sheets were, I realized I had been hugging them like a security blanket. Now all my protection was gone. I was handed a block of soap and told to lean over the side of the cold tub in between two others. 'Get scrubbing,' the elder boy said. I had never washed anything before so I watched the others rubbing their hard soap against their sheets. How did they know where the dirty patch was? It all looked the same colour in the water.

And how did they manage to keep hold of the soap? It was so slippery and much bigger than my hand that I struggled to keep a grip on it. If it slid under one of the other kids' sheets I wouldn't be able to reach it and then Aunt Ross would notice. The fear of that made me dig my nails into it for dear life.

Because it was summer I didn't mind standing there naked. The stone floor was still cold on my feet and the rim of the bath bracing on my chest and arms. I hoped that I would never have another accident like this in colder weather. More than anything, I hoped that I would never have to do it in front of Aunt Ross again. I didn't know how long I could escape her punishing hands.

Over the next few days my brothers and I tried to keep as close together as possible. In other circumstances they would have made fun of me for wetting the bed. But no one was smiling now. We weren't allowed to talk at breakfast, and certainly not during the inspection by the Superintendent that took place afterwards, but between dinner – what we would call lunch now – and tea in the afternoon we were allowed to play in the grounds or in the playroom. Even if it was raining a little, we took every opportunity we could to get away from the adults – especially Aunt Ross.

On that first full day we hid by the cricket field just behind our Cottage. I think the others were content just to be in the open air whereas I wanted answers.

'When's Mum coming back?' I asked.

'She's not coming back,' Robert replied.

I couldn't believe what I was hearing. 'Of course she is,' I said angrily. 'She said she'd never leave us again.'

'Well, she has done, hasn't she? She's broken her word already.'

'I wish she'd let us go with Grandad,' Richard added.

'We don't even know him,' Robert pointed out. 'And we'd have to live in Ireland. That's another country.'

'Better than living here,' I insisted.

We all fell silent. It would definitely be better than living here. Anywhere would be better than living here.

Even though they were older than me, I didn't believe what my brothers had said about Mummy. I knew she would come for us. She had before and she would again. I just didn't know when.

Nobody felt in the mood for playing and eventually we trudged back. Whatever our opinions on our mother, at least we had one another.

At least, that's what we thought.

We were woken as usual at seven o'clock the next morning. I'd had another rough night but at least I hadn't wet the bed. The first face I saw that day was that of the older boy who'd helped me. He was desperately trying to see if he'd be needed again. When he saw I was 'dry' he nodded silently and said, 'All right.'

A moment later Aunt Ross burst into the room.

'You, you and you,' she ordered and pointed at three boys. Two of them were Robert and Richard. 'Dressed and in the courtyard – five minutes,' she said. 'Move!'

I watched in confusion as my brothers clambered blearily out of bed and hurriedly dressed. All the while she shouted at them. It was such a rush I thought I'd woken up in the middle of a fire alarm. But it was for just those three. I still wasn't really awake when they left the room and the rest of us prepared for breakfast. By the time I sat down to eat I noticed they hadn't returned. Just as we finished, however, three new faces came in and the empty seats were taken. Whatever had happened to my brothers?

By dinnertime I was worried. Two hours later I was by

the cricket field again when I heard a voice behind me. It was Robert.

'Where have you been?' I asked desperately.

Robert shook his head. 'They moved us.'

'Why?' I asked.

'No idea. I'm in East 1. Richard's in East 2.'

They weren't even together.

'When are you coming back?'

I remember Robert swore as he shrugged his shoulders. His biggest complaint was the fact they had moved him so early. He hadn't even properly woken up, he said. We both decided it was probably done on purpose. We just didn't know why. In the meantime I told him that new boys had already taken his place.

'Don't worry,' he told me. 'I'll make sure we all see one another. We've got to look after one another.'

Over the next few weeks Robert worked hard to keep us close together at any opportunity. I even managed to see Philip and Janet a few times. He was our surrogate parent in many ways although Richard found that harder to accept than the rest of us. Once Robert told him off and Richard immediately turned on him.

'Don't order me around,' he said. 'You're not my father.'

We all went quiet. Richard had broken an unspoken taboo by using that word. It was like hearing other kids swear behind the houseparents' backs. They only did it to shock. Half the time, if not all the time, they didn't even know what the words meant. They just knew they weren't supposed to use them.

It was the same with that word 'father' for us. Mum had always made it clear we didn't need one so we never discussed it.

A short while later the argument was forgotten and Richard was soon being led once again by his older brother. Catching up with one another every day was better than nothing, but the main thing that kept me smiling was one thought: 'My mum will be coming to get me soon.'

I really believed it, even if the others didn't.

There were other changes shortly after we arrived. We were all given chores to do. I helped wash and dry up after breakfast. I was terrified at the thought of dropping a plate even though some of them were as big as my torso. I didn't dare think what would happen if I smashed a single thing.

Being separated from my siblings seemed very cruel. But it was still the loss of my mother that tormented me throughout the days and nights. I lost count of the times I woke calling her name. 'She'll be back,' I kept telling myself. 'She'll be back.' I think the worry of that contributed to my problem with sleeping which grew steadily worse. I also began to wet the bed more regularly.

Queuing to wash my dirty sheets never got any easier. If anything, it got more intimidating. I was such a regular visitor to the bathroom that an older boy didn't always have to accompany me. If others had wet the bed then I had to stand there shivering in my wet pyjamas while I queued.

But if I was on my own then it would just be me and Aunt Ross or one of the other staff and that was worse. I don't know how effective I was at cleaning on those occasions. I was so scared of dropping the soap I don't think it made much contact with the sheets.

The only good news was that Aunt Ross didn't seem to register how often I'd been down there. She was just the same to the boys who had suffered an accident for the first time as those who were daily visitors. I began to wonder if she could tell us apart.

After a few weeks of feeling thoroughly miserable and alone I began to notice that some of the other children had visitors on a Saturday. Saturdays were the one day the older kids didn't have school and there weren't as many chores for the rest of us, so we had more freedom to play in the grounds. As usual, nobody told me about it. I just happened to see strangers walk into the premises, then leave with boys I recognized. I couldn't believe it. Parents or other adults were allowed to come into the grounds and either play with the child nearby or take him out into Cosham for a few hours. Afterwards I'd see boys looking like the cat that got the cream showing off some little present they'd been given, no matter how trivial or cheap – it didn't matter what it was, it was a token of their parents' love. It was my dream to have something like that.

The more I watched the grown-ups coming in, the more I began to realize that it was usually couples. A woman – the mummy – and a man – he must be the daddy. I knew from as young as I could remember that I didn't have a father – at least that's what I was told by my mother and of course I believed her. She said the same thing to my brothers and sister whenever the subject came up – and she was never the one to raise it. What's more, she always made it perfectly clear that we were normal.

But watching these strangers walking in and out made me begin to question that. Every boy and girl seemed to have a female *and* a male visitor. It looked to me as though they all had fathers. I struggled to process the information quickly enough at first.

'All these kids have dads,' I realized slowly. 'And I don't.'

I'd always accepted we were a 'normal' family. Obviously, looking at all these other people, we were not.

At the first chance I brought the subject up with my siblings. The older ones had noticed the same thing. Janet and Philip hadn't thought about it. We'd led such sheltered lives, despite being dragged from pillar to post by our mother, and we had never really been exposed to many other people. But now all our minds were filled with the same thought: why didn't we have a father *like everybody else*?

I remember feeling as low as I'd ever felt that day. No one had hit me and no one had forced me to do anything against my will as punishment, but I felt absolutely dejected. A part of my life had been a lie. It wasn't normal then to only have one parent. Two thoughts shouted out at me. Number one was my mother had lied. Number two: who was my daddy?

I felt awkward discussing it with the others. Richard and Robert were even more uncomfortable. That didn't stop us positing possible father figures. The trouble was, with the war so recent, we didn't know that many types of men.

'I think he might be a general in the army,' I suggested.

'He might be a policeman,' someone else said.

'Or a sailor.'

'Or a spy.'

'What if it's the King of England?'

We laughed at that idea, but not for long. I think the wound was still too raw. Every time I thought about not having a father in my life I felt like I'd had the wind punched out of me. It gave me a sick feeling. I couldn't explain it to my brothers but it didn't feel right. We agreed not to speak about it again. Not for a while, anyway.

Just because we had managed to upset ourselves about our father, that didn't mean I was going to give up on the one parent I knew we definitely had. Thinking about all those other kids' mothers appearing every Saturday made me more determined than ever that I was going to be rescued from the Homes. Something was obviously preventing her from reaching us. But what?

I distinctly remember when the answer dawned on me a few days later. I felt like kicking myself for not spotting earlier how the visitor system worked – and where I had been going wrong all along.

'How can Mummy find us if we're not near the gate?' I thought. 'Nobody told us you had to be over there on a Saturday.' So I decided: I would sit at the foot of the driveway every Saturday and wait for her to arrive. She'd never miss us now.

I told Robert my plan.

'You're wasting your time,' he said. 'She's not coming.'

'You're wrong. She'll be here.'

'She's not coming,' he said again. 'And anyway, they'd tell you if she was.'

'How do you know that?'

'I just do.'

But I knew he didn't. He was making it up. Nobody told us anything.

The next Saturday I went out to the driveway at midday. I counted dozens of visitors but she wasn't among them. I was sad, but not beaten. The next week I returned again. Then again. Then again.

'I'm telling you – she's not coming,' Robert said.

'She's coming. I know she is.'

I was so sure. She'd found us once before and she would do it again.

By the end of the summer Robert and Richard were informed that they would be starting school. It came out of the blue. One day they were doing chores or playing with everyone else, the next they were walking into Cosham with all the other school-goers. After that it became harder for Robert to round us all up. The only time we were all free was on a Saturday – but I couldn't leave my post even if they wanted to play on the other side of the grounds near the orchard. I didn't dare leave my station for a minute. What if she came and I wasn't here? She'd have to go again without saying hello.

Since the day my brothers had been moved out of East 3 we'd had several new faces. Some stayed months, some just a few days. So far I'd been lucky. I was allowed to stay in Mrs Ingram's Cottage. I discovered she had lived in India for several years and occasionally she would regale us all at bedtimes, or in the playroom if she wasn't busy, with tales of tigers and tea. It sounded so exciting. More importantly, for those few minutes she was speaking I was distracted from the reality of where I was.

She was such a contrast to Aunt Ross. I didn't trust that woman one bit. I'd seen so many boys hit for no reason during mealtimes that I couldn't sleep if she was on night patrol. If anyone dared to get up for the toilet while she was on duty she couldn't resist hitting out. I lost count of the number of times I lay in bed, desperate to pee, too afraid to make a dash for the bathroom. I think a lot of those nights ended with me wetting the bed.

The other boys didn't stay around long enough to get close to them. And even if you did, there was hardly any time to talk to them. The upshot was that I was used to spending time on my own. Which meant that kicking stones around the driveway for hours on a weekend was no problem for me. I could do it all week if necessary. I would do it for weeks on end if I thought it would give me a chance to see my mother.

And then, after the tenth week of futile waiting, I saw her.

I will never forget that moment. I was standing by the gate – normally I waited closer to the Cottages. I saw a lady coming down the driveway and I knew it was her. I'd recognize that figure and that walk anywhere.

A huge, daft smile broke over my face. Then I started to run towards her. I've never moved so quickly. And all the while I called out, 'Mum! Mummy! It's me! Mum!'

I pelted along that driveway so quickly that my short little legs almost gave way a couple of times.

Moments later I reached her and, barely stopping in time, I flung my arms around her waist and hugged as hard as I could. I began to cry as I called out, 'Mummy!' and squeezed her even tighter. When she put her hand on the top of my head I thought I would faint. But then she said, 'I'm sorry, love, I'm not your mummy.'

The worst thing was I'd known. Just before I'd thrown myself into her arms I realized my mistake. But it was too late to stop then. I needed to cuddle this woman. I needed to feel the warmth of another human being for just a few seconds. And maybe I could even feel loved for that brief moment as well.

We embraced for a short while longer, which I'll always be grateful to that woman for. She could have pushed me off or called one of the staff to help her. But she didn't. She let me sob into her coat before walking me back towards the Cottages. In her own way she showed me more love than anyone else had done for months. Even if she wasn't my mother.

I spent the rest of the day thinking about that encounter. What if it had been my mother? I think I would have died with pleasure. That would have shown Robert and the others.

When I went to bed that night I had even more trouble sleeping than usual. I couldn't get the nice lady's face out of my mind. Every time I closed my eyes, I saw her – but I wanted to see my mother. The more I tried to picture my mummy, the harder it was and the more distressed I became. In the end I cried myself to sleep.

In the morning I had paid the price for my night-time anguish. My pyjamas were sodden and there was a large pool on my sheet. I had wet the bed again.

By now I knew the drill although I was still physically too small to be entrusted with all of it myself. Mrs Ingram sent a boy over to help me. As soon as her back was turned, he grabbed my arm and twisted it. 'Don't you ever make me do this again, understand?' he said. I was already so upset at being cold and damp that I felt my bottom lip begin to tremble. But I managed to control myself and not cry. I didn't want him to know he'd scared me.

As I walked down to the bathroom I could hear Aunt Ross screaming at another boy. I remember shuddering, sensing that she was on the warpath again. I also knew that I'd probably have to queue if there were too many people down there already.

It was her job to get all the boys washed and teeth cleaned, then have everyone down to breakfast on time.

The more kids who ruined their sheets, the longer the process took and the angrier she got. And when Aunt Ross became angry, everyone suffered.

All the baths were in use when I arrived so I joined a short queue. I was shivering in my wet pyjamas, but not as much as the naked boys pummelling their sheets in the tepid bathwater. I don't think they were moving quickly enough because all I could hear was Aunt Ross screaming, 'Faster, faster! What are you waiting for?'

I couldn't do anything but wait for my turn. I tried to block out the screaming. It wasn't my fault – there was nothing I could do.

But that's not how Aunt Ross saw it. I was suddenly aware that she was standing right next to me as she shouted at the other boys. I tried not to look at her. 'Just try to be invisible,' I thought.

I was so intent on not making eye contact that I didn't see her fist coming straight towards my head.

Her knuckles connected right on the side of my face and I was knocked clean off my feet. My head struck the door frame and then the stone floor. When I staggered to my feet a few seconds later I noticed spots of blood on the floor. My pyjamas also had specks of red. My legs felt like they were made of jelly and could give way at any moment. I had to stop myself from calling 'Mama!' but I wished with all my heart that my mummy was there to hold me steady, stop me falling, and make the pain in my head go away. The level of Aunt Ross's ferocity had caught me out.

I hadn't had time to move or even flinch. I didn't understand why the woman seemed to hate me so much.

I peered down at the mess and tried not to cry. Aunt Ross wouldn't like that.

She continued to look at me with utter contempt on her face and rolled her eyes in exasperation. As far as she was concerned, I was the reason she had so many problems. Not only had I wet the bed but now I'd managed to smear blood all over my clothes – and all over the floor. If she wasn't careful, she was going to get into trouble with the housemother Mrs Ingram for us being late into breakfast.

'Get a mop!' she yelled at the boy who had escorted me down. 'Get that cleared up.' Then she shouted to me, 'You, just get over there, out of the way.'

As I moved, I knew I could expect fallout from the boy made to clean up my mess. Still bleeding from my temple, I stripped off my dirty clothes. I knew the biggest mistake I could make now was to delay things any further. I had to wash my sheets.

'You'll give your clothes a soak as well,' Aunt Ross said, and I nodded. I would have to soak them along with the sheets to get the worst of the blood out.

My head still throbbing, I leaned naked over the bath and scrubbed the cloth. I heard Aunt Ross lecturing another boy elsewhere in the room. She hadn't flinched when I'd gone down. I don't think she'd even registered that I was hurt.

As far as she was concerned, nothing had happened – nothing abnormal, that is. Frustration with her workload had made her lash out and I'd been in the way. I don't think it was personal. She was shouting at everyone and I was the one she hit. I don't think she even wanted to make an example of me – she just needed to let off steam.

I remember putting the soaked bedding into the laundry basket and running off to get dressed. I wished my brothers were in the same Cottage; they would have looked after me. I was upset but I don't remember crying and I don't remember being surprised at what had happened to me. I'd been physically stunned and taken unawares by the explosive violence. But I really hadn't been shocked that she had done it. Which could only mean one thing.

I was used to it. As far as I was concerned, violence like this was normal.

This was the first beating I remember. But I'm sure it wasn't the first one that took place. There were probably others, while I was a toddler. I'd seen Aunt Ross smack teenagers, kids and babies plenty of times – we were all the same to her. No one escaped for long so it stands to reason I must have been punished before then. Almost certainly more than once.

Somehow all the other beatings had been blocked out of my mind, but the overall sense of dread had remained. That was why I recall having such a sense of trepidation when we'd arrived. I'd obviously been thrashed like this before, during our first stay at the Cottage. I'd just somehow forgotten about it. That's why I hadn't cried this time.

That's why I hadn't rushed out and told anyone what had happened.

I realized that day that only one thing could save me from more bloodied heads. More than ever I needed my mother to return. If I had to wait all year in the driveway I would. She was going to save me.

She had to.

FOUR: Who Do You Think You Are?

I found it very hard to tell one day from another at the Children's Cottage Homes. We weren't told it was Monday or Tuesday. We were just given orders about what to do next – and told how long we had to do it. We all knew what would happen if we failed.

The older I got, the more I began to understand weeks and months, but time like that had little meaning for me. We all lived on a day-to-day basis. Anyone who made the mistake of getting comfortable or assuming they knew what was going on quickly proved wrong. In my first six months in the Homes I was moved three times.

I remember the first occasion. It was exactly the same as the time my brothers were taken from me. There was no warning, just the sound of Aunt Ross screeching at seven o'clock in the morning that I needed to be quick getting dressed and outside with two other lads – or else. The rest of the dormitory carried on as normal, trying to avoid drawing attention to themselves. We'd all seen so many boys plucked from their beds and new faces slotted in their place, it wasn't news.

Still half asleep, I ran downstairs and lined up alongside the other selected boys. It was a crisp morning and I remember shivering in my shorts and thin jumper. Mrs Ingram appeared and told me to make my way to another block. On the way I passed another dozen boys marching in the opposite direction. They all looked as cold and as confused as me. I really looked forward to a bowl of hot porridge at the other end to warm me up, but by the time I reached my new Cottage breakfast-time was over.

'That's not fair,' I thought, but I didn't dare say so to anyone. The houseparents must have known the new boys would miss out. The morning moves always happened in exactly the same way.

Over the next few months I realized that I had actually been lucky with the crisp weather that day. It didn't matter if it was the dead of winter and there was snow up to your ankles – you moved when they said.

In East 3 I used to look at the new faces coming in and wonder what their stories were. Now I was one of the new boys, thrown into a different Cottage where I didn't know anyone. I hoped one of my brothers might already be there but I didn't recognize a single face. I didn't think it was possible to feel any lonelier than I had for the last few weeks, but that move achieved it.

'Don't they want us to have friends?' I thought.

I realized that it had been days since I had even seen one of my family. My sightings of Janet especially were few and far between. I couldn't remember the last time we had spoken. We were growing apart and there was nothing we could do to prevent it. I didn't have anything to tell them – there wasn't much to do anyway. But it was always better when my brothers and sister were around than when they weren't.

I began to panic.

'Will they recognize me? They might forget what I look like.' Either that or they would meet new friends. 'They won't want to talk to me any more.'

Sometimes the switch between Cottages seemed to take place in the middle of the night although looking back I suspect there was more to it. Because I had such trouble sleeping, I distinctly remember adults coming into our dormitory. I don't know who they were, and they may not have worked at the home, but they carried boys out while they were still in their pyjamas. The first time I saw it happen I thought I must have been dreaming. Then I realized I was awake and it was all too real and I froze.

The staff on night patrol never usually tried to walk quietly. They didn't seem to care who they woke up.

So why was someone creeping around now?

I didn't dare sit up, but I could definitely make out the figure of a tall adult – it was too dark for me to see if he worked at the home or not – come in and lift a boy called George out of his bed. George didn't wake up and neither did anyone else. I was the only one who saw it. I was terrified and it took me ages to fall back to sleep.

As soon as I woke the next morning I checked George's bed. It was still empty, but then so were a lot of the others because a lot of boys were already up. It was only at breakfast-time that I could see for sure. I looked everywhere round the room. George was nowhere to be seen.

I remember I wasn't in Mrs Ingram's Cottage at the time. I asked the housemother where George had gone.

'He's a bad boy,' she said. 'He's run away. No good will come of him, you can be sure of that.'

From the way she spoke I sensed I would be punished if I asked another question. I knew George hadn't run away but I couldn't think what else could have happened.

I don't know if the housemother knew more than she was saying but I felt that people were hiding things.

I was only ever moved during daylight. Apart from the upheaval I resented being taken away from Mrs Ingram. Of all the houseparents, she was the one who seemed fairest. She was strict and never stood for any nonsense and she would clip you round the head if she thought you deserved it. It never hurt and she always said the same thing when she did it: 'Bed early.' I remember playing with other kids and us all going up to one another and saying, 'Clip – bed early.' Another one of her habits was saying, 'Chop chop' whenever she wanted something done quickly. 'Pick up those plates, chop chop.' Whenever we heard this, a few of us would mime a chopping motion behind her.

Another trait was calling the children 'duckie'. I had never heard it before as a name but I quickly realized it was a term of endearment. I remember her leading us out of the Cottage for some reason, saying, 'Come along, duckies,' and behind her were thirty boys all saying, 'Quack quack.'

You always knew when you were in trouble with Mrs Ingram because she used your full name. I heard my full name a lot in East 3, but I was never scared of her punishments because she didn't seem to hate children like so many of the other staff did. She never lashed out with kicks and punches because she was annoyed.

Aunt Ross, on the other hand, I was happy to be rid of.

She was never nice to be near but mealtimes were the worst. That's when we were all seated and she was standing. Our heads were the perfect height for her hands.

Everything annoyed Aunt Ross. If she heard you whisper at the table, she struck. If she thought you were eating too slowly, she struck. I remember once not enjoying a piece of tinned beef but I was eating it because I was hungry. I was always hungry. But I wasn't quick enough for her.

I heard her first. 'Stop playing with your food!' she screamed.

I didn't realize she was talking to me but I still froze. Then I felt the palm of her hand square on the back of my head. My face shot forward and only just missed landing in my plate. My eyes stung with tears of humiliation.

I didn't say anything. I just stretched my sore neck and continued to eat. But Aunt Ross didn't care. She was already looming over the next table. She never looked back. She was always hunting for her next target, creeping up and hitting before you even knew she was there.

It was so regular, yet so unpredictable and so painful. But I always took it without complaint. We all did – because the alternative was even worse.

I once saw Aunt Ross so angry at breakfast that she dragged a boy from the table by his hair and pulled him into the hall. We all craned our heads to see what was going to happen and I heard him yelling, 'Not there! Don't put me in there! I didn't do it!'

I wondered what he meant. Where was he being put? The only door near him led down to the cellar. Aunt Ross couldn't have taken him there, could she?

She could.

I shuddered at the thought of being locked in that underground room. I had been down there twice to fetch provisions for the kitchen. Each time I was terrified that the door would slam shut and leave me stranded in the pitch darkness. It wasn't my imagination – there were definitely rats down there. Their teeth marks were all over the food crates.

Thinking about it now, being kept on our toes at mealtimes seemed to be part of a larger strategy. There was never any long-term planning. If there was, nobody informed us. We were like boats on the rough sea, thrown here and there without control. I had been at the Cottages for more weeks than I could remember but still no one had answered my questions about my mother. It was always the same response: 'Don't you worry about things like that' or 'All in good time.'

One of the ways they kept us in order was by emphasizing 'now'. Go there now. Eat this now. Put that on now. Whether it was a rare treat or a punishment, none of the staff was interested in tomorrow or the next day or the following week. Not where we were concerned. What was the point? Any of their kids could disappear without notice at any time.

I can only remember leaving the compound for one reason during those early months. Sunday was church day. We were never warned it was coming – no one ever said, 'Tomorrow we're off to church.' We just woke up and were told to get ourselves smart. After a while I worked out when it was and came to expect it. Church came the day after I looked for my mother.

I didn't have any opinions on religion at that age. Like everything else, I went because I was told to go. I wasn't encouraged to have a view on anything.

When you only have one outfit of hand-me-down garments it's hard to look smart. The older boys had blazers but the rest of us just had jumpers. I learned to be seen to make an effort, though. The daily morning inspection was always more thorough before church but if your hands were clean and your hair looked like it had been brushed, the Superintendent normally passed you by.

The first man in charge of the Homes that I remember was called Mr Marshall. His wife was the Matron. When I was four, this pair was replaced by Mr and Mrs Otterbourne. I remember being scared of Mr Marshall because he was strict and he looked so tall to me. But Mr Otterbourne was worse. He was even taller, and thin, and always dressed very smartly in a black and grey suit, whatever the weather. He was very well spoken, and with his glasses he looked and sounded like a gentleman, but when he grabbed my hands to inspect my nails I thought he would take the skin off. Everything he did was thorough and very painful. Sometimes he would check my ears for 'potatoes' and it felt like they were in danger of being ripped from my head. He always looked happier when he found a boy who wasn't up to scratch.

'This won't do,' he would roar. 'My office after dinner – we'll see if we can teach you some manners!'

Occasionally he would mete out his punishments on the spot – as I would find to my cost when I turned eleven – but generally he preferred to minister his most painful lessons in private.

Behind his back we used to call him 'Fishface' because he was such a cold person or 'Beanpole' because of his physique. We only dared say it when we could guarantee he was nowhere near.

Our local church was St Coleman's. It was a Catholic church but everyone had to go there. The best thing about attending was the fact we had to walk outside the Cottage Homes' grounds. I remember my first time. We all lined up in twos and marched hand-in-hand past the gate. It felt like I was escaping into the real world. I thought about running away but I didn't know anywhere else to go. The only other time I had ever been on the outside of these walls was when my mother had collected us that time.

When we arrived at St Coleman's I noticed there weren't any other people around. One of the houseparents entered first, then beckoned us to follow. Even though the church was completely empty, we were all directed to the very back pews. Only once we were settled did other people start to filter through. As the weeks went by I identified the same pattern and the reason behind it. We were actually delivered earlier so we could be seated and out of the way before the rest of the village congregation arrived.

It was as if the rest of Cosham was ashamed of us. They were embarrassed to share their religion with us. I didn't care.

'I don't want your stupid God,' I thought. 'Not if He's the one who lets me get hit every dinnertime and keeps my family all split up.'

Watching them all walk in in their 'Sunday best' was a painful experience for me. Some of the women were dressed so colourfully that they reminded me of my mother. I'd see a hat or a coat or a dress or a pair of gloves and think, 'Mummy has that.' I knew she would fit in perfectly in that congregation. She'd look better than all of them. But then I worried: 'Would she be ashamed of me dressed like this as well?'

Church wasn't the only place where we were publicly going on a bus with a group from the Cottages. We all made to feel inferior. I remember being excited about lined up neatly and quietly, waiting for this giant vehicle to arrive at its stop. I was actually excited. I couldn't recall the last time I felt like that. I'd been on a bus plenty of times with my mother. But not recently. Riding on public transport was something 'real' people did.

'I can't wait to get on,' I thought.

The doors opened and because I was at the front of the queue I stepped on. I found a seat near the driver and went to sit down when I felt someone's tough fingers and thumb clamp on to my ear.

'Up the back, Cummings. Who do you think you are – His Majesty the King?'

I was wrenched out of the seat and dragged squealing to the back of the bus.

'Now, sit down and behave.'

I never made that mistake again. All kids from the Children's Cottage Homes were expected to sit at the back of the bus. If someone from the village required a seat, we were told to stand.

'Let the lady sit down, Cummings!' Then *whack*.

It became clear on that first journey that we were second-class passengers. I thought of asking a smartly dressed man if he could help me find my mummy. But as hard as I tried, I couldn't catch his eye. In fact all the other passengers looked away when I tried to smile at them. I'd spent so long trying to blend into the background at the Cottages that I wondered, 'Am I really invisible?'

I knew I was being silly but there was a problem somewhere. They didn't want to look at us. We made them feel unhappy but I didn't understand how.

Sometimes when we walked to church families would cross over the road when we got near them. I wondered if they thought we were dirty. 'They think they'll catch something off our clothes,' I guessed. That made me sad. Again I thought of my mother. Would she have switched pavements as well?

If going to church was meant to be a treat for us, it never felt like it. Apart from feeling despised within the local community, it was just another exercise in time-keeping for us to fail. Week after week we marched to and from St Coleman's. Week after week several of us were cuffed fiercely for dawdling.

'I've told you before about dragging your heels, Cummings.'

Smack.

'We haven't got all day to wait for you, Cummings.'

Smack.

'No supper for you if you don't hurry up.'

Smack.

It didn't matter what words they used. The result was always the same.

Apart from its other associations, I soon realized that Saturday was also bath day. Everyone in the dormitory filed silently down to the bathroom and queued naked until there was space in one of the baths. As a four-year-old I was expected to share with other boys. As I grew bigger I got my own bath – but we all shared the same water, regardless of cleanliness or temperature.

Each Cottage had a boiler that heated its water, and an allocation of five wheelbarrows of coal a week to run it. Because of the high demand from the kitchen and the bathroom, we seemed to run out fairly often, especially in winter.

Washing was a painful ordeal. We used the same carbolic soap on our skin as they gave us to scrub the urine-stained bedclothes. It was so hard, like scraping a block of wood over your body. And if the water was second- or third-hand, it wasn't very warm anyway and became impossible to create a lather with. But if I didn't rub the soap all over myself, one of the staff might do it instead – and then I'd be lucky to escape without losing a layer of skin under their vigorous rubbing.

I didn't admit it to anyone but Saturday bath mornings were the only chance I had to cleanse my body of the traces of two or three nights' bed-wetting. Aunt Ross and her colleagues took a lot more care over cleaning the linen than they did us.

It wasn't a coincidence that we bathed on Saturday mornings. That was the day some of the children had visitors. The following day we were on show at church. It was made very clear to us that we all needed to look our best if we were going to be presented to outsiders.

I always tried to make myself as clean as possible, even though it hurt. I'd scrub for as long as I could bear it. I wanted to make myself look as good as I possibly could.

It wasn't because I wanted to impress anyone at church. It was because it was Saturday – and on Saturday I was going to see my mother.

I thought that every week. I'd clean myself, have my lunch, do my chores, then run and play as close to the driveway as I could. I could see the main gate from the large playing field and from outside the fire station, but my best view was from the cherry orchard. I loved to run around the trees in there. Sometimes I would join in some other boys' games of hide and seek among the air-raid shelters scattered among the trees. But I would never take my eyes off that driveway. Not even if it meant I was 'out'.

I lost track of time while I was in the Homes. I remembered that I'd arrived in good weather and now the Saturdays had begun to get shorter. Before I knew it, autumn had become winter. While most of the other boys spent their spare time in the playroom, I was the only one who ventured out in the worst conditions. I had to. I would never forgive myself if she came and couldn't find us.

Besides, in the worst weather being in the Cottages was almost as cold as being outside. I remember dreading having to run outdoors to use the toilet during the day – the inside ones were only to be used at night – but once there it was often the same temperature as indoors. There was no central heating as such. The dormitories relied on the pipes that ran along the walls carrying hot water from the boiler to the taps. At best the pipes took the edge off the extreme conditions. But they were no match for the freezing temperatures of December and January and they were sometimes turned off to conserve fuel.

During the winter days I used to look forward to going to bed and being wrapped up in my blanket but it was never as good as I dreamed. The bedclothes often felt damp because they were so cold, but getting changed from our threadbare clothes into pyjamas while standing on that cold floor was the worst part. For those brief moments we were totally exposed to the frosty air. Although it was against the rules, some of the other boys occasionally slept in their work clothes for extra warmth but I didn't dare. I knew if I wet the bed and ruined my shorts I would be severely punished.

Once we were all tucked up in bed I was often too cold to sleep. I'd lie there, watching my breath visible in the air, listening to the other boys shivering around me. The sound of teeth chattering would eventually stop as one by one they dropped off to sleep. I was always the one left on my own. Always the last one awake in the cold and the dark.

There were two fireplaces, one in the dining room and the other in the playroom. The dining-room fire was lit regularly in the worst weather. However, the one in the playroom was used only on Christmas Day. That was our gift from the Homes, regardless of how cold it actually was.

Our meals also improved slightly at Christmas. I remember that instead of the 'bully beef' and vegetable pies that we were often served, we actually got real meat from a chicken or a turkey. One of the gardeners kept chickens but these were only used for fresh eggs. I'd often dreamed of eating one, though, while I'd been waiting by the driveway.

I was too young to remember Christmas with my family so I didn't have anything to compare it to. Santa Claus didn't visit us, but we were all given a 'new' book. Well, it was new to us. They had all been donated, as usual, from local charities. Once the day was over, they would all be taken and added to the box in the playroom for everyone to share. It didn't matter to me. I couldn't read anyway.

We benefited from the generosity of others in another way. The first time I realized this was when I noticed a crowd of boys near the empty fireplace in the playroom. Pinned to the wall above was a sheet of paper, which they were all reading. I'd never seen a message delivered like that in the months I'd been there.

The sheet of paper contained lists of boys' names. Various organizations within the local community had offered to host a party for some of us. The lists told us whether we would be invited to celebrate with the Royal Navy Club, the Gas Club, the Firemen's Club or one of the others. I was confused by the gesture. I was so used to people in Cosham pointing at us and taking our seats on the buses that I suspected it might be a trap. I don't know how I thought the trap would work exactly, but I couldn't see what other point there was to these parties. After so many months living in the Cottages it never crossed my mind that these strangers were just being nice.

My name was on the Royal Navy Club list and I remember waiting along with a dozen other boys by Mr Otterbourne's office on Christmas Eve. As usual we were sent out to wait early, even though the cold was almost unbearable through our winter jumpers. At the designated time a bus appeared at the gate and we were instructed to board.

The next few hours took me entirely by surprise. I realized after a while that I was enjoying myself. I was happy, even. I couldn't remember the last time I had genuinely felt like that. We were taken to a small hall where lots of men and women in Navy uniforms offered us jelly and ice cream and played games with us. There was even a Santa Claus later in the day, although he didn't hand out any presents. But I was just so happy to be in a room with a proper fireplace and people who didn't want to hit me just for being there that I didn't need anything else. I was content and I felt safe.

I hadn't felt like that since I'd last seen my mother.

After Christmas it was business as usual. The older boys went back to school, while the rest of us did our chores and tried to keep out of reach of the more volatile staff. And then one day Mrs Ingram took me aside.

'You've got a visitor coming tomorrow. Be smart, there's a good boy.'

I couldn't believe it. A visitor? Me? But why was I being told now? That meant tomorrow must be Saturday.

I was too nervous to sleep very much that night but at least I did not wet my bed. The next morning I was the first boy from the dormitory into the bathroom, which meant I managed to have some warm water for once. I struggled to eat any breakfast. Only the hovering hand of Aunt Ross forced me to finish my bowl of porridge.

Normally I resented being sent places early but not this time. As soon as I had finished drying up the breakfast dishes I ran as fast as I could over to the driveway. I promised myself that I wouldn't take my eyes off the gate for one second. I knew visitors only arrived in the afternoon but what if the rules had been changed? I wasn't going to risk it.

But the longer I waited, the heavier my eyes felt. The lack of sleep the night before was catching up with me. I could feel myself getting tired.

Suddenly a thump on my back woke me up. It was Robert. Not far behind him was Richard, carrying Philip. Skipping behind them was Janet. I was so happy. I hadn't dared think it. But if they had all been told that a visitor was coming, it could only be one person.

'I said she'd come back for us,' I said quietly. And then again, loudly, almost shouting in Robert's face, 'I told you she'd come back.'

I was going to see my mother. She was going to take us away. I couldn't be happier.

I was so nervous every time I saw the gate open, but then we'd identify somebody else's parents and look away again and start to chat among ourselves. I couldn't remember the last time I'd seen my sister. She'd grown so much. But all the while we spoke I never took my eyes from the driveway. I was so used to doing one thing while monitoring the comings and goings of visitors that I'd forgotten how much practice I'd had over the last few months. It was easy for me. I could play and keep watch for hours.

I just didn't expect to do it that day as well.

I don't know how long we had been waiting when Robert announced, 'She's not coming.'

I leapt at him. 'Of course she's coming. Don't say that.'

But he shook his head and began to walk away. 'You can stay here all night but you won't see her.'

I didn't want to believe him but I had no choice. Even if she turned up now it was too late. The last visitors had left and all the children who had been taken out had returned.

Why hadn't she come? I didn't understand it. When I woke up that morning I thought I would be walking out of that gate and never coming back. I had even thought of swearing at Aunt Ross, then running away. 'I can say what I like because I'm escaping here today,' I thought. But it hadn't turned out like that.

The next few days were utterly miserable. I tormented myself at church by thinking I saw her every time I looked around the congregation. Dejected, I also fell foul of Aunt Ross's temper more than usual. I seemed to get through a pair of pyjamas every night – and have to wash bedsheets the next day – and I couldn't eat food quickly enough for her satisfaction. I was being punched every other hour and I didn't even care.

That was when she decided to do something else instead.

I'd seen other boys taken to the cellar but I prayed it would never happen to me. On this day it did. Steep wooden steps ran down from the hallway into the darkness. On her way down Aunt Ross pushed me so hard off the top step I stumbled down the first half, then completely missed the others. Instinctively I put my arms out to break my fall but I couldn't see the floor so I didn't know when to tense. When it hit my hands I thought my elbows and wrists would break.

It got worse. Once she was satisfied I could walk, Aunt Ross climbed back up the stairs and – 'No!' I cried.

But she stepped out into the brightly lit hallway and locked the door all the same. I looked around. Nothing. I held my hand to my face. Nothing. I was terrified. I tried to remember where I was in relation to the walls and the boxes of kitchen provisions. But I didn't dare move anywhere. I was too scared. What if I trod on a rat? What if a rat trod on me? I felt my heart begin to race and I had an overwhelming urge to go to the toilet. I closed my eyes and began to cry. I just stood there like a statue and let the tears flow down my face. 'Let me out,' I said between sobs. 'Please let me out.'

About an hour later the door at the top opened again. From watching her punish other boys, I knew Aunt Ross rarely kept anyone locked up much longer than sixty minutes. Often it was less than that. She obviously knew that just ten minutes in that horrible room was unbearable enough although maybe she was worried we might actually grow to enjoy it. Probably she just needed someone to do skivvying work upstairs.

As I staggered into the daylight I swore to myself that I would never get punished in that room again. If it meant running away from Aunt Ross all the time then that's what I'd do whenever possible.

Even as I made that pledge to myself I realized how impossible it would be to keep out of her way for good. I remember Aunt Ross hitting me three times in the course of one meal. Once in the food queue, once at my table and again during the washing up. I thought she might have restrained herself because I'd been hit before. But that was not her policy. She lashed out every time she was annoyed. She could have pummelled me all night. I don't even think she realized she was doing it. I think we all looked the same to her.

Then, during every break I got, I drifted diligently towards the gate. The trees in the cherry and apple orchards didn't have much to offer by way of coverage, but they were big enough for me to hide behind and cry and still keep an eye on the driveway. Even though it wasn't visitor day, I was still hopeful. Maybe she'd got the days wrong? What if she came on Tuesday instead of Saturday? Or Wednesday, Thursday or Friday.

She didn't come on any of those days. But then, on Saturday, she did.

When Mrs Ingram told me on Friday to expect a visitor again I nearly blurted out, 'You said that last week and no one came.' But I didn't. I truly believed it would be different this time. The next morning I was the first child bathed and waiting. And waiting. And waiting.

Eventually the visitors started to arrive and there she was. I didn't dare believe what I was seeing. The woman talking to the gatekeeper was definitely her. She thanked him and started walking down the long drive. Before she'd even covered a yard I had left my hiding position and dashed towards her.

I'd felt like this before, when it had turned out to be a false alarm. But I knew this was the real thing. Behind me I heard other footsteps running. Still sprinting, I turned my head and saw my brothers and sister not far behind. I don't know where they came from but I knew where they were going. And I knew that I was going to get there first.

Mum didn't get very far at all into the grounds. We didn't let her. We were like five young tiger cubs trying to feed, pushing and scrabbling around, desperate to be the one to get closest to their mother. I think she was shocked. Even above the noise we were making, I remember her squealing with laughter as she knelt down and tried to kiss and hug us all equally. As soon as we'd squeezed her half to death we all turned and walked towards the gate and freedom.

Memories of the last time she'd met us here came

rushing back. She was going to put us all on a bus and take us to our new home. It didn't matter if it was a house or a room or a box in the road – as long as we were together that was all I cared about.

Everyone was too excited and emotional to make much sense, but I noticed once we were outside the perimeter fence that we had walked past the bus stop.

'I hope she hasn't moved to Cosham,' I thought. 'I'd hate to see the Children's Cottage Homes every day. I want to live as far away from it as possible.'

We walked for another ten minutes, everyone taking it in turns to hold her spare hand while she clutched Philip with the other. Once we were in the centre of Cosham she said, 'I hope you're hungry.'

I was confused. We were outside a small café and she was opening the door. Were we going on such a long journey that we needed to eat first?

The next couple of hours are a blur to me now. I remember that we all sat down and I ordered beans on toast and a glass of milk. I remember that we all cried a lot and I remember that Mum told us she loved us all and that we were going to be one big happy family again, just like before.

But I don't remember what else was said. I don't remember her telling us where she'd been or what she'd been doing. I don't remember if she told us where we were going to live now or whether she had found a job.

The only thing I remember with certainty is that at the

end of the meal she walked us back to the Children's Cottage Homes, kissed us all, and then walked back up the driveway again.

I ran crying back to East 3 and threw up everything I'd eaten that day.

This should have been the happiest day of my life but instead it was the worst.

FIVE: *It's Only for One Day*

For my fifth birthday I was given four squares of chocolate by the Superintendent, Mr Otterbourne. It was 17 March 1949 – the day I was told to celebrate until I was eleven – and that is the first birthday present I remember ever receiving. I don't remember my previous birthday although it probably followed the same pattern. I know this time I didn't get a gift from my mother, or a card. n fact I hadn't heard from her since her visit a month earlier.

Before that day I sometimes used to wake up thinking, 'I'll be leaving today.' I truly believed it. I don't know why, I just did. And even though my mother had returned us to the Homes that Saturday, I still believed it. Although maybe not as much.

Shortly after that day in the café, Robert had found me by the cricket field. I was on my own, shivering, but it was better than being indoors.

'I told you she wasn't coming back for us,' he said.

I didn't answer.

'She's never taking us back.'

'Do you really believe that?' I asked him. Robert had

known her for longer, and lived with her longer, than the rest of us. 'She said she would, didn't she?'

My brother just shrugged. 'She says lots of things. If she wanted us, why hasn't she got us already?'

We walked together for a few minutes, then he ran away to do his chores. We both knew what would happen if he was late.

I had always spent a lot of my time in the Cottages thinking about my mother. Now I was asking myself different questions about her. She hadn't told us where she had been all this time. But she did say she was back for good and that we were all going to be together again. So why did she bring us back here? Why didn't we all go home then, like we did last time? Why did she bring us back here where men and women kept hitting me all the time? I didn't wet the bed before I arrived at the Children's Cottage Homes. I needed her help to make that stop. Why wouldn't she take me away?

I think it was the hope that she would walk in one day and rescue me that had kept me going so far. I took each blow that came my way, tried not to cry and got up again ready for more. I'm convinced it was believing that my escape was imminent that gave me that courage to keep bouncing back.

But I was only fooling myself. In daylight I looked like a normal kid because I tried to hide my anxieties. At bedtime, however, all my fears came out. More often than not I struggled to get to sleep. When I did drop off, I was often awoken by terrifying nightmares. Sometimes I was being held somewhere, in darkness, and I couldn't escape. Or I might be struggling, unable to scream, while I was carried away by men I didn't know. Other times I was cowering and some faceless stranger was about to strike me. I would wake up sweating and petrified just before the hand or weapon made contact with me.

I knew it was silly and I wished I could have made them stop. After all, in my nightmares I usually woke up before the violence actually took place. What I suffered during the day was actually worse. But still the nightmares kept happening.

And I continued to wet the bed.

Some of the other boys did this as well. I was rarely alone when I queued in the cold bathroom to clean my sheets. No one did it quite as often as me, though, which soon made me self-conscious. I began to worry that something was wrong with me. Why couldn't I control it?

I started to become less sure of myself, almost jumpy. Any noise behind me or something glimpsed out of the corner of my eye and I flinched. I was always worried it might be Aunt Ross or one of the other houseparents creeping up on me. I didn't find it easy to mingle with other boys, either. We didn't have much time away from adults and when we did, the older boys usually led the way. There were several boys in my Cottage who were more than double my age. They normally controlled playtimes and arranged games in the grounds or in the playroom. Sometimes I joined in. More often I hung around on the sidelines or wandered off by myself. I was too young to read any of the books we'd been given but I managed to keep myself busy with my thoughts. I knew I couldn't share those with anyone.

Being on edge all the time didn't help my sleeping. Where other boys managed to take naps in the fields during playtime, I never could. I couldn't relax while other people were walking around, even though it wasn't against the rules. My head was always too full of questions. Or worries.

What if someone creeps up on me?

What if Aunt Ross catches me?

What will they do if they find me like this? I thought about the cellar and prayed it wouldn't be used.

Nervous as I was just thinking about the staff, being near them was worse after the meeting with my mother. Mrs Ross's vicious hands seemed to sting more. The Superintendent's criticisms during inspection were more cutting. And considering I was now more openly nervous around them, I appeared to be on the end of even more whacks. I remember playing in the orchard when one of the housefathers walked past. I hadn't done anything wrong apart from run too close to him. Without saying a word he just swung his leg and kicked me in the shin. The other boys looked away until the man had gone, then they carried on as normal. We all did. But I couldn't understand it. When I didn't care, I'd had my share of punches. Now I seemed to be attracting more than ever – and definitely more than everybody else in my dormitory.

Why though? What had I done wrong?

Why me?

Had my faith in my mother returning given me strength? Now that was beginning to wane, was I more vulnerable to the attacks? Or was there another reason?

By the time I had been in the Homes for about a year I was considered old enough to take on harder chores. One of them – 'spud bashing' as we called it – I didn't like because I had to be in the kitchen near the cook and Aunt Ross or Mrs Ingram while I did it. But another job was more fun – at least, if you did it right.

One of my new tasks was cleaning the floors in the Cottage. Downstairs the cold stone dining-room floor required a mop and bucket. Considering the mop handle was taller than me, it wasn't an easy job, but normally there were two or three of us doing it so you could pretend your mops were swords. We never played pirates or St George and the Dragon. The only person I ever pretended I was stabbing was Aunt Ross.

Polishing the wooden dormitory floor could be even more fun. We had these heavy things called 'bumpers' that we wrapped in rags covered in polish. Then we put a long stick handle in the bumper and pushed it across the floor. This was another two-person job, but as soon as the adults weren't around one of us would stand on top of the bumper and the other would push him along. I was smaller than a lot of the other boys so I was easier to push, but I struggled to move them very quickly.

I knew that if we were caught I'd be in for a good hiding. But as far as I could see, it was worth it. 'They hit

Les Cummings

me whether I've done anything or not,' I thought. I might as well try to have fun whenever I could.

I remember playing the bumper game with a boy called Henry. He was my age but larger and a lot heavier. He could push me along really fast, though, so I didn't mind the effort of shifting him.

We did one dormitory one day and were scheduled to finish the second one the next. When I turned up the following morning, however, I noticed Henry wasn't there. I waited for as long as I dared but then I had to start working. The bumper was a lot heavier when you weren't having fun with it. I trudged up and down the long room, getting as far under the beds as I could reach. They were slotted so close together it was hard. The main area to clean was the walkway up the middle of the room.

I was struggling along when I heard a voice in the doorway. It was the Cottage's housemother, Mrs Perrin.

'You're not meant to be doing that on your own,' she shouted.

'Henry should be helping me,' I called back. 'I don't know where he is.'

While I was speaking, she marched into the room and studied the floor where I had already rubbed. 'Henry's run away,' she said.

'But he was here yesterday. He said he'd see me today. We were looking forward to—' I stopped myself. I couldn't tell her our plans for playing with the bumper.

'Henry's a bad boy and he's run away,' Mrs Perrin said again. 'So get on with your work and no more cheek.'

And as she said it she smacked me across the side of my face. It wasn't the hardest blow I'd received but it smarted. I think she must have been wearing a ring. My face was cut just below the eye.

A few weeks earlier she had poured boiling water over another boy – and he still has the scar today. I was lucky to escape so lightly.

I desperately fought back the tears as usual but I was worried. I didn't know Henry very well but we always got on when we did chores together. He would have told me if he was planning to leave when we were playing yesterday. I was sure of it.

Suddenly I remembered the boy called George whom I'd witnessed being lifted out of his bed at one of the other Cottages.

'I wonder if Henry's been taken as well?' I thought. Now I was scared. I didn't know where George had gone but that only made it worse. I couldn't imagine it was anywhere nice.

I finished polishing the dormitory floor in a record slow time. I was too lost in thinking to put any energy into it. If I were lucky the houseparents would not punish me for taking so long because I wasn't supposed to be doing it on my own. But I knew from experience that I couldn't count on it.

I still watched the main gate every Saturday, but I began to turn up later and leave earlier. Sometimes I wouldn't hang around there all the time, but play elsewhere and pop back every half an hour or so. I still believed my mother would save me, but something had changed. My brother's words haunted me.

'If she wanted us, why hasn't she taken us already?'

What if that were true?

I pondered that question many times over the next few months, especially when I was allowed to play outdoors in the open air. I never concluded a satisfactory answer – but there had to be one. I knew it.

One day, towards the end of the summer, Mrs Ingram came over to me during breakfast. I naturally tensed as I heard footsteps approach and only relaxed when I could see it was her. It was a habit I couldn't switch off.

'When you're finished here you need to go and see the Seamstress,' she said.

I was confused. We only went to see the Seamstress if there was a tear in our jumper or shorts. She would either stitch a repair there and then while we stood in our underwear or shirtsleeves or she would hand us a replacement from the rows of identical clothes behind her chair. But as far as I knew, there were no more holes in my clothes than usual.

'Why do I have to go, Ma'am?'

I wouldn't have dared ask anyone else but I trusted Mrs Ingram not to explode.

'You need to pick up your school uniform.'

And that was the first I heard of this thing called 'school'.

I really didn't know what school was. I knew some of the boys went to a building in the village every day and I knew there were lots of other kids from other places who went there as well. I also knew my older brothers had been going for some time although we hadn't ever spoken about it. So no one had ever described to me what went on there.

And no one had told me I would have to go.

The only advance notice I ever remember was for the Christmas parties in Cosham. At any other time of the year we were informed of things at the last possible minute. I hadn't been told I was going to live in the Homes the first time. I hadn't been told how long I would be there. Even when it was time to leave, no one had tipped me off. The events just happened with no warning.

And it was the same now. I was in the Homes but I didn't know for how long. Every day I woke up not knowing if would be my last day there or the first of another thousand. I didn't even know which Cottage I would be sleeping in the following night. We weren't told anything.

The Seamstress's room was in the same building as the assembly hall so I knew how to find it. It was also the closest block to the main gate so I'd spent many hours hanging around it while I monitored the comings and goings on the driveway. Whenever I went near it there was always the same whirring noise, like a giant bumble bee, coming from inside. It didn't matter what time or what day it was, the Seamstress always seemed to be at her sewing machine. When you consider she had more than 100 boys and girls to make trousers and dresses for, as well as do repairs for, it was no wonder she was busy. She was the one who made our shorts and trousers and jumpers out of the coarse material she seemed to have an endless supply of. All the girls wore frocks made from yards of material donated by the community. It didn't matter where we went, people could always tell we were from the Cottage Homes by the clothes.

As I approached the building I noticed there were already several other children there. A tall boy called Paul walked near us and yelled, 'You're all going to school. Trust me – you'll hate it.' He laughed as he wandered away.

I remember thinking that it was an odd thing to shout as an insult. I didn't know what went on at this 'school' place, but I knew it wasn't inside the Homes grounds, which meant I would probably enjoy it. I hated the people I saw inside the church every Sunday, but I would rather have looked at their sneering faces than spend the afternoon in my Cottage. Whatever this 'school' thing was, I imagined it would be just as nice.

The next morning was even more unpleasant than usual. I was told to get up, as usual, wash as usual, dress as usual, then get down to breakfast. All within about fifteen minutes – as usual. After breakfast it was different, though. Normally I would go straight into the kitchen to help dry the dishes but Aunt Ross pulled me aside by the scruff of my neck as I went to pass her.

'Upstairs, in your school uniform, now.'

I fled out of her grasp, but I still felt the tips of her fingers on the back of my head as she swung her hand.

The clothes I had to change into were almost identical to my play clothes – or 'work clothes' as some kids called them – but a bit smarter. For the first time in my life I had a little jacket, like a blazer. The grey jumper and grey shorts didn't have many stains on at all. I wondered for a moment whether they might even have been new. I had never had anything new before. Not even when I lived with my mother. When you've got two older brothers, everything they've finished with passes to you, even if it has seen many better days.

There were half a dozen other boys getting changed as well. One of them was my age, the rest had probably been doing this for a year or more. I had never noticed where they disappeared to after breakfast.

Next we had to report to the pathway outside the Superintendent's office with everyone else. For the first time I noticed how many of the other children were wearing these slightly smarter versions of our normal clothes. After Mr Otterbourne's terrifying scrutiny I was then led through the woods along with the others of my age. We were ordered into double file. A boy I hadn't seen before was pushed alongside me.

'Hands!' an unseen adult barked, and the boy next to me immediately hooked my hand in his. On another command we all walked forwards through the trees to a smaller gate in the fence.

I didn't have a clue what was going on and no one was about to tell me. All I understood is that a boy I didn't know was holding my hand and dozens of us were marching in pairs to the perimeter of the grounds. As soon as we were through the gate it became even more confusing. The boy next to me dropped my hand and moved quickly away. The ordered lines of a moment earlier disappeared. It was a free for all but everyone seemed to know where they were heading.

Shortly after we'd left the Homes we reached the bridge which crossed Southwark Road. The front boys ran up the steps two at a time and then tried to block the way for the rest of us. Everyone was so excited to be out of the sight of the houseparents. By the time I got up to the top step there were two lads hanging over the edge of the handrail, dangling their legs above the road beneath. Looking back, it was very dangerous. But at the time it was the funniest thing I had ever seen. It had been so long since I'd laughed like that.

It took about fifteen minutes to reach the school. One of the other boys said that it was a mile's walk. I'm sure we could have covered the distance in half that time if we'd wanted to, but nobody did. It was so exhilarating not to have houseparents looming over you, I could have walked for another ten miles.

The walk wasn't the same for everyone, however. Cosham is quite a small town, but the Portsdown School was very big, encompassing separate buildings for boys' and girls' primary and secondary schools. With all the individual schools built in a line, some people had a lot less distance to cover than others. The first building was the senior girls; then a playground, an assembly hall, then the primary girls. Then the same layout for the boys the other side. In other words, new boys like me had the furthest to walk.

I discovered on the first day that my time at the Children's Cottage Homes had programmed me well for the ritualistic rigours of school. If the adults told me to do something, I did it. Bells sounded every day at the same time, which I found strangely comforting. But the Homes had also prepared me for something else: being treated like a second-class citizen.

The infants' school was divided into ability groups. Without a single question being asked, every pupil from the Homes was placed in the lowest – Class C – and ordered to sit at the back of the room. It was made very clear on day one that the teacher expected us to try to cause trouble – but he also made it very clear he was not going to tolerate any misbehaviour at all from us.

My heart sank. After the excitement of the walk there, I had almost believed we were going to be treated like other people. But it was just like being in church again, or travelling on the bus. Other children were more important. People took one look at our clothes and made a judgement.

I looked around the classroom. There was no uniform as such but the other boys were undoubtedly better dressed. It seemed so unfair to me. Their nice clothes might as well have been labels that read: 'I live with my mummy and daddy'. I was full of sudden envy and resentment of them.

After a morning's teaching that seemed to drag on for ever, the bell sounded for lunch. Nobody explained why, so I just followed the other boys who were dressed as shabbily as me. They all dashed out the door and across the playground to the school gates. I followed immediately and quickly realized we were heading back to the Homes. No one was messing about this time.

As soon as we got back inside the grounds we all headed to our individual Cottages. I remember being so hungry after the long morning and the fast run back, but before I could reach the dining room Aunt Ross appeared.

'Where do you think you're going in your school clothes?' she roared. 'Upstairs! Changed! Now!'

With each single word she cuffed her hand at my head. The first one caught me at full speed. The second and third attempts I half dodged as I ran towards the stairs fuming. I'd just set foot back in the building and she was on me already. At least at school nobody had hit me. Not yet, anyway.

By the time I got back downstairs it was half past twelve. We had to be back at school by one, and it was a fifteen-minute walk away. Which left a quarter of an hour to eat our dinner of boiled cabbage and potato, get changed back into our school clothes, and get out the door.

I was so miserable as I ate. Why did we have to change clothes before we could sit down? Did they think we'd embarrass the Homes if we turned up at school with food down our jumpers?

'Ah well, it's only for one day.'

I can't believe today how naive I was then. For some reason I didn't appreciate that school wasn't a one-off, like the Christmas party at the Royal Navy Club. Thinking about it, perhaps it's not that surprising. After all, no one at the Homes had taken us aside to explain what school was or how it affected us. We didn't even get any warning that we were going to be starting our formal education. The other kids at school got help from their parents. They'd probably been preparing for months. I noticed that some of the boys in my class could write their names and a few words. I'd never picked up a pen in my life.

I couldn't even ask my brothers what school was like. I was seeing them less and less these days, and when we did meet it was usually to argue about whether our mother was coming back.

For some reason I was angry at the lack of information. I shouldn't have been. I'd lived in the Homes for so long I should have been used to it.

The following day I was horrified to find I was expected to do exactly the same as on the previous one. And that meant changing my clothes half a dozen times and going back to that school. At least I could look forward to the freedom of the walk, I thought. For a while that cheered me up.

When I got outside for the inspection parade I changed

my mind. The fine late summer weather of yesterday had vanished. It was raining hard. And still we had to wait while the Superintendent marched up and down, looking for signs of insubordination. He was wearing a hat and raincoat while we only had on our thin jackets and short trousers as usual. After a couple of minutes my clothes were soaked through and I began to shiver. Was it my imagination or was Mr Otterbourne taking longer than usual?

The walk to school was horrible. I ran as much as I could, but the water was running down into my eyes and my soggy jumper got heavier with every stride. When I finally arrived I realized that for once I'd be grateful for a change of clothes. The school had no heating on that day and we had no choice but to sit at the back and drip. I was told off for letting my teeth chatter too loudly.

I thought it couldn't get worse but it was still raining at lunchtime. Not only did we have to sprint back in the wet, but after changing into our dry work clothes to eat we were forced back into our dripping school outfits. And then came the journey back.

I did not learn much academically during the next few months but I vividly recall one valuable lesson.

It wasn't long after my first day that my teacher took umbrage at my behaviour. I was guilty of dropping my sheet of paper on the floor and scrabbling too noisily to pick it up. I didn't see it coming until it was too late. His wooden blackboard cleaner, thrown from the other side of the room, cracked against the side of my head and set my ears ringing for the next half an hour.

That in itself didn't shock me. I had suffered worse at the Cottages. If anything, it underlined my mistrust of all adults. A few days later, however, I thought of it again.

One of the boys from 'the good homes' did something wrong and the teacher immediately pulled out his cane. The boy cried as he took half a dozen whacks on his hand. I remember thinking I would never have given the teacher the satisfaction of letting him see he'd made me cry. But then, I'd had a lot of practice at hiding my emotions. This other kid looked like he'd never even been told off in his life.

The next day I thought I was going to burst with excitement. We had all just settled down into our seats when a man came storming into the room. He wasn't particularly big but he was angry. He took one glance around the class, spotted the teacher and dived at him. I couldn't help smiling. The man had one hand around the teacher's neck and was jabbing his fingers into the teacher's face with the other. I quickly understood it was the father of the boy who had been caned the day before.

'Don't you ever touch him again, you understand!' the man was shouting. 'If he does something wrong again, you give him a note to give to me and I'll deal with it. But you never touch him again – or else!'

And then he left. I think the teacher had to have the rest of the day off but I never saw him hit that boy again.

And that was the lesson: boys with parents have someone to stick up for them. And I didn't.

I heard a while later that the police were sent to visit the father who had attacked the teacher. He was warned about his behaviour and he agreed not to take matters into his own hands again. I don't know if he was threatened with prison, but it didn't matter. His boy was protected. No teacher would cane him after that.

That was the first time I ever considered that something was wrong. From before I could remember, I'd been hit by some of the adults in charge of the Homes. Sometimes it was punishment, other times I might just have been within reach when they were frustrated.

It didn't matter to me what the reason was. The effect was always the same.

I had never thought to question this behaviour before.

It was only when I saw that parent threaten the teacher that I realized not all adults were like that. I was being beaten because of who I was rather than anything I'd done.

'If I my mummy was here they wouldn't hit me. If I had a daddy they would be too scared.'

It was such a simple piece of logic but it had never occurred to me before.

I had honestly never considered the idea that some of the houseparents and the Superintendent were being 'violent' towards me. They were just doing their job. I didn't like it, but I had to accept it. Just like I had to accept preparing vegetables in the kitchen, cleaning the bathroom floor or being separated from my mother. I didn't like any of those things. Why would I think that being punched by Aunt Ross was any different?

Once I realized this, I began to spot similar signs within the Homes. A young boy called David seemed to go out of his way to infuriate Aunt Ross sometimes. But she never laid a finger on him. Not while I was there. And now I knew why.

His parents came to visit him every Saturday.

Part of me wishes I'd never worked it out. Before that day I had been content just being unhappy because it was a horrible place to be, if you see what I mean. I was thoroughly miserable but at least everyone else was suffering as much as me. I thought the elbow blows to the side of the head at dinner, the kicks on the back of the leg, the backhanded smacks across your face were all random. I knew now they weren't. A lot of the other kids were treated immeasurably much better than I was – and it was just because they had parents.

'It's so unfair,' I cried. 'I'm being punished for not having a family.'

I was kept away from my mother, which was bad enough. On top of that – in fact, as a direct result – I was being treated as the personal punching bag of a lot of the staff.

I realized that day that being hit by them was wrong and they knew it too. And yet they still did it.

I started to hate them all more than ever. And now for the first time I began to blame my mother as well.

'She could get me out of here if she wanted,' I thought. 'She could stop them from hurting me.'

I think something changed in me that day. I could even say something in me died. Young as I was, I was aware that this new knowledge had to have an effect. It just had to. But would it be for the better – or for the worse?

SIX: *I'm Rich*

I struggled at school. I don't think this was a surprise to anyone. All of us from the Homes were mostly overlooked by the teachers. At the time, I think I relished the freedom it gave me. The teacher didn't care if I scored 100 per cent or 1 per cent in a test so there was no pressure in that area. But that didn't stop us being hit for talking out of turn or running in the corridors.

We were left alone a lot. I quite enjoyed drawing and sometimes an art teacher would come in for an hour or two and give us things to paint or colour in. Unfortunately she was just as inattentive to the kids on the back tables as the other teachers and spent most of her time helping the 'normal' pupils. If she looked over at us it was usually to say, 'Shut up!'

Looking back, I should have hated school but I didn't. In fact, I probably enjoyed my time at Portsdown a lot more than all the kids from proper families. There was a clock at the front of the room and as we grew old enough to tell the time I used to enjoy watching the other kids staring at it. I knew they were wishing the hands would go round faster so they could leave. I didn't feel that way.

I would have been happy if we stayed till eight o'clock instead of three. As far as I was concerned, it was better to be there than at the Cottages. We didn't have chores at school and the level of violence was considerably lower. The only time I ever longed for the end of class was if I was hungry.

I liked school for other reasons. The first was the freedom it gave me to explore the local area. Most of the boys ran the same route every day but after a while I began to deviate off the usual paths. I felt like an explorer. A lot of Portsmouth had been bombed during the war and by the time I was six or seven there was still a lot of rebuilding to be done. There were entire gardens filled with rubble on some streets, where houses or shops had been destroyed. If I thought I could get away with it, I'd dart in and climb up the brick mountains and pretend I'd discovered a new country.

Wherever I went I wasn't normally alone. There were too many boys and too few roads to disappear completely – not if you wanted to reach school within the allotted time. If I found a new bombsite or a hidden shell hole, there was always another lad or two around to enjoy it with me. I think I made more friends during those fifteen-minute journeys than I ever did in the Homes.

Sometimes I saw my brothers or sister on my route. Occasionally we went out of our way to walk together. Usually we just waved and carried on talking to whoever we were nearest to. I knew I could count on them in an emergency but apart from being family we didn't have that much in common any more because we were all kept in separate Cottages.

We were losing touch with one another and nobody seemed to notice – or care.

There was another advantage to going to school as I discovered one Saturday morning. I had endured my weekly bath and had just finished eating breakfast. Before I could leave the room, Mrs Ingram called out, 'School-boys, stay where you are.'

The rest of the room emptied. I'm sure I heard some boys giggling to themselves. They obviously thought we were being held back to be punished for some indiscretion. To be honest, so did I.

But that wasn't the case. Aunt Ross made us all line up by the door, then Mrs Ingram walked along and pressed something into everyone's hand. I had no idea what it was although the older boys looked like they were expecting it. As she got closer to me, I still couldn't make it out. Even when I looked in my hand a few minutes later I remained confused.

Mrs Ingram had given me 9 pence. But why?

'It's pocket money,' she told me. 'You'll get it every week – if you behave.'

I pressed the coins in my palm and smiled. I'd never had money in my life before.

'I'm rich,' I thought. 'Now, what am I going to do with it?'

That Saturday afternoon was the first for as long as I can remember that I didn't monitor the gates religiously.

Mrs Ingram had announced that all school-age boys were allowed to leave the grounds for a couple of hours on a Saturday. It gave me the perfect opportunity to spend my new-found wealth. I was so excited. I couldn't wait to get out into Cosham. I had formulated my plan within seconds of hearing the news. I would dash into the little sweet shop on the High Street where I had often seen other children with their parents. Then I would run to the old air-raid shelter near the park and eat them all. I couldn't wait.

It was only as I ran through the gate that another thought occurred to me.

'What if Mummy comes today?'

I stopped walking. How could I have forgotten what day it was? I had never missed a Saturday by the gate. I thought about it for a second. Then I turned and ran as fast as I could towards the town. I didn't look back once. That afternoon I ate my first ice cream in a cone. It made quite a mess but it was only as I wiped my face that I remembered my mother.

'If she comes today she'll miss me,' I thought.

The following week I was amazed to receive the same amount again. Once more Mrs Ingram reminded me the pocket money was dependent on my good behaviour. I was grateful to receive anything. I was prepared for the previous week's generosity to have been a one-off. I was given it without warning; I knew it could be stopped without warning as well.

It wasn't long before I suffered my first penalty. Aunt Ross – of course – told Mrs Ingram that I'd been messing around when I should have been cleaning the stairs and I was fined accordingly. What Aunt Ross didn't report was that she'd nearly killed me in the process.

We were all getting changed for dinner when I heard Aunt Ross scream up the stairs. She was saying someone had spilled water on them. Nobody moved but seconds later she burst into the room.

'You two, get the mop. Clean this mess up!'

I was one of the chosen ones. With Aunt Ross in this mood it never paid to look less than urgent. We ran to fetch the mop and bucket and I dived on to my knees to start the clear-up. I remember really trying to get the job done quickly and well. But it wasn't good enough for her.

I don't even recall what she said. I just remember her shoving me so hard that I fell backwards down the last half-dozen stairs. I couldn't remember pain like it. I could see blood on the floor and on one of the stairs. I thought I'd broken every bone in my body. Suddenly Aunt Ross appeared next to me. She was so angry I couldn't even understand what she was screaming. It was just like the time she'd knocked me over in the bath queue. In her mind I was to blame for lying winded at the bottom of the stairs. It was my fault my face and arms were cut and bleeding.

She didn't know what to do so she did what she always did – and kicked me in the stomach. She missed my ribs but it took all my concentration not to throw up on her shoes. Maybe I should have done. But who knows what she would have done to me then.

She still wasn't finished. My fall had caused more mess. As I staggered to my feet, she swung her hand once more at my head and knocked me on to the stairs. Then she grabbed my hair and dragged me up to the spilled water.

'Clean this mess!' she was raging. 'Lick it up, you nasty boy!'

She rammed my face so hard into the wet mess that I thought my nose would break. I was choking, I couldn't breathe. Worst of all, the harder she pushed down, the more blood from my head smeared the floor. Even with so much going on, I knew, 'When she sees that, I'm dead.'

But before she could do any more damage I heard Mrs Ingram's voice from another room.

'What's going on out there?' she demanded.

Without even letting go of me Aunt Ross said, 'Cummings is up to no good again.'

I didn't hear what Mrs Ingram said next but suddenly my head was released. I was told to take myself to the sick bay. It wasn't the first time I'd been there. The Matron cleaned me up and said she was going to write in the care book: 'Cause of injury: fighting.'

I didn't question her. I didn't dare. She was Mr Otterbourne's wife, after all.

Mrs Ingram never actually rebuked any of the Aunts or other houseparents for punching us, but no violence ever took place in her presence.

That week I only received 3 pence pocket money. But at least it was something. In my eyes that was Mrs Ingram's way of telling me she didn't believe Aunt Ross's story but she had to be seen to. And more importantly, it still allowed me the opportunity to escape into Cosham that afternoon.

My excursions outside the grounds quickly became the highlight of my week. I began to hang around with other boys a lot more and we played imaginative hide-and-seek games among the bombsites and shelters of the town. Even though unexploded bombs were being discovered around the country all the time, I still preferred to take my chances among the rubble than with Aunt Ross or the Superintendent. I was still slightly small for my age but I was adventurous – at least when there were no adults around. I couldn't believe the weight that lifted from my shoulders as soon as I crossed the perimeter of the grounds. The contrast between inside and out was immense. Sometimes I actually felt elated. The last time I remember being truly happy was when my mother had arrived to visit. But that was a long time ago. Thinking about it now only made my mood darker.

I spent a lot of schooltime and mealtimes daydreaming about what it would be like to leave the Homes permanently. I thought, 'If I save all my pocket money, I could run away.' But where would I go? I didn't know anyone. In any case, the intimidating environment of the Cottages was second nature to me. I wasn't even sure I could survive in the outside world.

Soon, however, I would get my chance.

I hadn't been shifted from one Cottage to another for ages – I thought the reason for all that upheaval, whatever it was, had been ended. A few months after my seventh birthday I noticed that dormitory changeovers seemed to be getting more frequent. It was some time after that before I realized that the boys weren't just walking out of my Cottage. They were leaving the Homes themselves.

The more I studied the activities, the more I learned. Boys were disappearing left, right and centre. At least it was going on in broad daylight – not mysteriously in the night like before.

Through chatting with the other boys I discovered that some of the kids were being sent back to their parents. Others were put on boats to a country called Australia. A few of the older ones were given train tickets and sent to work in the coalmines of Scotland and Wales. For some reason the Homes couldn't get rid of us quickly enough.

I was thrown into an unexpected panic. I had wanted to escape the violence in the Homes for so long but I'd always known where I wanted to go: to my mother.

'What if they send me to Australia?'

I didn't want to go to another country I'd never even heard of. That would be worse. I'd never see any of my family again.

Over the next few weeks my sleeping problem grew worse. I had such vivid nightmares of being torn out of the arms of my sleeping mother that I kept waking myself up. Always terrified, always soaked in sweat. And then I'd just lie there until Aunt Ross woke the rest of the room.

My bed-wetting increased as well, which brought its own problems. Aunt Ross persuaded Mrs Ingram to dock my pocket money again and again. Just to guarantee I'd got the message that she was displeased, she made sure to smack the back of my head every time she saw me.

All the time I was thinking, 'Don't send me away. Not again.' Much as I hated the Children's Cottage Homes, at least they were close to my mother. If I stood a chance of living a normal life like the kids I saw in church and school, I needed to stay near the rest of my family.

I began to suffer what I now know were panic attacks. My chest would tighten and I'd struggle to breathe for a few minutes. I'd feel light-headed and not really know what was going on around me. If I was standing, I had to sit down before I fell. If I was in bed I would feel myself shaking uncontrollably. My mind would be filled with so many worries, all surging round at the same time. The only thing I knew for sure was that I was not in control.

The first time it happened I thought I was going to be sick. For a few moments I even imagined I was dying. But I didn't tell anyone. I didn't want the attention. It was safer, I felt, to suffer in silence, but the sensation of being suddenly scared was never far away.

I understood how the Cottages operated. I knew they wouldn't give me any advance notice. One minute I'd be here, the next I'd be on a bus going somewhere else. I couldn't relax for a moment. Every time Mrs Ingram walked into the room I panicked she was going to send me away.

As the weeks of worrying passed, I learned from talking to others that the long summer holidays were about to end. For some reason this comforted me. It made some sort of sense to send the boys away when there was no school to worry about. 'Once I'm shuttling backwards and forwards to Class C, they'll leave me alone,' I decided.

I was wrong.

I received a lot of my bad news immediately after breakfast. This August day was no different. I was summoned over to the Super's office. When I got there I noticed a man wearing a black suit standing alongside Mr Otterbourne.

'Leslie, this is Mr Maynard.'

The man nodded towards me and said nothing.

'Go and get your things. You're going with him.'

SEVEN: *I'm on My Own*

Whenever I waited by the Children's Cottage Homes gate for my mother, I was always looking for a lady approaching on foot. There were hardly any cars in those days, and certainly, people like my mother had no access to them. During the war fuel was scarce and money for such luxuries was tight for years afterwards. Unlike a lot of the other boys at the Homes I had travelled in a car twice in my life so far: both times it was a police car, and both times it took me to the one place I didn't want to go. Now I was in a car again and I was being taken to a new destination. Wherever it was, it had to be better than the Homes.

'I just hope it's not Australia,' I thought. But the butterflies in my stomach suggested it might be – or worse.

Mr Maynard told me as little about himself as he could get away with. He was the placement officer for the Homes. I didn't know they had one – or what the job involved. He said it was his responsibility to find new families for the children like me.

'But I have a family,' I said.

'I'm going to give you a family that loves you and wants to look after you,' he replied.

I was hurt and confused. How could he give me a new family? Is that why I wasn't allowed time to say goodbye to my brothers and sisters at the Homes? And what did he know about my mother? Hearing a stranger voice my innermost doubts was hard. I felt a sudden surge of guilt at doubting her recently. 'I know she loves me,' I told myself. 'She wants to look after me but she can't.'

We drove for about ten minutes and then he stopped the car. We were in Queen's Road, a suburban residential street in the Buckland district of Portsmouth.

'This is it,' Mr Maynard announced. 'Get your things. And remember to behave. These people want to help you.'

I didn't realize I needed help. I just wanted my family.

My 'things' consisted of a set of work clothes and a couple of books. I didn't have another possession in the world. Nervously I waited next to him as he rang the doorbell. It was opened by a large woman who at first glance looked similarly dressed to the housemothers at the Homes. She was wearing a housecoat and a hair net. She was very fat and didn't have a very friendly face. She smiled at Mr Maynard but didn't even look at me. When she moved away from the door to let us in, I noticed a boy, a few years older than me, clinging to the back of her waist. He was trying to cuddle her but his arms wouldn't reach round. He was a lot skinnier than his mother and his face didn't look at all like hers although the expression was the same. He didn't take his eyes off me for a second but he didn't say anything or smile. He looked scared of me but I didn't know why.

We sat down at a table in the kitchen at the back of the house and Mr Maynard made introductions.

'Leslie, I want you to say hello to Mrs Baker,' he said, as the large woman began to boil water for tea.

'Hello, Ma'am,' I mumbled.

'And this must be your delightful son, Peter.' Mr Maynard reached over to ruffle the boy's hair paternally but he cowered out of reach behind his mother's large skirt. 'I'm sure you two will be the best of friends in no time.'

As I looked at the boy's wary eyes I wasn't so sure.

For the next half an hour we all sat around the table drinking tea. While the adults chatted about paperwork and schools and meals and other practical things, I stared at the floor, or the ceiling, or the teapot in its colourful cosy. I felt lost and nervous – especially with Peter's eyes still boring into me. Occasionally I was asked a question but when I was too shy to answer instantly they carried on talking without me. Outside school I wasn't used to being asked anything. At the Homes I was only told things. My opinion didn't matter.

'I don't like it here,' I thought as I sat silently on the large plastic-cushioned chair. I couldn't explain it. I was wary of adults anyway and usually tried to keep at least an arm's distance from them. The staff at the Cottages had taught me that. Strangers terrified me and here I was trapped between three of them. More disturbingly, I realized I had never sat down at a table with grown-ups before. Not for a cup of tea and a chat. The situation felt awkward and too 'new' for me and I found it impossible to relax. I couldn't explain why. No one was being horrible to me. The adults were actually being as friendly as any I had ever been around. The worst they were doing was speaking about me as though I wasn't there but I was used to that. I liked it normally. It made me feel invisible, safe. But the butterflies in my stomach were getting busier and I didn't enjoy the tea. I knew the next phase of my life was being decided there and then and as usual I didn't have any control at all over it.

Years later I learned what the paperwork involved. Mrs Hilda Baker was legally fostering me – which meant she was taking me into her care, to be looked after 'as one of her own family'. She agreed to clothe me, feed me, monitor my health, ensure I attended school and church and train me in habits of 'honesty, obedience, personal cleanliness and industry'. In exchange for all this, in particular to cover the expense of feeding an extra mouth in the difficult post-war years, she would be paid 20 shillings a week.

I wasn't aware of being part of a financial transaction as we sat there that day. I didn't realize I was effectively being sold across that kitchen table. But I definitely sensed agreements were being made by people who weren't interested in me. And as soon as Mr Maynard left the house a short while later, I was proved right.

I was given the tour of the house – at least, the parts of it that were open to me. 'That's Mr Baker's room,' Mrs Baker said as she gestured towards a closed wooden door at the front of the house. It was the first time I'd heard of her husband. 'You won't be going in there.' I was led up the stairs to a small boxroom which still had heavy black-out curtains.

'This is Peter's room,' Mrs Baker said. As she spoke, her son left his hiding place at her side for the first time and ran into the room.

'Don't touch my things,' he said emphatically.

'I won't,' I replied. But I was confused. It looked the same as a dormitory at the Cottages. I always imagined that normal homes had pictures on the walls, toys on shelves. These brown walls were bare and there were just a few puzzles balanced on top of a thin wardrobe.

'You sleep over there,' Mrs Baker said.

I followed her pointing hand. There was only one bed in the room. Then I noticed just below the window what I had originally thought was a small pile of laundry on a set of drawers. It wasn't. It was a pillow, a sheet and a blanket on top of a large metal trunk. The truth slowly sank in.

'That's my bed.'

'Don't get too comfortable there,' Mrs Baker said as she left the room. I didn't dare answer but I thought, 'How can I get comfortable here? There's no mattress.' I would later realize that wasn't what she meant.

My room-mate was torn between wanting to stay and guard his non-existent possessions and to follow his mother out of the room. In the end he stayed long enough to say, 'I hate you and I want you to go,' and then ran noisily after his mother. I was left alone. Alone in a room where I wasn't welcome, in a house where I felt very uncomfortable. It was a new sensation for me. I had suffered in many ways at the Children's Cottage Homes but I'd never felt so alone. There were always people around. Even when I was being beaten I could take some comfort from knowing others were often suffering too. But here it was just me.

'I'm on my own,' I thought.

I climbed on to the high trunk bed and tried to lie down. It was cold and too rigid to get very comfortable on but I closed my eyes anyway. The butterflies in my stomach had been replaced by a feeling of sickness. I had a terrible feeling about 258 Queen's Road and I didn't know what to do. I hugged my bag of clothes to my chest, curled up on my side and shook silently in tears.

A noise made me spring to attention. I was just in time to see Peter Baker's deepset eyes disappear from the doorway. He laughed as he ran down the stairs.

Also upstairs was a small bathroom. The house's toilet, like most places at the time, was in the backyard. The Cottages all had outside toilets for use during the day, but there had been internal ones as well. Nobody wanted boys traipsing around the grounds at night. I didn't realize how fortunate we were in that respect until that day.

The other difference between here and the Homes was that there I could hide. Other boys were always around to distract the staff. In this house, as I soon found out, I was on my own and I had nowhere to run.

'Boy!' Mrs Baker's voice blasted up the stairs.

I ran down and found her in the kitchen. I didn't even stop to question how she'd addressed me.

'Time for tea,' she said. Peter was already seated at the table so I climbed into the chair opposite. That was my first mistake.

'Who told you you could sit there?' Mrs Baker shouted. As she spoke, she swung her short, fat arm at my head. She was slower than Aunt Ross but so much heavier I think she would have really hurt me if I hadn't swerved away to soften the blow. 'That's your place over there.'

She pointed to a smaller table with one chair by the wall. Still stunned by her smack, I ran over to my new seat.

'I can see we're going to have to teach you some manners,' Mrs Baker said as she dropped a small bowl of soup on to the table in front of me. I didn't dare start eating until she and Peter did. They each had a slice of bread with their meal. I wasn't so fortunate.

I was lucky to eat as much as I did. My table was next to a dog basket and its owner, a black and white mongrel called Patch, kept trying to lick my spoon and bowl. He was a scrawny creature whom I immediately liked the look of, but I had to twist in my seat just to protect my food from him.

At the other table mother and son slurped their soup wildly until it was all over their faces. Every so often they would just wipe their mouths with the back of their hands, then smudge their hands on their clothes. I tried not to look at them while I ate but they made so much noise it was hard not to. Peter's jug ears, sunken eyes and skinny frame were in complete contrast to his mother's round features. She had dark eyes and thin lips. Burst red blood vessels covered her face, her colourful headscarf only highlighting her complexion.

I couldn't wait to get out of the kitchen but the rest of the afternoon and evening were just as unpleasant. I was told to wash up and then get out of Mrs Baker's sight because I was cluttering up her kitchen.

'I'll be grateful of some space to myself while you're at school tomorrow, boy,' she said. I had only been there a couple of hours.

After the stress of the day's upheaval I was looking forward to bed. Even with my track record of sleep problems I thought I would be out like a light as soon as my head hit the thin pillow. But I was wrong. The second I climbed on to the hard box my head started buzzing. Wild thoughts and questions swirled around.

I could hear Peter Baker was still awake. I decided to try to make friends with him.

'Where is your father?' I asked.

'None of your business.'

'Have you got a father?' I said. For me that was an innocent question. I didn't have a father. I had never lived with a man who called himself my father. I didn't even know who my father was. I thought that Peter could be in the same position.

'What sort of a stupid question is that?' I saw Peter sit

up in bed angrily. 'Of course I've got a father. I'm not like you.'

I was so used to living without a father that if Mrs Baker hadn't mentioned her husband's existence, I wouldn't have questioned the fact that he wasn't around. I didn't think much of it when Mr Baker hadn't come home. I wasn't even confident that's what fathers did.

I managed to establish that Mr Baker was in the Navy. Peter didn't know how long he'd been gone or when he'd be back. But he was certain of one thing. 'You're going to be for it when he gets back. I'm going to tell him what you're like.'

He wouldn't explain what he meant by that. But he'd said enough to worry me. I'd already been hit by Mrs Baker for nothing. What if Mr Baker was even bigger? If he was in the Navy he could kill me. Increasingly dark predictions cluttered my mind. With the blackout curtain keeping out all moonlight I felt like I was having nightmares while I was awake. There was no way I could sleep with these worries filling my head.

Eventually I managed to get off but not for long. I was suddenly aware of a giant wave capsizing the ship I was in. I realized it was a dream. But something had roused me. As I came round, I was aware of Peter Baker running back to his bed.

I hadn't been shipwrecked. He'd shoved me until I'd woken up.

That happened twice more before morning, each incident taking me longer to get back to sleep. The last time

I was woken up I was in the deepest sleep of all. But this time it was Mrs Baker standing over me. And she was angry.

'Get up, boy! I can't believe they've sent me such a lazy good for nothing.' I felt like I hadn't slept for more than ten minutes all night. Why was she waking me up? I sensed Peter hovering menacingly just behind his mother's housecoat as usual. Slowly his part in my terrible night's sleep came back to me.

'He kept me awake with all his shouting,' Peter said.

'Did you hear that, boy? How dare you keep my precious awake? Can't you even sleep like a civilized person?'

I knew I only had a few more seconds before she stopped standing over me and did something to actually get me out of bed. I pulled the blanket off me – and then wished I hadn't.

My pyjama trousers were soaking wet. So was the sheet. I'd wet the bed and because I was so tired I hadn't even noticed. I tried to pull the blanket back but Mrs Baker grabbed it first and threw it on to the floor.

'What's this, boy? What's this?' Not even Aunt Ross could scream that loudly. It must have had something to do with her size. 'Are you an animal? Have they sent me an animal?' She was shaking her head in disbelief. 'Get up, animal! Get up!'

Before I could move she reached around my throat and lifted me upright so quickly I tumbled out of the bed and on to her feet. She jumped back. 'Don't dare touch me, you dirty boy,' she said, and kicked me in the ribs.

I didn't know what to do. I ran to the bathroom and started filling the bath to soak my sheets. Mrs Baker had other ideas. 'If you think I'm wasting water on your nasty body, you're mistaken,' she said. 'Get dressed. If you act like an animal you can smell like one for all I care.'

I wasn't given any breakfast but at least I didn't have to wash my own sheets. I would have given anything to control my bladder but I couldn't. It was embarrassing and it always got me into trouble.

Queen's Road was too far away from Portsdown for me to walk there so I was moved to a nearby Catholic school called Corpus Christi. Mrs Baker told me which way to walk and then warned me not to be late. Along the way I bumped into a couple of friends from the Cottages who were bunking off school. I didn't tell them anything about the Bakers, though. They lived at the Children's Cottage Homes. They had it worse than me.

At least, that is what I honestly thought. It wasn't very long after that I changed my mind. Later that same day, in fact.

I was so hungry throughout the morning class. For once I couldn't take my eyes off the clock. I was wishing for twelve o'clock to come round so I could get back to Queen's Road for some food. I sprinted all the way back, praying that Mrs Baker wouldn't make me change into work clothes just so I could eat. When I knocked on the front door, she didn't look happy to see me.

'What are you doing here?' she demanded.

I couldn't think of an answer quickly enough for her. She filled the entire doorway so I couldn't even walk in past her.

'Well?' she shouted.

'It's lunchtime,' I mumbled. I couldn't bring myself to say, 'I've come home.' I didn't know if this was my home or not.

'If you think I'm feeding you, then you're mistaken,' Mrs Baker said. 'I don't feed animals at lunchtime.' And then she shut the door.

It all happened so quickly. I sat down on the step and looked at the road. What now? I hadn't eaten since that bowl of soup the night before. I was starving.

The rest of the day was torture. I could only think about food. Whatever the teacher said, my mind wandered to images of sweets, dripping, bread and jam. What if Mrs Baker didn't give me any tea either? Or supper? How long could I last without food? My imagination began to run wild. I pictured myself being found as a skeleton in the bed the next morning.

That evening I was given food but Mrs Baker hadn't forgotten the morning episode – and she was still in no mood to forgive me. As I went to sit at the small table by Patch's basket, she cuffed me firmly around the head.

'Animals don't need chairs, do they, boy?' She pointed at the dog. The next thing I remember is Peter sitting down in the small chair – my chair – as I was handed a small plate of potatoes and gravy and some meat. They couldn't want me to sit on the floor, could they?

They could.

I spent the next five minutes kneeling on the hard kitchen floor as I ate my dinner from the little table. All the while I felt Patch's cold nose nudging my arm, trying to get a mouthful of my food. I hated depriving him, but there was no way he was getting a sniff off my plate. I was starving. He would have to look after himself.

Things got worse after supper.

I was told to wash up again, which I didn't mind doing. I only wished Mrs Baker would leave the room while I got on with it. She preferred to fuss around the kitchen noisily, occasionally making remarks like, 'I'm so lucky you're a good boy, Peter – not like him.' Afterwards I assumed I would be allowed to go to my room. I was wrong. Mrs Baker met me in the hallway before I could climb the stairs.

'Where do you think you're going, boy?' she asked.

'To my room.'

'This is your new room,' she said. She was standing by the wall beneath the stairs and holding a small door open. I hadn't noticed that cupboard before. It was painted the same colour as the rest of the wall. I noticed it now, though. The entrance was only three feet tall. I didn't dare get too close but I could see it would be dark inside if the door was shut. Why was Mrs Baker trying to scare me, I wondered.

Then I realized she meant it.

'Well, what are you waiting for? Get in.'

I was frozen to the spot. She couldn't be serious. I couldn't clamber in there. It was a cupboard. This was worse than the cellar at the Homes. I looked from the intimidating black hole back to her face. She had a look of intense hatred on her face. And she wasn't messing around. Somehow I found the voice to resist.

'I'm not going in there,' I said.

'Yes you are,' she ordered, and before I could move she lunged an arm towards me. I felt her stubby fingers grip into the top of my arm as she pulled me towards her. I grabbed hold of the kitchen door frame. I couldn't let her do this.

'Come here!' she shouted.

I clung on with all my strength. I couldn't let her win.

'Peter, help me!' I cried. I didn't know where the boy was but I assumed he was nearby. Even he couldn't let her go through with this. But he could. I felt teeth sink into my hand and I was forced to release my grip on the jamb. Peter had bitten me just to please his mother but I was the one she was calling 'animal'.

I started screaming and flailing my arms. I don't think I tried to hit Mrs Baker – I didn't dare – but I needed to keep her away from me. Unfortunately my puny arms were nothing compared to her strength and size. She had an arm around my neck and she was just walking me towards the cupboard. It was like a lorry pushing a bicycle.

'Stop it! You can't!'

She didn't say anything. Just pushed. Then one final effort, a huge shove, and I fell smack against the inside wall. The next thing I knew it was dark. She'd closed the door – and locked it.

'Let me out! I'm sorry! I'm sorry!'

I was desperate. I couldn't apologize enough. I didn't know what for, but saying sorry was the only thing I could think of.

'Mrs Baker, please! Please!'

I don't know how long I screamed. I don't remember stopping. Eventually I must have done because Mrs Baker didn't come back. Not that night. Eventually I must have slept.

My next recollection is a crashing noise as Peter kicked the door, again and again, yelling. I didn't know where I was but I could feel pain all over my body. Then I realized I was hunched over a box. I must have slept like that, my head in my arms like on a school desk. And it was so dark. I couldn't tell if it was day or night. Only the fact that Peter was making so much noise gave me any clue.

I was allowed to go to the toilet outside and then have a wash. I was so relieved I hadn't wet myself. I couldn't understand why not. I was sure it only happened when I was particularly upset. If anything was going to cause me distress, a night in that dark cell should have done it. For breakfast I was given a bowl of porridge and once again made to sit on the floor. Then it was time for school. I couldn't wait to get there.

Over the course of the next few weeks I spent nearly

every evening, some nights and most of the weekends in the cupboard under the stairs. Every time I was pushed in I found myself scared in a new way. In the darkness your worst fears seem more real. I tortured myself with thoughts that I would never be let out again. Or that the house would burn down and the firemen wouldn't know I was there.

Sometimes I felt more confined by the blackness all around me than by the actual walls which I couldn't see. It was so dark that if I shut my eyes it made no difference. I'd open them quickly then screw them tight again, but I couldn't escape the black. I felt the familiar squeezing in my chest as my heart pounded faster and my breathing grew louder. And all the time I couldn't tell if I was locked in the darkness – or the darkness was locked in me.

Years later I began to read about how armies have used sensory deprivation to torture prisoners. A person who is denied sleep and detached from his surroundings can quickly go mad. Many innocent confessions have been extracted in this way, I have learned. I can understand how. Even though I was surrounded by very close walls, being in my cupboard sometimes made me feel as though I was exposed on a firing range. I couldn't tell where the boundaries lay. And all the while I was conscious of every response my body was having. Every itch in my arm or hair, every faint brush against some unseen object or piece of wood made me jump. What if there was someone else in there with me?

Or *something* else?

And with nothing to do, my feelings of hunger grew stronger. I could hear my stomach rumble and churn and there was nothing I could do to stop thinking about it. When other physical functions began to stir my body it was even worse. Even if I'd just used the outdoor lavatory, knowing that I couldn't made the desire to go even greater.

On my third or fourth time in the cupboard I realized I could use this to my advantage.

After I'd screamed her name for long enough, I heard Mrs Baker outside the door.

'What do you want?' she shouted.

'I need the toilet.'

She knew I had trouble controlling my bladder and so she unbolted the lock and dragged me blinking into the light.

'Hurry up,' she said. 'I'll be waiting here.'

I made my way into the backyard and caught my breath. I was so grateful to be out of that box. Cold as the wooden toilet building was, at least it wasn't pitch black out there. Even at night there was usually the moonlight or lights from the house.

I stayed there for as long as I dared, then slunk slowly back to the hallway. Mrs Baker hadn't moved.

'Think you can pull one over on me, do you?' she said.

'I don't know what you mean,' I replied.

'You didn't need the lav at all. You lied to me, didn't you? No one spends that long out there.'

She wouldn't believe I had been really desperate. That

123

was the last time she ever let me out for a call of nature. I was thrown back into my cell to face my waking nightmares once more.

Even if I dared to sleep, it was very hard to get comfortable. There was so much junk in the cupboard that it was impossible to stretch out properly. I think if the space had been empty I could have lain down. Sometimes I was allowed to sleep in Peter's room. I was never given any warning – just as at the Homes, I could never get into a pattern. On those occasions Peter did his best to keep me awake by flicking me or punching me while I slept. As soon as I wet the bed, however, I'd be banished back to my prison. I think if I hadn't been hardened by my experiences at the Cottages I might not have lasted so long. That still didn't explain why it was happening to me. Mrs Baker kept saying I'd been naughty and she was punishing me. I thought she did that enough with all the smacks to the head I received. But what had I done? If I was so much trouble, why didn't she send me back?

On the occasions when I was not confined to the cupboard I still had to do my chores. I would clean the floors, sweep the yard, wipe the windows, scrub the dishes – anything that Mrs Baker didn't want to do, I was left with. It had been the same at the Cottages so I was used to it, but at least there I was never the only one working. At the Bakers' Peter would hover near me, gloating at not having any jobs himself. Even though he was three years older than me, I knew that I could have beaten him in a straight fight. He knew it too. That's why he was especially mean to me when his mother was around in case he needed the protection.

He annoyed me so much once that I told him, 'My mother is going to come and get me and I'm going to tell her what you've done to me and you'll go to prison.' I regretted it instantly. It was one more piece of ammunition he could aim against me.

The next day I heard a knock at the front door. I was forbidden from answering and Mr Maynard was my only visitor anyway so I ignored it. Peter came rushing into the kitchen and said, 'It's your mother – she's come for you.'

I ran into the hallway, my hands still dripping with dishwater. Where was she? How did she find me? I knew she would. But where was she? They hadn't made her wait outside, had they? But there was no one there. Peter had knocked on the door himself before rushing in. At that moment I wanted to kill him.

I fell for that trick a lot more after that. I know I should have learned, but I was clinging so desperately to the hope that my mother really would come that I let myself be hoodwinked every time. Sometimes I would be under the stairs when the knock occurred so I'd be anxiously straining to hear her voice – not that I would have recognized it necessarily. It was difficult enough trying to remember her face.

I'd be shouting, 'Mum! Mum! I'm under here – I'm a prisoner!' Then I'd hear Peter's voice as he began to laugh.

Sometimes real women would call with nothing to do with Peter. I never gave up hope that one of them would be her. I always tore through the house to catch a glimpse of the visitor but it was always one of Mrs Baker's unpleasant-looking friends.

My mother never came but it didn't stop me hoping. I would cling to any belief, however flimsy, to escape. I even tried to go through official channels.

Part of Mr Maynard's job involved checking up on the children he had placed with other homes. When he came to visit after my first few months, he sat down with me in the kitchen while Mrs Baker busied herself upstairs. Safely out of her hearing, I told him I wasn't happy.

'And why is that?' he asked, but not looking up from a handful of paperwork that he'd pulled from his briefcase.

'Mrs Baker beats me and she makes me live under the stairs,' I said angrily.

At this Mr Maynard stopped reading and picked up his pen.

'Does she now?' he said, and wrote a note on one of the sheets of paper. 'I'm sure you must have done something to deserve it.' I learned later he had to report on each child for the committee who ran the Children's Cottage Homes. That was what his notes were for.

I also told him that I had been having pains in my left ear. He was happier with this complaint and before he left he spoke to Mrs Baker. A few days later I went to see a GP and was referred to Treloar Hospital with a condition called torticollis.

I had been suffering stiffness and spasms in my neck for some time. I hadn't mentioned it to anyone for obvious reasons: who would care? Every pain or bruise or cut or niggle in my body was normally an injury caused by being attacked by my foster mother. What was the point of showing her her handiwork?

My earache had been with me for some time, however, regardless of whether or not I had been recently thumped. I was glad I mentioned it to Mr Maynard – but why had he acted on this and nothing else?

A few weeks later he came to Queen's Road to tell me I could expect another GP's appointment to investigate my sleeping problem. He said he was also concerned about what he called my 'constant screaming'. I was surprised to hear this. I hadn't told him I screamed whenever they locked me in the cupboard under the stairs. I'd never told anyone that sometimes I'd been so scared of what was in the darkness with me that I'd hollered until I was hoarse. *How did he know?*

Years later, when I was eighteen, I bumped into a woman who lived on Queen's Road near the Bakers. She immediately recognized me and we soon got talking about the old days. She told me how they used to hear me screaming every other day. I wonder now whether she reported it to Mr Maynard. I can't imagine Mrs Baker did. Either way, I'm grateful that someone did. I always felt that if I could tell the right person what was happening to me I would be saved. And apart from a policeman, who was better than a doctor?

First, though, I had my other problem to get through. I think a lot of children would be horrified at the idea of being admitted to hospital at the age of seven, but I was delighted. I didn't understand what they were going to do to me, but I was certain of one thing – I would be safe from Mrs Baker for a day or two.

It turned out to be a lot longer than that. I was admitted to Treloar Hospital on 24 January 1952, some weeks before my eighth birthday. According to my file held at the Children's Cottage Homes, I was discharged on 2 March. During that time I had to undergo an operation called a mastoidectomy, which involved removing bone from behind my ear. It was not a straightforward procedure back then, which is apparent from the amount of time I was kept in for observation.

From reading up on the subject as an adult, I have learned that torticollis often occurs during birth. Sometimes a trauma to the neck can induce the same characteristics, however. I do not know for sure, but I think the number of times my head was smashed against the floor or a wall or with a fist was to blame.

I remember feeling groggy after my operation but my main recollection is the exhilaration of being away from Queen's Road. I had more than a month of freedom. Five blissful weeks. During that time nobody visited me. But that meant nobody hit me, either, and I was also given three decent meals a day. Mrs Baker was not a bad cook, but on the rare times I was allowed to eat, the portions she gave me were never filling. Peter always had twice as much, as he was delighted to show me.

Even though I experienced feelings of safety for the first

time in that hospital, I was still a child of my environment. I couldn't really relax while I was there because I wasn't told at the start that I'd be staying for so long. For the first fortnight I was too drowsy to worry. After that I dreaded that every day could be my last.

A mastoidectomy just before my eighth birthday wasn't my last brush with the medical profession but it remains the most successful. The pain behind my ear disappeared, although you can still see where the bone has been removed to this day. However I contracted torticollis, its physical impact remains a permanent reminder.

When I was signed out, nobody from the Baker family came to collect me. The hospital arranged for a nurse to accompany me to Queen's Road in a car. Once again I was in that mode of transport that only ever meant one thing: I was going back to hell.

What I didn't know was that there would be a new person living in the house when I returned. And things were about to get a lot worse.

EIGHT: *You Need to Be Taught a Lesson*

On the drive back to Queen's Road the nurse tried to make polite conversation with me but I was too busy staring out the window, trying not to cry at the thought of being returned to the place I hated most in the whole world. Imagine how I would have felt if I'd known I had a new problem to deal with.

Mr Peter Baker was the physical opposite of his wife. Where she was overweight and imposing, he was lean and considerably shorter. Where Mrs Baker's features disappeared under the fat of her face, he was hard-faced, with chiselled bone definition that hinted at past good looks. Dark, beady eyes gave him a hawkish expression. Lank, thinning hair sharply parted was reminiscent of all the pictures of Adolf Hitler I had seen over the last couple of years.

I had no idea he would be there when the car pulled up outside the house. I didn't understand that he had been demobbed from the Navy and would now be working closer to home. Even when I went inside it took me a few moments to realize there was an extra body there. I was so wary of Peter and Mrs Baker, studying how they reacted to the arrival of the nurse, that I quite overlooked him at first. It was easily done. He had little physical presence. And he didn't speak once, at least not to me.

After the nurse left I was given jobs to do. I expected Peter to follow me, quick to goad me after the weeks I'd been away. But he didn't. If anything, he clung to his mother more than when I'd first arrived. Was it possible he was actually guarding what he saw as his territory from his own father? The closeness of the maternal relationship had always disturbed me. Partly because I was envious and partly because they were both so unpleasant to look at. Peter would sit upon Mrs Baker's wide lap at every opportunity he got, and she sometimes even fed him like that while I scrapped around on the floor. Neither of them acted like he was ten or eleven years old. If I hadn't always been so hungry I would have found it hard to keep my food down while they giggled like teenagers together. They'd walk hand-in-hand down the street and he'd sing made-up songs of how much he loved his mummy. I used to think he did it just to annoy me, but it was the same even when they thought I wasn't around. When Mr Baker returned, it seemed to get worse.

I didn't know what to expect from the man of the house. My gut instinct was to be wary of him. That was my default emotion with any adult I came into contact with. He wasn't very big but he looked powerful. Years in the Navy had probably made him very fit. I knew that if he hit me as viciously as Mrs Baker I would be in trouble.

But hitting me seemed to be the last thing on his mind. If anything, he seemed more nervous of me than I was of him.

When I cleared the table after dinner, I heard him say to his wife, 'What's he doing?'

When I had sat on the floor to eat he'd asked, 'Why's he doing that?'

It went on like this for a couple of days. He enquired about me as though I wasn't there. Yet all the while he couldn't take his eyes off me. Everywhere I went I could feel his dark glare following me. Sometimes I would be dusting the shelves in the parlour and he'd be so close I could feel the heat from his breath. But he didn't say a word.

As time passed Mr Baker became more adventurous. If he saw me coming towards him he would raise his hand to smack me, then laugh as I flinched. Still, though, he said nothing.

I still hate being watched today. It reminds me of him. He was tormenting me in a new and subtler way and I felt physically sick every time. But it was a lot better than actually being hit. That was still a real concern where his wife was concerned and so I did my best to avoid it whenever possible.

During my years at the Homes I had developed the art of being invisible in a crowd. I employed similar tactics at Queen's Road. The first thing I did upon waking each day or returning home was to listen to the house. I needed to gauge exactly where the other three were at all times. I was always in potential trouble if we were in the same room long enough, but if I could keep out of their way it was safer. It bought me time.

I would do whatever it took to stay out of my prison under the stairs, anything to dodge Mrs Baker's fists. If I heard movement coming towards me, I would quickly dive into hiding. Anywhere would do, stand behind something, crawl out of their sightlines. If they yelled for me I'd pretend not to hear or suddenly walk into the room with a broom and sweep up, to distract their train of thought.

That was a tactic that worked more often than not. The only way to ensure I wasn't attacked was not to engage in conversation with any of them. If Mrs Baker asked me a question, nine times out of ten she wouldn't like the answer, so I developed a way of changing the subject. If she asked, 'Why can I still see dust on this floor?' I'd say, 'I think I left the soap on the floor upstairs' and run out of the room. Sometimes I'd start to cough and choke and dash out for a glass of water. I wasn't always successful but if I could dodge a kick once or twice a day, it was a tiny victory for me.

Mr Baker didn't hit me, not at first. But he never stopped his wife from thumping me when the mood took her. I think he was almost as scared of her as I was. If she called him he would actually run to attend her. Even with her he rarely communicated in much more than a series of grunts, nods and occasional words. She definitely ruled the roost.

If I thought my life would improve now Mr Baker was

in the house, I was wrong. Mealtimes deteriorated even more. Apart from having now to listen to three people eat like chimps at a tea party, my own allowance was gradually reduced. I was already allocated meagre portions of whatever meal Mrs Baker was putting in front of the others. Slowly, though, I began to miss out on entire helpings. Sometimes she wouldn't call me for dinner or supper and then say, 'You missed your chance.' When I began to turn up at my place on the floor without being summoned she went a stage further. I remember watching her serve up a stew in three plates. I assumed I would be given the pan to eat from as occasionally happened. Not this time. She put it back noisily in the sink and sat down to eat. I was given nothing.

'What about me?' I asked.

Mrs Baker stared at me. 'Did I ask you to speak, boy?'

I shook my head, but I couldn't just sit there. 'What will I eat?'

'Do you really think you deserve to eat?'

I couldn't answer that. Obviously she felt I didn't. I racked my brains – what had I done wrong? What was I being punished for? I couldn't think of anything. She couldn't have done it out of spite, though, could she?

Could she?

The next day I realized that she could indeed be that malicious. I was given nothing for breakfast, nor let into the house at lunchtime, and ignored again in the evening. Not one scrap of food all day, just the daily glass of milk at school. This continued the next day and the next. Even Patch the dog ate better than me.

This was no exaggeration. Even though I wasn't given anything to eat, I was still expected to sit on the floor and watch them stuff their faces. Peter often looked at me, sneered, then crammed an overloaded forkful into his mouth. Worst of all, though, was that they all threw scraps under the table for their faithful mongrel. As I missed out yet again on a proper meal, I dreamed of overpowering the dog and eating his dinner. It was my only chance.

That day I hatched a plan. When I came in to eat the next time I didn't quite sit against the wall as usual. The next meal gave me the chance to squat even closer to the table. Each time I sat down in the room I edged closer and closer towards them. Even though I was only eight I still appreciated the danger of letting them guess my plan. I had to be subtle. If any of them twigged what I was up to then I would be thwarted.

Writing these words now is very hard for me. Recalling how degraded I felt as I was forced to scheme like this sends me into a sweat even today. But that was my long-term plan. In the meantime, if I didn't eat I would become seriously ill.

Even after all the beatings I'd taken, by far the worst feeling was that of starvation. Your body yearns for food twenty-four hours a day. It's hard to sleep, hard to think, hard to concentrate, hard even to walk sometimes. I was like a zombie at school and not much fun for any of my friends to hang around either. Lunchtimes were the worst. Mrs Baker refused to give me any dinner money but she also warned me that I wasn't to return home till teatime.

I was being tortured through hunger and I'm ashamed now of the lengths it made me go to to eat. I remember the first time I scraped up a piece of discarded chewing gum from the pavement, just to get something in my mouth. I remember the first time I stood on the street corner near my school and held my hands in a begging shape, and said, 'Please help me, I'm so hungry.' And I remember the first time I stole food. Occasionally a boy would bring some fruit into class and I would pinch it while he was distracted.

Sometimes I plundered the local sweet shop when other kids were being served. I even began to creep into the Bakers' kitchen to hunt out leftovers and I developed a new trick at school. I would ask permission to go to the toilet then, as soon as I was out of the teacher's sight, tear around the building on a feeding frenzy. Sometimes I got lucky and grabbed a handful of potatoes or baked beans or even meat from the school kitchens. At other times I was reduced to climbing into the giant waste bins in the playground and grabbing handfuls of congealing rubbish. This was food destined for pigs on the local farms, but that didn't stop me. I remember the first time I ever did this. I had a handful of slops from dirty plates and I just closed my eyes and put it into my mouth. I didn't care about whether it was hygienic. I didn't even worry about the taste. I just had to get something in my stomach.

At least once a week I would be caught and then I would be punished. If I was lucky, I would get a detention – which I liked because it delayed the moment before I went home. On other occasions I would be banned from having my glass of milk in the afternoon. It was a gamble I couldn't avoid. I had to steal scraps to get by but risked being punished by more starvation.

None of this was as bad as my behaviour if I was locked up during one of these 'nil by mouth' periods. All these years later I can't believe I actually did this, but the images are so vivid I know it all happened. Once I was so faint with hunger that I actually experimented with chewing the wooden beams in the cupboard under the stairs. I'd scratch bits off with my nails and chew. I can't imagine I got much more than a couple of splinters but I was so desperate to get sustenance of any description inside me. And I know it happened more than once.

Meanwhile, my plan during mealtimes continued. After a week or so, I had moved so far across the kitchen floor that I was now underneath the dining table.

'I can't believe they haven't noticed,' I thought. Then I got a kick in my back. 'They've noticed,' I realized, 'but they like me down here with the dog.'

For a while it was a novelty for the family to kick me while they ate. I grew quite adept at dodging their feet. But I'd have taken a few blows to get what I came for: the dog's food.

All three Bakers were in the habit of reaching under the table with stripped leg bones and the like and letting Patch devour the leftovers. Whenever I saw him line up to take food from their hands, I acted. If the bone fell on the floor I dived on it before he could. If it was fed directly into his mouth I grabbed his jaws in both hands and prised them open. I felt so cruel doing it. It wasn't Patch's fault that I was hungry. There was no reason why he should suffer. But he did. That poor dog didn't get a lick some days whenever I was underneath the table.

When Patch realized that I would be there every day stealing his food he became territorial. Before I could get my hands on his scraps he stood there baring his teeth and growling. He made it very clear: touch this and you're dead. On that occasion he won – but I wasn't going to give up that easily. When it was time for the next meal I came armed. I reached into my shorts and pulled out an old wooden hairbrush. At the first growl from Patch I cracked him hard on the nose. He opened his mouth and the food was mine.

To my eternal shame I discovered that I even began to look forward to this animalistic ritual. I actually enjoyed hurting him. It turns my stomach now to admit that. Monsters like Aunt Ross and Mrs Baker had a lot to answer for.

I was becoming like them.

In their own way, the Bakers did want me to become like them. They were a Catholic family and had already sent me to a Catholic school. It was a lot further to walk to than Portsdown had been, but at least that gave me longer away from the house.

They attended church every Sunday and sometimes they took me. Even though I still wasn't exactly smart it made a change not to be abandoned on the back pews. Every service I went to contained something called the Lord's Prayer, which the entire congregation seemed to be able to recite off by heart. I'd heard it plenty of times at St Coleman's but had never taken any notice before. It had just been one more tedious thing to get through. Now, though, I heard it with new ears. I was struck by the line: 'Give us this day our daily bread.' I wondered if I'd imagined the words and so I made a point of listening out for it the following week. But there they were. What's more, I watched as Mrs Baker pronounced them as loudly as everyone else in the church. I was very confused. She never gave me bread – or meat or vegetables or anything. In fact, thanks to her I was beginning to scavenge in people's rubbish bins on my way to school in the hope of finding a few scraps. What did the Lord's Prayer mean if it wasn't that?

After I had been to church a few times Mrs Baker announced that I was to be baptized. I didn't know what this meant and I was afraid to ask but the following week the priest at the church explained everything. The ceremony took place shortly afterwards in front of the regular Sunday crowd. I don't think the Bakers invited anyone to watch. As far as I could tell, Mr Baker had no friends at all and his wife's tended to go to church anyway. I wasn't consulted at all, just told to stand at the front and let the priest perform the ceremony.

I found it very embarrassing being the centre of attention in front of all those strangers. I was concentrating so hard on trying not to blush that I wasn't really following the priest's words. Suddenly, though, he caught my attention. I was stunned.

'Did he really say that?' I thought. 'Did he just say that my name was Leslie *Peter* Cummings?'

It was true. The Bakers had baptized me and given me the middle name of 'Peter' – the same name as the father and son of the family. I wanted to shout out, 'That's not my name!' but I didn't dare. All those years of not standing out in the crowd at the Homes had taught me well. Just the thought of drawing attention to myself now made me sweat. All those faces watching me, those men and women in their suits and hats – what would they think if I dared speak out? Maybe that woman with the blonde hair and brown hat would listen sympathetically? Perhaps that man with the white moustache would demand the priest undo the baptism. Or maybe they would all be angry and hate me and try to hit me.

My heart was racing. I felt cold and hot at the same time. But I knew I couldn't do it. I couldn't risk saying anything.

Not in front of all those people.

Mrs Baker told me that they eventually wanted to get me confirmed as a Catholic. This entailed learning prayers and studying the Bible. I didn't enjoy it but I knew that if I took an interest she would be pleased and less inclined to hurt me.

Before I could be confirmed I had to attend classes with the priest. During one he explained that I would soon qualify for a ritual called Holy Communion. 'It's a wonderful ceremony,' he said, 'but you have to fast before it can take place. Do you think you can do that, Leslie?'

I asked him what fasting meant and he said it was the forgoing of food before a religious service.

'That will be easy,' I said. 'I don't have any food to eat anyway.'

The priest looked at me for a second and said nothing. Then he turned his attention to the other children in the group and didn't speak to me again. I could see from his expression that he thought I was obviously a liar and a troublemaker.

Telling the truth also got me into trouble at school. My teacher asked me why I had so many bruises on my arms. I explained, 'That's where Mrs Baker twisted my arm when she was trying to lock me in the cupboard under the stairs.'

'Are you telling the truth, Cummings?'

'Yes, sir.'

The teacher nodded and we continued the class. I struggled to concentrate for the rest of the day. An odd sensation was flowing through me. I think it was relief. The teacher had looked as though he genuinely believed me. For the first time in my life, an adult had listened to me. I didn't know how to respond. But would the teacher do anything to help me?

When I got home that afternoon Mrs Baker was waiting for me.

'What lies have you been telling that school?' she shouted.

'I haven't told any lies,' I said defiantly. I could see that Mrs Baker was in one of her furies. Whatever I said to her now would make no difference. When she was like this none of my tricks to distract her or make myself invisible stood a chance. I flinched and waited.

She hit me first with her hand, then picked up a rolling pin. She swung it at my head as she yelled at me to get into the cupboard under the stairs. I couldn't get there quickly enough. If she made contact with that heavy piece of wood I thought I would have died.

My teacher never asked me about my bruises again and I was careful to keep them hidden in future. He may have believed me once but he was accepting their word now. Whatever explanation the Bakers had given when he confronted them had obviously proved satisfactory. Once again I was seen as the villain.

'Is it my fault?' I wondered. Was there a reason why adults treated me like this? In desperation I dropped to my knees, pressed my palms together, closed my eyes and spoke.

'Dear God, I don't know if you listen to boys like me, but please, please, please can you make Mrs Baker stop hitting me? I don't like it and it hurts. I promise to be a good boy if you can do this.'

I had never prayed before and I have never prayed since. At the time I didn't know what else to do.

I don't know if it was related to the teacher's conversation or our neighbours' intervention or maybe even my prayer, but Mr Maynard's note about my 'constant screaming' was addressed when I was informed I had another visit to a GP. When we arrived, the doctor was already aware of the problem. 'I understand you're having trouble sleeping and you scream in the night?' he said.

I looked at Mrs Baker and nodded. The memory of confessing to the teacher was still fresh in my mind. I don't know if I would have said more if Mrs Baker hadn't been in the room, but on that occasion I just sat mute. It was enough for the doctor, however. He scribbled a fast note and handed it to Mrs Baker. 'That should do the trick,' he said. 'Come back in a few weeks if there's no change.'

That night I was allowed to sleep in my normal bed. Mrs Baker brought me a glass of water and handed me my first sleeping tablet. I was only eight years old.

I didn't scream that night but then I usually didn't when I was allowed to sleep upstairs. When I was woken by nightmares in that room it just made me panic and cry quietly to myself until I could drop off again. The screaming only took place when I was awake. When I was trapped inside the cupboard downstairs and I thought I would never see daylight again.

Mrs Baker knew this, but she still gave me the tablets.

Shortly after, the screaming stopped for good although the tablets didn't have anything to do with it.

Every so often the Bakers would give me a treat, which I found very confusing. I can't remember if it was at

Christmas or perhaps my birthday but we were all taken to the Portsmouth cinema in Copnor Road to see *The Phantom of the Opera*. This was the first time I had ever seen a movie on the big screen and I couldn't believe how thrilling the whole experience was. As for the film itself, I was terrified. Peter spent the whole evening shielding his eyes and clasping his mother's arms. I wished I could have held someone. It really was amazing.

When we got back to the house that night, though, I realized I was still shaking with fear. Everywhere I looked I thought I could see disfigured phantoms in the shadows. I really needed to go to the toilet before bed, but I couldn't face going out to the dark garden on my own. Mrs Baker told me to get out and stop being so ridiculous, but the more I thought of making my way through the blackness to the cold wooden box in the yard, the more petrified and hysterical I became.

As she shouted at me to get a move on, I felt the unmistakable sensation of my bladder letting go. There was nothing I could do to prevent it. I wet myself right there, standing in the hallway.

As soon as it happened, I started screaming, 'Don't hit me! I'm sorry! Don't hit me!' But I knew it was too late. Mr Baker started moving towards me but his wife reached me first. With her first whack she knocked me to the floor. With her second she winded me. The next thing I remember is being kicked, by Mrs Baker, then by Mr Baker and by Peter Baker.

Each kick sent a searing pain through my body. I felt a

powerful toe in my ribs but before I could scream another shoe planted itself against my shoulder. Another hit my neck, then crashed against my spine. I tried to curl up into a ball but the kicks were too quick. Every time I moved they kicked harder.

'Why are they doing this?' I thought. 'Why won't they stop?'

I managed to wrap my arms around my head but that was it. The rest of me was unprotected and the kicks showed no sign of stopping. Then one made contact with the back of my head.

And after that – nothing.

I think I must have slipped into unconsciousness. When I woke up I was in Peter's bed. I was wearing pyjamas and I was dry. My head was throbbing and I couldn't face opening my eyes. I could hear my foster parents arguing as I came round. She wanted to call an ambulance but he was saying they couldn't. I don't know where Peter was.

The memories of being hit came back to me. I tried to cough and instantly regretted it. I thought my stomach would split. It also alerted the Bakers that I was awake.

'See if he can walk,' Mr Baker said. I was lifted into an upright position and dragged to the side of the bed. Mrs Baker put her sweaty arm around my waist and pulled. I staggered to my feet but as soon as she let go I toppled backwards on to the bed. I think my legs were working fine although my head was whirling too much to keep my balance. But I was alive.

The Bakers realized this too. 'He's fine,' Mr Baker said.

I might have broken every bone in my body but he could see I wasn't going to die there and then and that was good enough for him.

I wish I'd had the foresight to fake serious injury. I really wanted to be taken to hospital. Those weeks recovering from my mastoidectomy were the calmest of my life. Now they could see I had survived their attack, the Bakers returned to their normal scary selves. Mr Baker leaned into me and said, 'Remember this night, boy. Remember this is what happens when you scream. You understand?'

I nodded. It was one of the first times he had ever spoken directly to me. I could never forget those words. I knew that he meant every one of them.

That was when I decided I had to run away.

It wasn't the best of plans. I went to school the next day, tried to steal food at lunchtime, then just didn't go home. I didn't have anywhere else to go so I ran as fast as my injured body would let me to the only place I knew: the Children's Cottage Homes. The air-raid shelter in the woods was the only place I could think of where I could sleep.

Adrenalin was running through me as I arrived. Sneaking over the fence without anyone noticing was the easy part. After all, I'd been sneaking out of it since I was five. Negotiating inside the grounds was trickier. It was still so light and any boy spotted playing in this area would arouse suspicion because tea was almost certainly being served in the Cottages. As I got near the shelter I froze. Voices. I could definitely hear voices.

I strained my ears. There was the snap of a twig. Then a movement in the trees to my right. The footsteps were getting closer. Someone was walking towards me. If it was Mr Bone or Mr Stanley, the gardeners, I was done for. I looked around desperately for cover but I was exposed. Any second now I would be seen. So much for running away.

'Oi, Cummings! What are you doing here?'

The relief in my chest when I heard that boy's voice! He was a friend of mine from East 3 Cottage. The other voices were those of more boys hiding in the shelter. I recognized one of them as my friend Ralph Mitchell. I told them I'd run away and they asked to hear stories about the monstrous Bakers, so I told them some. As darkness fell they had to leave but some of them promised to smuggle me out some food. As far as they were concerned it was an exciting adventure. As far as I was concerned it was survival.

They were as good as their word. Shortly after eight in the morning I heard footsteps running through the leaves. The boy had two slices of toast. I couldn't remember the last time I'd had such a hearty breakfast. I nearly cried with gratitude. I didn't see anyone else until six that night when another boy appeared with a pocketful of potatoes. He apologized for the poor choice but I was so grateful.

My first night was thrilling. I couldn't sleep easily but I knew this time it was through excitement, not fear. Even though it was pitch black inside the shelter, the brightness of the moon illuminated the narrow window hole enough to tame my apprehension. I felt so comfortable I even walked around. I couldn't get over how tranquil the woods were and how beautiful the moon was in the dark sky. I'd honestly never noticed either before. The heavens had never seemed important in my life. That night it was the most important thing in the world.

The next night was less peaceful. Now the initial excitement had worn off I couldn't help being reminded of how similar the shelter was to my cell in Queen's Road. The room seemed smaller than it had done the night before and the darkness was blacker somehow. A fierce gale blew through the woods and the howling from the wind and the regular cracking of branches torn to the ground exacerbated my fears and ensured a nervous and restless night. Not once, though, did I think, 'I wish I was at the Bakers'.'

On the third night the weather was balmy and I decided to be bold and sleep outside the shelter. For the first couple of hours I just stared at the stars and marvelled at the changing shapes of the clouds. If I stared long enough, I could imagine they were faces or buildings. Then I started to pretend they were toys for me.

I was in heaven that night. I thought I was the happiest kid in the world. Then a noise behind me shattered my calm. In a split second I went from daring adventurer to timid schoolboy. The noises – what were they?

'What if it's Germans hiding after the war?' I thought. A second later I was scrabbling inside the shelter and leaning against the thick wooden door. I fell asleep like that. I had been bent in the same position so many times in the Bakers' cupboard that it was second nature to me.

That was my last night in the woods. A boy was followed running down the next morning with my breakfast and within an hour Mr Maynard had arrived to pick me up. He always looked so scary to me because he wore a suit and carried a briefcase. That morning as he dragged me back to the main entrance, Hitler himself couldn't have been more threatening.

'What do you think you're doing, Leslie? Do you have any idea what you've put us through?'

'No one's worried about me,' I sulked.

'Don't be stupid, boy. The Bakers have been very upset,' he said. 'I don't suppose you thought about all the people your selfish behaviour was hurting? Do you have any idea of the trouble you've caused me?'

In awe of Mr Maynard as I was, something about this conversation gave me the nerve to respond. Before I could stop myself I blurted out, 'I ran away because Mrs Baker beats me and makes me sleep in a cupboard. Why do you think I came here? I hate this place. But it's better than there.'

I was shaking with rage as I shouted. Months of pain and resentment came pouring out. All the while Mr Maynard tutted and tried to calm me. I think he was worried about other people at the Cottages hearing. Eventually I ran out of words and he marched me to his car.

'If I were you, young man, I'd be grateful that a good family like the Bakers are prepared to take you in. Now, don't let me hear another word about this. And make sure you apologize to Mrs Baker for the aggravation you've caused her.'

I arrived back at Queen's Road just in time to leave for school. Mr Maynard stayed to talk to Mrs Baker while I was gone. I dreaded going home that night. 'What on earth is she going to do to me now?' I thought. But when I got in Mrs Baker let me sit at the small table in the kitchen and even gave me a small meal. I couldn't understand it. 'I should run away more often,' I decided.

Whatever had caused my foster mother to tolerate my escape that night, it was quickly apparent to me that things were back to normal in the Baker house as soon as I woke up the following day. I tried my best to keep out of their way, I really did. I think, though, that they resented me even more for the inconvenience caused by my absconding and they went out of their way to trick me into warranting fresh punishment. It was Peter who succeeded. I watched him leave the kitchen with a glass of water. As soon as he saw me he tipped the glass and let the water splash all over the linoleum floor. I knew from the look on his face what he was planning.

'Mum!' he yelled, even though I could hear Mrs Baker behind him. 'He's spilled my drink.'

Mrs Baker flew out of the kitchen as though she was in a race. I've never seen her move so fast. She took one look at the damp patch on the floor and pointed at the cupboard under the stairs.

For once I didn't dare resist. I walked slowly over to the door and climbed inside, broken. Before she shut the door Mrs Baker said, 'If I hear one word out of you – if you so much as scream once – you will regret it.'

I knew she meant it.

As I sat in the darkness, scenes from *The Phantom of the Opera* kept coming into my mind and I wanted to cry out. But I didn't dare. It was as though they were hoping I would give them an excuse to punish me again.

'They want to kill me,' I thought. 'But I'm not going to let them.'

I concentrated so hard on biting my lip to keep my fears in check when I was in that cupboard that I actually drew blood. Another tactic to ward off a panic attack was to drum my fingers on the stairs above my head. Tap-tap-tap, over and over again, just to keep my focus on something other than my pain and fear. At other times I invented friends to talk to in there, or I'd rock myself backwards and forwards as though I was on a seesaw.

Every time I grew used to one of my distraction tactics I had to concoct another one. I went through a phase of counting the knots in the wood by running my fingertips along the beams as if I was reading Braille, then trying to name each and every one of them. I also became proficient at taking my clothes off in the dark, placing each item on the floor in front of me, then putting them all back on, one by one. It was so cramped in there that just stretching my arms or legs to pull on clothes took minutes. That exercise kept me quiet for hours.

Not everyone was happy that I was so obedient. I think Peter was terribly disappointed that my beatings had dried up to such an extent. He did his best to lure me into crying out, mainly by kicking the cupboard door when I had fallen asleep. He hoped I would wake up crying so he could bring an angry Mrs Baker down on top of me.

There was a thin crack in the cupboard door. Hardly any light could get through it but if I propped my head at the right angle I could just about see out. Once I was peering through when Peter decided to kick the door again. I didn't see his foot coming until it was too late. It sent the door flying back into my face and gave me a black eye for the rest of the week. I didn't dare tell anyone how I'd come by it. The Bakers would cover the crack if they knew I could see out.

After a few days in the cupboard I was allowed back into my bed on the metal trunk. This gave Peter the opportunity to throw things at me to keep me awake but at least I could stretch out and get a few hours' sleep. It wasn't long, however, before even this privilege began to get me into trouble.

I remember washing in the bathroom when Mrs Baker called me angrily into the bedroom. I knew I hadn't wet the bed so what could she want? When I found her she was standing by the bed and holding my pillow.

'What's this?' she demanded. She pointed to a small damp patch on the pillow.

I honestly didn't know. I had probably dribbled in the night during one of my nightmares. How was I meant to know?

'I know what it is,' she said mysteriously. 'You're a dirty, dirty boy. I'm going to get Mr Baker for you.'

A few minutes later Mr Baker was in the room as well. They both pored over the pillow. 'He's been playing with himself, that's what that is,' the man said after close scrutiny. I heard the words but I didn't know what they meant. I hadn't played with anyone.

Mr Baker edged over to me and spoke quietly. 'This won't do, boy, this won't do at all. You need to be taught a lesson. Come with me.'

I followed him out of the room and downstairs. My head was awash with ideas of 'playing with myself'. I couldn't work it out. What games can you play on a pillow?

I realized that Mr Baker had stopped outside the front room. In all my time at Queen's Road I had never seen that door open.

'In,' he ordered. I stepped inside and saw a neat room with a brown sofa and a large armchair, plus a few pictures on the wall. The window looked out to the front yard and the linoleum on the floor was the same as in the hallway. It didn't look as if people ever came into the room.

I noticed that Mr Baker had seated himself in the

armchair. He looked different, more menacing than usual. He was glaring at me, just like he had when he'd first clapped eyes on me. I felt uncomfortable and he could see it. Maybe that was the punishment he had in mind for me.

I soon found out it wasn't.

'Take your clothes off, boy,' he ordered. Take my clothes off? Why? I hadn't wet myself. Everything was dry.

'I said, take your clothes off!'

I hastily yanked my pyjama top over my head so I was only wearing the bottoms. Mr Baker stared at me, just like he had first done when he came back from the Navy. 'And the rest,' he said. I made pulling my trousers down take as long as I could. It was cold but that's not the reason why I started to shiver. Whatever punishment he had in mind was going to hurt if it hit my bare skin. I looked furtively around for a weapon. There was no stick or anything it looked like he could hit me with. 'It must be here somewhere,' I thought.

Mr Baker shuffled in his chair and said, 'Come here, boy.' I stepped forward slightly. As soon as I was within reach, he sprang up and grabbed my arms and pulled me against his chair. Instinctively I started wriggling to escape. 'Stay still,' he hissed but I struggled even harder. He began to grunt with the effort and froth appeared on his top lip. I had no idea what he was doing. Why wasn't he hitting me? Why was he making those funny noises?

I threw all my weight backwards and caught him off guard. I felt my arms burn as I slipped out of his grasp but before I could turn, he had me again, this time in a proper grip. I felt a kick in my shins and I fell to the floor, crushed by his powerful hands. Only then did he release one of my arms. As I struggled to my feet I noticed his breathing had changed. His face was full of an expression I'd never seen before.

Panic hit me like a jab in the ribs. I needed to run but I couldn't move. I had a terrible feeling about what was happening but I couldn't explain what it was.

All I knew for certain was that Mr Baker had undone his trousers and his right hand was pulling something out of his underwear.

'Come here,' he said. 'You need to be taught a lesson.'

NINE: *Leave Him to Me*

For the first few years that I was being hit at the Children's Cottage Homes, I didn't realize anything was wrong. Growing up without a father didn't strike me as odd either. That was the only life I knew. I thought it was the same for everyone. Those were the rules and it didn't occur to me to question them.

But when I saw Mr Baker masturbating himself in front of me I knew instinctively that it wasn't right.

I had never seen an erect penis before. It took me a few seconds to realize that was what I was looking at. I knew from overhearing playground talk among other boys that penises changed shape at certain times although I was too young to have experienced it myself.

That's why at the time I couldn't comprehend what I was being punished for. I didn't understand it then but Mrs Baker had thought I had used my pillow to climax. Yet I was physically too immature to do anything of the sort. Whatever the damp stain was, it wasn't my semen.

Mr Baker was moving his hand up and down his penis and started shouting how dirty I was and how he was going to make me repent. It was so loud it must have been heard all through the house. At the same time he dragged my arm towards his lap.

'Hold it,' he said quietly, and sank his fingers into my wrist to make sure I understood. I resisted but he twisted my arm until I thought it would snap. I had no choice. Gingerly I reached out. 'What does he want me to do?' I thought. Whatever it was, I knew it was wrong, wrong, wrong. But what were my options? At the same time as he yanked my arm downwards, he bucked his groin up in his seat until my small hand was wrapped around him. His own rough fingers clamped over the top of mine and he forced me to mimic his rhythm. Up and down, up and down.

I was scared. I knew I shouldn't be doing this. Why was he making me?

I thought I would be sick but I hadn't eaten anything to throw up. I had never been so close to him and I hated it. His face was sweating, and he kept frowning. He would shout insults about me one minute, then whisper. Sometimes I couldn't make out the words. They were more like little grunts, animal noises, sometimes drowned out by his rasping, loud breathing. I had no idea what was going on. I didn't know what I was supposed to be doing. And I didn't know when it would stop.

From where I was standing, it looked as though Mr Baker was actually in pain. His face was contorted in discomfort and his eyes were closed. Now I had a new worry. 'Is he going to punish me for hurting him?'

But my problems were about to get worse. Much worse.

Suddenly his eyes opened and through gritted teeth he said, 'Put it in your mouth, boy.'

'No.' I barely heard my own voice. It was so puny with fear. But I couldn't just give in.

'Do as I say!'

His right hand shot up to the side of my head and grabbed my neck. Then he pulled. It was no good. I couldn't fight him. I tried but he was too strong.

I think he was only in my mouth for less than a minute. He kept telling me, 'Keep still you little bastard, stop struggling,' but I wouldn't listen. I was in a blind panic. I began to choke. I didn't care what he did to me, I had to get away. In the end he let go of my head and I fell backwards and crawled quickly to the edge of the room, coughing and spitting, just trying to get the taste of him out of my mouth. I tangled myself trying to get my pyjamas back on too quickly. I thought my heart was going to burst through my chest.

When I dared to look back white liquid was coming out of Mr Baker's penis.

His eyes were closed and he was perfectly still. Was he dead? I was fixed to the spot with fear and fascination. 'I need to get Mrs Baker,' I thought.

Then the slumped body moved. Mr Baker wiped his hand on a handkerchief and fastened his trousers. He slowly eased himself out of the chair and went to the door. For a moment I thought he had forgotten about me as I sat pressed against the front wall. But as he opened the door he yelled, 'I hope you're going to think about what you've done, boy,' and marched straight over to the cupboard under the stairs. For once I didn't wait to be ordered inside. I shot past Mr Baker and climbed in while he was still shouting at me. The door slammed and he kicked it for good measure. I didn't care. For now my little prison was my sanctuary. He couldn't make me touch him if I was in there.

I hugged my knees up to my chest, closed my eyes and cried. What had just happened to me? Why did he make me do those things? Why didn't he just punch me? I understood it when they punched me. None of this made sense.

A short while later I heard him leave the house to go to his job as a labourer at the docks and my door was unlocked.

'You'll be late for school if you sit in there all day,' Mrs Baker scolded me. But I didn't move. The door hung ajar for several minutes and I ignored it till Mrs Baker returned and threatened to drag me out. I couldn't explain to myself what had happened. I didn't want to leave the cupboard. My whole world had turned upside down. 'I'm safe in here,' I thought. My biggest nightmare had suddenly become the only place I felt safe. I crawled out, my head still spinning with sickening images of what I had seen that morning. I was still short of breath. 'I've had enough,' I thought. I had to do something, but what? And then the answer came to me.

That was the day I would try to kill myself.

I went to school hungry as usual, but for once I didn't

forage through neighbours' bins or look for discarded drink bottles. I couldn't have kept a thing down, not that day. I don't remember what was taught or how I got home or what I did during the afternoon. All I recall is going to the bathroom at bedtime and picking up the box of sleeping tablets that my doctor had prescribed for my insomnia. I shook the box. There were several in there, although not as many as I hoped.

I don't think I planned to end my life. When you're that young you don't understand suicide and life and death. All I wanted to do was to hide, and the only way I could think of doing that was sleeping.

Normally I was given one tablet a night. I thought, 'If one tablet makes me sleep for one night, then ten tablets will make me sleep for ten nights.'

I knew the Bakers would call me lazy and shout at me later but I would deal with the consequences when I woke up. It seemed so simple to me. I didn't appreciate that an overdose of those tablets would mean that I might never wake up again.

The next thing I remember is Mrs Baker shaking me. I was lying in bed and her face was suspended over me like a big, red moon. I could see her mouth opening and shutting quickly. She looked as though she was shouting at me but I couldn't hear a word.

My next memory is of being in the kitchen. I don't know how long after taking the sleeping tablets this was. It's just the next event in my memory. Mr Maynard was there. That wasn't unusual – he called fairly regularly, although usually I was kept away from him. But there was someone else with him this time. It looked like my brother Richard.

That's when I knew I was still asleep.

I heard Mrs Baker tell Mr Maynard I had swallowed the sleeping tablets because 'he thought they were sweets'. Mr Maynard said he would put it in my report. In the meantime, he said, my brother Richard was going to move into Queen's Road with me.

It was true. He was really there, sitting at the table drinking a cup of tea, just like I had done on my first visit. Peter Baker was hanging around his mother's neck as she sat. I couldn't wait for the chance to speak to my brother. I just wanted to tell him, 'Run away! Don't come here!' but I didn't dare. In any case, I selfishly hoped he would be able to look after me now. He couldn't do that if he was living somewhere else.

Before Mr Maynard left he told us that my other siblings, Janet, Robert and Philip, were all being moved into another house nearby.

'You're all going to be together,' he said to us. 'You'll like that. Might even keep you out of trouble.'

I think he was trying to be nice. I don't know if it was his decision or that of the Children's Cottage Homes committee, whom he reported to, but the fact that all the Cummings children were to be within walking distance of one another seemed like a good thing. I think he was disappointed that I didn't look happier. Why should I? The five of us had all lived close together at the Cottages but someone had made it impossible for us to even see one another.

The next day was a mixture of emotions for me. I was excited to have Richard there but I soon realized we didn't have much to say to each other. Apart from looking like an older version of me, he was almost a stranger. He had suffered at the Homes like I had and that had hardened him. He had learned to put himself first just to survive. Just like I had. And now the two of us were under the same roof, why would anything change?

I didn't tell him about what Mr Baker had made me do to him. Partly because I was ashamed. Partly because I thought if I never spoke about it I could pretend it was a bad dream. But there was a third reason: I didn't think he would care. We were children of the Homes. We never spoke about our punishments, not even among ourselves. That's how we survived.

The only thing Richard and I had in common was that we were both hated by the Bakers. Apart from that, we just happened to be thrown together. We might have been flesh and blood but where survival was concerned we were rivals. At mealtimes I watched enviously as Richard was allowed to sit at the small table while I was on the floor fighting Patch for scraps. He could have saved me some of his food but he didn't. Peter had moved into the spare room so Richard was given his bed while I had the metal trunk but he never offered to swap for one night. He could have stepped in when I was locked under the stairs but he never did.

He was looking out for number one and I couldn't blame him. I would have done exactly the same in his position.

When we were outside the Bakers' environment our behaviour towards each other improved. It was less 'every man for himself' than 'us two against the world'. Richard was given more food than I was but it was no amount for a growing lad, especially with the three-mile round trips we both had to make to school. If I could scavenge something in the street I would often share it with him and vice versa. For some reason Richard was sent to a different school to me, so we had an agreed meeting spot where the routes home converged. Many a time I remember approaching with empty hands praying that he would be holding something edible. I'm sure there were days when he devoured his finds by himself. I admit I was sometimes so desperate I couldn't wait to share. But we tried.

We earned a bad reputation in the town as thieves. I was banned from a couple of places. The local baker suffered the most. If he was lucky, I'd stand outside the shop just to smell the aroma of fresh bread. Other times temptation would get too great. I'd watch salivating through the door as loaves were piled up in the window, thinking, 'I'm going to have one of those.' A customer would go in and be served and while the baker was making the sandwich or taking the money I'd dash in, grab a loaf and scarper. At first he used to run after me, but once that bread was in my hands Jessie Owens couldn't catch me. I didn't stop running till I saw Richard waiting for me.

Sometimes the baker would see me hovering and chase me away with a stick before I could pounce. Once in a blue moon he did manage to lay his hands on me – but only by chance. My school route took me past the bakery and I was walking past on the opposite side of the road when I felt a heavy hand grab my neck.

'Gotcha, you ruddy little thief!'

I think he expected me to run or at least put up a fight, but I preferred to save my energy for races I could win. Still shouting, he swung his spare hand and cuffed me round the ear. It stung for hours but I didn't care. That's what I was used to. I'd trade a slap for a decent meal any day of the week.

A few weeks later I had my collar felt again. This time, though, Richard was walking behind me with a couple of his friends. Before the baker could really get a grip, Richard ran up and planted a kick square in the man's shin. He fell over and we both took off, laughing at the ripe language pouring out from behind us.

'If he does half the things he's threatening to do to me, it still won't be as bad as Mrs Baker,' I thought.

I don't know if it was because he was older and bigger or whether the Bakers just hated me more, but Richard was never treated as viciously as I was. Not while I was there, anyway. Sometimes, though, his age counted against him.

One day Peter Baker announced he wanted a cat so shortly afterwards he was given one by his adoring mother.

He loved that cat for a while but I think it scratched the furniture or bit him and he went off it. Mrs Baker told my brother to drown it.

'I don't want to,' he said. Seconds later she was chasing him around the kitchen with a rolling pin, shouting at him. I hid under the table, terrified for the poor cat, watching their legs crash past me. Eventually Mrs Baker grabbed hold of Richard and I saw him hit the floor across the other side of the room. He was still shouting 'No!' even as Mrs Baker punched and kicked him.

It was horrific to watch. I couldn't believe anyone could be so angry with another human being that they would hurt them so much. I remember my next thought vividly:

'I'm glad it's him and not me.'

I'm not proud today when I remember that. I was witnessing an assault on my own brother and it turned my stomach but I knew too well that if he weren't made to be the victim then I would be. I cry now thinking of that realization. When did I learn to not care about others? Was it in the Homes or with the Bakers?

Mrs Baker picked up the poor cat and shoved it into Richard's lap. Then she dragged them both over to the sink, which she'd already filled with water. It seemed to go on for ever. Even though he was still being smacked, Richard kept resisting. He'd dunk the cat for a few seconds then give in to its dreadful twisting and mewing cries. Then she'd hit him again and force him to do it properly. I could hear the cat fighting for its life underwater and I knew my brother's hands were going to kill it.

I watched transfixed and horrified. And grateful that it wasn't me.

Afterwards Richard was told to bury the cat in the garden, which he did, sobbing with every scoop of his shovel. I know he suffered a lot from the trauma of that afternoon yet I didn't envisage how it could get worse for me. But it did.

Peter Baker realized how terrified I'd been watching that poor animal's execution. I can't say he enjoyed seeing the cat's life snuffed out, but he definitely didn't mind it dying, and he always took pleasure seeing Richard and me beaten. While we both watched the garden burial he whispered to me, 'You're next.'

I span round. 'What?'

'Your brother's going to drown you and bury you in the garden. I heard Mum telling him to.'

Everything that I knew about Peter Baker should have told me it was another piece of malicious troublemaking. Unfortunately everything I knew about his mother told me it was not only plausible – it was probable. I begged Richard not to drown me and he told me not to be so stupid. But I'd seen the way he had held the cat's head underwater on Mrs Baker's orders. I became a nervous wreck for the next few days. It was no surprise to me when I wet my bed shortly after. I was banished to my cupboard for the entire weekend where at least I thought I would be safe. It didn't last.

There was a noise outside the door and I heard Peter's voice.

'He's coming to get you,' he said. 'He's already digging the hole in the garden.' Then he ran off, screaming with laughter.

I was crying in fear.

One of the techniques I developed at the Children's Cottage Homes was to recover as quickly as possible from each new attack and move on. If I dwelled on a problem or an argument or an injury I felt it would get into my dreams. I tried to con myself that some events never took place in the hope that they never would again. It was one of the reasons I was able to get up every morning.

I continued that approach in the Bakers' house as best I could. I used to cry myself to sleep at nights because of Mrs Baker's savagery but by the next morning I had put it out of my mind. Each new day always brought new problems. I needed to be alert to face them. I had to focus my energy on finding food for the day, whether it was stealing from the boys at school or raiding the Bakers' pantry when I thought I could get away with it.

It was different with Mr Baker's punishment, though. Try as hard as I could, it would not leave my mind. I could be thinking of anything else – stealing sweets, hiding from Peter, running away – but as soon as I closed my eyes I saw Mr Baker's perspiring face gurning at me. It was like being trapped in a nightmare. I am struggling to pull away from his lap and he's tugging me down, forcing my mouth on him. I open my eyes and realize it's not a dream. It's a memory.

Every day I thought about that event. I thought it was

the worst thing that had ever happened to me. I thought I would remember it until the day I died.

But I never thought it would happen again.

Mrs Baker and, before her, Aunt Ross always seemed to take delight in finding new methods to hurt me. It was like they planned it sometimes. They derived extra pleasure if I was caught unawares. I was rarely tormented the same way twice if they could think of something worse. I never thought about it but I assumed it would be the same with Mr Baker. When he summoned me back to that front room a few days later, my blood chilled. I couldn't speak. Every thought vanished from my mind. 'No, no, no,' I thought. 'Not again.'

I remember feeling numb as I stood there this time, naked once again. I could hear Mr Baker shouting about how dirty I was and why I needed to be punished but the words meant nothing to me. I felt him wrestle me into submission and I know I fought back, but it was as if I were watching myself being attacked. I think I was trying to pretend it wasn't happening, but there was nothing I could do to stop him.

He made me use my hand again, then he made me use my mouth. I remember the sensation of not being able to breathe, of wanting to be sick, and all the while his powerful hand on the back of my head trapped me there.

I couldn't see his face, but I didn't need to. I could picture it sweating and grimacing. I remember the smell of his vile, hairy body so close to me and I can still hear the hissing of his grunted commentary all these years later. 'Stop fighting, boy, that's it, that's right. Good boy.'

I was aware of Mr Baker's other hand landing on the top of my head but instead of pushing me down further he began to stroke my hair slowly. I was trying not to choke but I remember thinking his touch was surprisingly gentle. With every stroke he said again, 'You're a good boy, you're a nice boy.'

It seemed to last for ever this time. I couldn't escape, his grip was so tight. And then suddenly it got tighter as both hands grabbed me. I felt the man's entire body tense and a new, horrible sensation hit me. I knew instinctively that the white liquid I had seen on his hands yesterday was in my mouth. And I thought I was going to die.

Ten minutes later I was once again in my prison sanctuary, the foul taste still contaminating my mouth. After so long with the Bakers I never thought my life could become more painful but I knew that day it had. The punishment Mr Baker had dealt me was worse than anything Aunt Ross or Mrs Baker or the Superintendents or any teacher had ever subjected me to. And the most devastating aspect of it was the realization now that it wasn't a one-off. It was a ritual. I recognized the signs. He had punished me twice in a week in exactly same way.

This was going to be my new life. And there was nothing I could do to prevent it.

TEN: *Babes in the Wood*

The Bakers were guilty of starving me of food but they were also guilty of denying me something more important: affection. At the Children's Cottage Homes I always felt that the housemother Mrs Ingram was fond of me. She liked all our family. However unfair or vicious the other staff were, I could usually rely on her for warmth. She treated us respectfully, if not with actual love. She didn't pick on anyone or lash out if she was experiencing a bad day at work. It proved to me that bringing up children could be done with kindness, or the minimum of force.

This was brought home to me when I went to church with the Bakers and I would see all the 'normal' families enjoying one another's company. No one seemed scared. I'd dawdle home from school and watch as immaculately dressed boys and girls were helped into ostentatiously large cars by their equally well-turned-out parents. I'd hear them talking about the day's classes and quietly mimic their conversations to myself.

'Did you have a nice day at school, Les?'

'Yes, thank you, Mummy, it was delightful.'

It was silly, and if anyone heard me they probably

would have thought I was mad. It made me feel better, though.

Some days there were so many beautifully dressed children in Portsmouth that I couldn't face being near them. But it wasn't their clothes I was envious of, it was what the clothes meant. I'd see kids and parents take one look at me, dressed like some sort of street urchin in my oversized jumper and shorts, and either look away or – and this was the worst feeling in the world – look right through me. Again and again it happened, as though I didn't even qualify as a person.

'I've done it – I've really become invisible,' I thought.

Then I stopped letting it hurt me and I wove them into my fantasies. I'd see pretty girls with hair so beautifully groomed and shiny I wanted to reach out and touch it as they walked past me holding hands with some lucky boy. It hurt to realize I'd never be able to get that close. The best I could do occasionally was use my invisibility to my advantage and walk as close to a girl as possible and pretend she was accompanying me. 'Look at me,' I'd think, I'm not a nobody, I have a beautiful girlfriend and a family who loves me.' In this eight-year-old's dreams I was just like them.

One day I was leaning against a shop window daydreaming when a girl actually spoke to me and I froze. I remember just staring at her, in awe of this young goddess with perfect skin, hearing the words coming from her mouth but not understanding them. She was being nice to me and I wasn't used to it. Any other day I could stand by that window for an hour without anyone noticing I was there. But she had seen me, and I was so shocked I could barely reply.

By the time I spluttered an answer her elegantly attired mother, wearing lily-white gloves, had appeared and called her away. I remember kicking myself.

'Why didn't you talk to her, you idiot? She might have wanted her family to adopt you.'

It was a long shot, but I viewed anyone who showed the slightest kindness towards me as potential new parents. This didn't happen very often but it didn't stop my idyllic dreams. I spent hours in my cupboard under the stairs imagining being in the arms of a mother who would hold me close and whisper, 'I love you so very much' again and again. She'd pull my bedcovers over me, kiss me goodnight and say she couldn't wait to see me the next day. This mother actually creeps into my bedroom at night just to see if I'm all right.

Occasionally I dreamed of a father as well. I always struggled to picture a face but in my imagination he would hold my hand as he taught me how to fish or play tennis. He would tickle me when I wasn't looking and at night-time when he tucked me into bed he would tell me a story filled with pirates and pillow-fights.

In reality I knew full well I didn't have parents who loved me. But at least I had my brothers and sister and thanks to Mr Maynard they were all living near me again. When I heard the news I had hopes of us reuniting again.

Unfortunately Robert, Philip and Janet's foster home was no better than mine.

Once again it seemed to be run by the woman of the house. Maybe it was a result of women having to cope alone during the war, but their foster mother was as intimidating as Mrs Baker. The two women used to visit one another for tea during the afternoons and once my siblings had moved in I looked forward to them all coming over but their foster mother had other plans. I remember the first time she came after fostering the others. She took one look at me and said to Mrs Baker, 'Is he as lazy as my lot?'

'Lazy? He wrote the book on it. And he's nasty too. I advise you to beat it out of them before they cheek you. His brother's no better.'

I wondered why they both kept us if they hated us so much. It couldn't all be about the 20 shillings they received for each child, could it? But it was the only reason I could think of.

Shortly after that I tried to visit my siblings. Their foster mother answered the door.

'Oh, it's you. Did Mrs Baker send you?'

'No. I wanted to see my family.'

'Oh, did you now? Well, you can't. And if I see you in my house again I'll call the police.'

She slammed the door so hard I thought it would hit me. We were then told we weren't to speak to one another under any circumstances. We all knew the punishment if we were caught.

Two days later I bumped into Robert on my way to school. He was pleased to see me but we didn't have much to say. They were hardly fed anything, he said, and they had to do more chores than at the Homes. We were like two old soldiers comparing war stories although neither of us wanted to go into details. I think if you talk about something you make it real. We were both in some level of denial, trying to pretend our horrible lives weren't really happening, all the while knowing they were very true. We didn't crack a smile between us that morning and I didn't see him again for a few weeks.

The next time I saw him he was with Philip and Janet. They were all standing outside their house, facing the front door. Instead of giving them a key their foster mother made them wait outside after school, even if it was raining, until she came home. Once I came home from a school detention very late in thick snow and they were all standing there shivering.

It was a sickening sight. None of us ever looked healthy but the young ones seemed to be in a terrible state. Philip looked so pale and small as he hung on to Janet's hand. We were raised by our foster parents and the Cottages in a 'dog-eat-dog' environment but at that moment I saw that this was my family and they were the most important people in the world. I wanted so much to go over and kick the door down so they could all get some shelter from the weather, but I knew I never would.

'Who am I kidding?' I thought. 'We're all prisoners together.'

The best I could do for any of them was pass over tips on where to find food. I'd lived in the area the longest so I had a better grasp of which shops you could steal from without being caught. I had a list in my head of the shopkeepers who were the slowest runners. The local bakery lost even more stock shortly afterwards.

There was, however, one other thing I could suggest.

The first time I ran away from home was just after the *Phantom of the Opera* episode. I lasted three nights. The next time I tried to get away was less successful. I was walking past another school and I just slipped into a line of children queuing to go in. I don't know what I was hoping to achieve but I managed to sneak into the classroom. A few children stared at me but nobody said anything. When the teacher called the morning register I ducked and I even managed to stay long enough to get the daily glass of milk before I was discovered. Then I was given a clip round the ear and told to get back to my own class. I wandered once more to the safety of the Cottages but Mr Maynard knew where to find me this time.

Although my escapes had always ended quickly, I ate surprisingly well when I was away from the Bakers'. When I saw my sister Janet and brother Philip suffering so badly, I thought it was worth trying again – but this time with them.

We all did the usual trick of not going home after school one day, instead running straight to Victoria Park. I was so happy to be doing it with other people. It was suddenly a great adventure – and at eight years old I was the leader. We fashioned ourselves a small burrow under the railway bridge to sleep in and then I ventured back to the fish and chip shop in the town centre. I stood there for an hour begging for food, and eventually I took a decent haul back to the others.

It was a bizarre yet idyllic set-up. I suppose if we'd bumped into Robert or Richard they would have come along and taken charge. But as it was, Janet was naturally mothering Philip and I found myself in the role of provider – almost a father figure in the little woodland family we'd created. Janet even showed a talent for housekeeping. When I returned with food for breakfast the next morning I discovered her using a large branch to sweep the ground around our den.

I was quite successful in getting food as I'd recently discovered a new source. If I lurked near the railway station's tea vendor I could pick up quite a few crusts and leftovers from the staff's sandwiches. If I was really lucky, I could steal something more substantial from time to time. The fact that our base was under the railway bridge also paid dividends. Every so often we'd find half-eaten apples or cakes that passengers had discarded from the train windows as they approached the station.

I was exhilarated by the challenge of supporting my siblings. I couldn't remember clearly ever living with them before. I think Janet enjoyed it as well. Philip, though, was still too young to appreciate his freedom. Even though we all cuddled together at night for warmth and courage, the bitter chill meant sleep was intermittent at best. No amount of leaves could keep my toes from freezing. Philip suffered the most.

'I'm cold,' he complained. 'I want to go home.'

We both cuddled him and tried to explain that the struggle was worth it, but even though he'd taken his fair share of beatings at the foster home, his memory was too short-term to believe us.

'I just want to go home,' he kept saying. Soon the decision was taken out of our hands.

On our third morning as we lay under the leaves we were awoken by two policemen. Instinctively we all thought we would be told off but I remember clearly how they both just laughed at the sight of us.

'If it isn't the Babes in the Wood,' one of them said.

We were taken to the police station before being picked up once again by Mr Maynard. Even he managed a smile when speaking with the original officers before we left.

'Babes in the Wood, indeed,' he said. 'That's going in your file.'

Something the file didn't get, I'm sure, was how Mrs Baker hit me so hard on the back of the head when I got home that I thought I would pass out. My mind went black and I felt sickness well up from nowhere. I staggered silently towards the doorway to the cupboard and climbed in meekly as Mrs Baker shouted in my face. I didn't hear a word she was saying. I was concentrating too hard on not throwing up.

I didn't know what normally went into Mr Maynard's

files but I imagined my adventures took up quite a lot of space. As well as trying to run away from my foster home, I had complained to him several times about my treatment at Queen's Road. I had serious bed-wetting problems, the Bakers accused me of masturbating, I was known for screaming a lot and a GP had prescribed me a course of sleeping tablets – on which I had later overdosed. On the other hand, maybe he didn't write any of this down.

'That would explain why he still lets me stay here,' I thought. No other reason occurred to me at that time.

Mr Maynard would also have received increasingly bad reports from my school. If I wasn't being held back for detention after school I was being sent to the headmaster's office to receive the cane. I didn't mind either, really. The detentions kept me longer at school, which reduced the time I might spend at home, and the cane made no difference to my life. Part of its usage was as a deterrent and I could see it working on other boys. If they knew they had six of the best coming their way at lunchtime, by the time they knocked on the head's door they were gibbering wrecks. The cane had done its work before it even hit them – although it was still used anyway. That didn't work on me, though. Pain was part of my normalized daily life. At least I knew it was coming. At the Bakers' and at the Cottages, I never had any warning that I was going to be assaulted. It was almost a relief having such a structure to the punishment system.

The caning itself usually brought water to my eyes but I never cried out. Not like the other boys who I'd hear begging and screaming as I waited for my turn. If Mrs Baker saw you hurting she did it harder. I always hid my feelings for as long as I could bear it and getting through half a dozen lashes of the strap or cane was relatively straightforward.

I was always in trouble. Sometimes it was because I'd been caught raiding the bins again. Occasionally it was for stealing someone else's food. As far as I was concerned, these were all things worth risking punishment for. Sometimes, though, I distinctly recall not wanting to go home and so I would actually swear or throw my books around just to provoke teachers into holding me back after class. I didn't realize at the time that all these breaches of regulations were written down and passed to Mr Maynard. He was always well informed about my latest escapades.

He was even informed about my constant 'masturbation'. I denied it but he didn't believe me. He never listened to a word I said in Mrs Baker's kitchen.

Mrs Baker was such a dominant person, even with her own family, and she very much called the shots. She never laid a finger on her beloved Peter, but he never questioned anything she asked him to do. It was the same with her husband. He would always come running if she so much as clicked her fingers. The only time she gave him uninterrupted space, in fact, was when he went into the front room. Once that door was closed, she never entered. She wouldn't even try to speak to him from elsewhere in the house as usual. And that meant that I was always trapped in there with him. I could stare at the door all day and I knew that no one would open it. There was only one way to leave the room and that was when Mr Baker had produced his white stuff.

The first few times I was dragged into the room happened after my supposed 'semen' had been discovered on the pillow in my bed. After that he became more methodical. Two afternoons a week were put aside for my 'punishment'. I would come in from school and he would tell Mrs Baker he was going to educate me on proper behaviour. It didn't matter if I had detention or not. He would always be waiting for me. I couldn't get out of it.

I couldn't work out why he always punished me like this. When his wife hit me, she got pleasure from it. I could tell. But in that front room, Mr Baker always seemed to be as uncomfortable as me. His face was always so vivid and sweating.

I don't know when I began to suspect that what we were doing was a type of sex. I didn't understand the subject at all. It must have been to do with hearing schoolfriends discuss the birds and the bees and working it out from there. The only problem was they were always talking about men and women. I wasn't a woman – I wasn't even a man yet. What did he want from me?

I asked myself the same questions for weeks. What did he want from me? What could I do for him?

After a few months it became even more confusing. It was a Saturday. I remember washing the kitchen floor while Mrs Baker was out. Richard and Peter were also elsewhere. As soon as I'd finished I was planning to raid the larder for something to eat. I'd spent the night under the stairs and missed lunch and supper. I was just dreaming of what I'd find when Mr Baker came into the kitchen and walked straight over my clean, wet surface. I didn't look up but I could sense his eyes penetrating me like they always did when I worked. I didn't wait for him to say anything because he never spoke to me outside the front room.

This time was different.

'You hungry?' he said.

I didn't answer. He knew I was hungry. I was always hungry.

'I've got fish,' he said.

I looked up. What was he talking about? Why was he telling me this?

'I've got fish,' he said again. 'In there.' He pointed to the front room. 'Want some?'

Then I realized.

He'd never given me a choice before. No one ever gave me a choice on anything. I was only given instructions. But I knew what he was asking now and for the first time I knew I could say, 'No.'

But I was so hungry. And he stroked my hair so gently sometimes in that front room and told me I was a good boy. No one ever touched me like that. No one ever complimented me.

So I said, 'Yes.'

I've never admitted that story to anyone before. I think I've worried that people will think, 'I don't care how hungry you are or how starved of affection – I could never go through with that.' I agree. I can't imagine being so broken that I would think of entertaining that proposition. But I know it happened. And I know it happened many times after that, especially at a weekend when I could be made to go for two days without being fed and without the chance to steal food. Mr Baker traded food for sexual pleasure and I went along with it time after time.

Nothing else changed, however. An hour later I was always still locked in my sanctuary beneath the stairs, disgusted with myself. Yes, I hated the feeling of being trapped in that tiny space. Yes, I hated Mr Baker. But I hated myself as well.

Once they began, my punishment sessions always followed the same patterns: the same threats, the same squeezing so hard and so long that I felt cramps well up in my body, the same pressure on my neck, then the same caresses, the same gentle words, the same hand and mouth forced on to his penis. Only on two occasions that I recall did it deviate.

I was still subjected to the usual claustrophobic hugs and he made me masturbate him for a while. Then he pushed me away. What was going on? Had I done something wrong? Was he going to hit me?

'Get on the floor,' he ordered.

I sat down.

'On your stomach. Face down. Do it.'

I obeyed.

I didn't know what to expect. I could hear Mr Baker

moving behind me. I felt the rough fabric of his knees plant either side of my legs. I tensed instinctively.

Then winced.

He was touching my naked bottom. But it wasn't his hands. Something hard and very cold was being placed between my legs. I had no idea what it was. I didn't know what he was trying to do. Then I felt a sharp tearing pain and it was inside me, suddenly red-hot.

'No!'

I couldn't help crying.

'Quiet!' Mr Baker spat. 'Or else.'

I bit my lip like I'd done so often before, just to prevent a scream. The burning sensation inside me was so painful but I was helpless.

Eventually he stopped. I was pulled to my feet and we continued where we'd left off. My whole body felt different, unnatural almost. I scoured the room for the mysterious item that had penetrated me but I couldn't see anything. Whatever it was, he had put it away. For weeks later, every time I was ordered into the room I dreaded it being used again. Apart from one later occasion, it never was but Mr Baker had succeeded in making me feel almost 'lucky' to only masturbate him with my hands and mouth.

I don't know if Peter Baker knew what took place during that room but from some of his behaviour I began to suspect he did. I always tried to think of other things while I was being subjected to Mr Baker's wishes and I often thought I could hear someone outside the door. Was it him peeping through the keyhole? Maybe he just listened and worked it out for himself. Or perhaps he had his own experiences?

From the day I had arrived in the house, Peter had loved nothing more than stopping me sleep. Usually this took the form of kicks and prods and shouts. Now, though, he developed a new tactic. I was awoken dozens of times by a pain in my groin. He would never be there, but I'd gradually piece it together. Peter was groping my penis in my sleep. I don't know why. Had he seen his father do it to me? Had anyone ever done it to him? Or had he thought of it all by himself?

There was another trick he lifted straight from Mr Baker's book of torture. I was clearing the fireplace at the time when he came into the room with a sandwich.

'Are you hungry?'

Those exact words were an electric jolt through my brain.

'Why?'

'I've got this sandwich. Want a piece?'

Of course I wanted a piece. I would have eaten his leg if I'd thought I would have got away with it. He held the sandwich out. I could smell the horseradish and beef filling. I felt my mouth salivate. Then, just as I was about to take a giant bite, he pulled it away and ran off laughing.

The next time he pulled that stunt there was a variation. He really did let me eat the food – but in return for something.

I didn't think he was capable of punishing me in the way his father had but what else could he mean?

'What do you want?' I asked.

'I want you to knock that vase on to the floor.'

I looked over to where the glass vase was standing on the kitchen table. I could nudge it easily. It might even work if I just brushed accidentally into the side of the table. But why would I do that?

We both knew the reason. I would smash the vase, Peter would immediately then tell his mother. And she would exact her revenge on me as painfully as possible.

And that's exactly what happened.

But at least I got to eat.

I can't remember where my brother Richard was during these times. He never seemed to be around when I was punished in the front room and I don't think he saw half the beatings I took in the house. He was old enough to be out later. Maybe that was the reason. One thing that troubles me half a century later is whether the attacks by Mr Baker would have taken place if my brother had been in the house. I genuinely don't know.

On one thing I was adamant, though: none of this would have happened to me if I'd been allowed to live with my mother. I couldn't understand how she had let it happen to me. When I arrived at the Bakers' house, I'd been blissfully ignorant of how I'd ended up at the Children's Cottage Homes in the first place. It was Peter Baker who put me straight. Mr Maynard must have told Mrs Baker, who had of course shared it with her son.

I remember being informed by him, 'Your mum's been in prison. She's a nasty criminal.'

I worked out with Richard that he wasn't joking for once. We'd suspected, of course, and as I'd got older the memories of those scary men who'd taken us to the Homes had crystallized. The men were policemen. And policemen got involved when someone had broken the law. Robert had worked it out ages ago but I think we all chose not to believe him – even though if Mum was in prison she had an excuse for not rescuing us. Hearing Peter call her a criminal now made it seem too real to ignore.

I wanted to hit him as hard as his mother hit me, but I was too dazed to move. These days the only thoughts in my head were food, food and running away to get food – in that order. All the questions that burned me up every day I lived in the Homes had been relegated to further back in my mind. Suddenly they all came jumbling to the front. As far as we knew, Mum wasn't in prison at the moment, so why were we forced to live like this while she was out there, in another house, without us? Didn't she love us? Was it something I'd said to her? Something I'd done that made her not want to find me?

Richard and I spoke about it for the rest of the day but we didn't get anywhere and neither of us felt happier. As bedtime approached, my regular concerns became more pressing and angry thoughts of my mother were consigned to the backburner once more. Until the next time.

A good day for me was one when I had at least one meal to eat. A great day meant I managed to eat and not get beaten. There were very few of those.

My attempts at running away from the Bakers were

always short-lived but that didn't stop me scheming. I was always alert to a new hidey-hole where Mr Maynard wouldn't think of looking. Then one day after school I had a brainwave. I couldn't believe I hadn't thought of it before. I would tell the police.

It wasn't something I planned to do. I was walking along with my eyes fixed on the pavement as usual, desperately wiling a Sunday roast to appear on the floor in front of me, or at least a discarded pastry. I reached a busy junction and waited for the policeman who was directing the traffic to signal for pedestrians to cross. I watched him on his box for ages, and the more I stared, the more I marvelled at how important and powerful this single man was. With one wave of his hand he could make a dozen cars roar to life. Everyone listened to a policeman.

That's when it occurred to me.

I looked right, then dashed across the road to where the policeman was stationed in the middle. It took a few seconds for him to notice me.

'I want to report a crime!' I shouted.

'Pardon, young man?' he called down.

'I said, I want to talk to you about some people who are hurting me and making me do things to them that I don't want to do.' In about sixty seconds flat I poured out everything that the Bakers had done to me – and made me do to them.

It must have looked bizarre. Any driver being summoned by that point officer would have done a double-take when they saw this skinny kid standing there as well, in floods of tears and haranguing this poor policeman who had to keep directing traffic throughout.

'Look, I can't talk now,' he said. 'Wait on the kerb and I'll come over in ten minutes.'

I hadn't expected that. I picked my way back through the free-flowing traffic and waited. Would he really stop directing the traffic just to speak to me? I wouldn't hold my breath.

But he did. He walked over to where I was perched on the kerb, lifted me up and carried me to a police phone further up the street. He was a giant of a man, really smart in his dark-blue uniform, and as I listened to him speak I experienced an odd sensation. I actually felt safe. After the call he held my hand and we walked to the police station. All the while I gabbled my story, throwing random horrific memories up at him but feeling the happiest little boy in the world.

'He believes me,' I thought. 'He's actually going to help me.'

Seconds later I had the same thought I always did when I met a stranger I felt comfortable with. 'I wish he could be my father.'

I was very nervous going into the police station. All the men there were dressed the same as my hero but they didn't look half as friendly. He sensed I was worried and told me to relax. I was taken into a room and we sat there talking to another officer while a lady brought us drinks. After a while the other man left the room. My policeman said, 'Don't worry, we're going to sort everything out.'

My heart leapt when I heard those words.

In my mind everything was so straightforward. The next time that door opened I would see Mr and Mrs Baker and their son all in handcuffs. They would be crying and the policeman would force them to apologize to me. That was definitely what was going to happen. I could barely contain my excitement as I waited for the door to swing open once more.

When it did I couldn't have been more disappointed. Standing next to the other policeman was the unmistakable figure of Mr Maynard.

How had this happened? I thought the policeman had believed me. From the way he was looking at me, he still did. I watched him speak to his colleague and then they both left the room. I stared incredulously at Mr Maynard. How had the Bakers talked their way out of this one? I couldn't believe it when he told me. Apparently I was angry because I'd been kept in late after school and so I had concocted a mass of wicked lies about my loving foster family.

On the journey back to the Bakers' I feared the worst. I honestly imagined I would be dead before Mr Maynard's car had pulled away from number 258. But nothing happened. I wasn't beaten, just sent up to bed with no supper. That actually passed as a not bad day.

The only reaction I got from them the next day was

silence. Nobody put a finger on me. They all just ignored me, which I enjoyed. Over the next few days, however, my treatment from Mr and Mrs Baker gradually returned to its usual levels.

One thing was different, though. A few weeks after the policeman incident Mr Maynard arrived to take me away with him in his car. He told me we were going to see a special kind of doctor called a psychiatrist who would help me with my problems. I couldn't imagine what kind of doctor could help me with those, but I was happy to speak to him. The medical profession in the 1950s ranked just below royalty. A lot of people felt honoured to be seen by them.

I was confused as soon as I arrived at the St James Hospital. The psychiatrist, Mr Haffner, seemed to believe I had run for police aid because I had been given a detention at school. I quickly told him the real version of events and he wrote lots of notes on his pad. He was also aware of my sleeping problems and the overdose I'd taken. He even knew I'd told my headmaster about my problems at home and that I'd been called a liar. It was all there on my records. Other people had concluded I was a 'difficult child'. It was this man's job to work out why.

It didn't feel like being at a doctor's because as soon as I got there I was given a lot of toys to play with.

'Just play with them,' Mr Haffner said. 'Have fun.'

At first I could sense him watching everything I did, and memories of Mr Baker stalking me silently around the house came into my mind. I was soon distracted by the planes and cars. I'd never seen so many great toys and after ten minutes I was disappointed to be interrupted by lots of questions.

'What is your favourite toy?'

'This one.'

'What do you like about it?'

'It's fast.'

'Is there any toy you don't like?'

'I don't like that one.'

'Why don't you like it?'

It went on like this for some time. Then he said, 'Leslie, do you know where your mother is?'

'She's dead.'

Somehow being an orphan sounded better than being abandoned.

'According to my notes, Leslie, it says here your mother placed you in care.'

'Yes,' I said, 'then she died the day after that.'

I don't know how, but at the end of the session the psychiatrist reached a conclusion. Years later I discovered what it was: 'He is of course basically a deprived and affectionless child'. He was most clear, however, that 'the present foster home is, I think, a very good one'. All of my problems, in his view, could be pinned on what he called my 'habit insomnia'.

I was told nothing of this at the time. As far as I was concerned I wasn't going to be helped by the medical community any more than I was by the constabulary or the committee who ran the Children's Cottage Homes. I certainly couldn't trust my school. I remember being called into the headmaster's office and interrogated about my behaviour.

'What are you trying to prove, Cummings? You don't listen, everyone says you're rude, and you're always running out of your lessons without permission.'

I stared at my feet and let the words wash over me. He couldn't say anything to hurt me. But then I thought, why not? So I answered.

'It's because I'm so hungry all the time.'

'Don't you eat your dinners? Have you got a problem, boy?'

'I'm not given any food here and I don't get anything at home,' I shouted. 'And if I take anything I get punched and kicked and locked up in a cupboard under the stairs. If you don't believe me, look!' And I lifted up my jumper sleeve to show a large black bruise.

I was shaking as I pulled my jumper back down. It had taken a lot for me to be so honest.

The head thought I was a liar and gave me detention.

In the weeks following my brush with the police and the psychiatrist my behaviour deteriorated. I didn't plan it. I certainly didn't set out to be a pain. I can only put it down to feeling let down first by the police and then by the medical profession. They could both have rescued me from the Bakers. They both elected to look the other way.

I began to steal for fun as well as of out of desperation. Pens, watches, toys, newspapers, hats – anything that would be missed by its owner. I swore at nice-looking people just to shock them. My lowest point came one afternoon as I walked back from school. On the other side of the road I saw a boy of about nine, the same age as me. Unlike me, he looked happy. Something in my brain clicked, and I ran across the road and as the boy began to smile a friendly 'hello' at me, I punched him in the mouth. He held his face and didn't make a sound. We both stood there looking at each other for what seemed like an eternity. He slowly walked away, nervously checking over his shoulder every so often. I waited until he was out of sight and then laughed. What had I done? Why had I done it? Why didn't I feel any remorse for this random act of violence?

I shuddered as I contemplated the answer. I was becoming like the Bakers. Picking on Patch the dog was one thing – attacking another human being was something only Hilda Baker would do.

I was more determined than ever: 'I have to get away from them. I don't want to be like them. This isn't right.'

I still couldn't work out an escape plan that would work. Then unexpectedly one fell into my lap.

One beautiful day in January 1954, Mrs Baker told me I was going to be sent back to the Children's Cottage Homes because they couldn't tolerate my bad behaviour any more. I assumed it was a trick, like Peter pretending my mother was at the door, so I didn't bother to get excited. The next day I was thrilled to see Mr Maynard enter the house.

'Come on, Leslie, get your things,' he said.

I disappeared and returned two minutes later with a small bag.

'All of them, boy – you can't be coming back here every five minutes to pick things up.'

I looked at the bag. Obviously Mr Maynard expected me to have more clothes but Mrs Baker hadn't bought me a stitch to wear since I'd arrived. The clothes I'd arrived in had been so baggy I'd actually grown into them and I had a pair of Richard's old trousers. That was it. I certainly didn't have any other possessions.

'That's all he's got, Mr Maynard,' she cut in. 'He tore everything else up in one of his temper tantrums. You know what he's like.'

Mr Maynard rolled his eyes. I wanted to scream out the truth but there was no point. No one ever believed me and on this occasion it might even delay things. I didn't want to be in that house another second longer than I needed to be. I didn't even want to risk waiting to say goodbye to Richard in case Mr Maynard changed his mind.

As we left I didn't look back. I didn't need to. Every single floorboard or speck of dust in that building would remain etched in my memory for as long as I live. The Bakers' faces would haunt my nightmares for years to come.

I felt a smile break over my face as I climbed into Mr Maynard's car.

I was two months short of my tenth birthday, and being sent back to the Children's Cottage Homes was the best present I could think of getting. Would I live to regret it?

Would I survive at all?

ELEVEN: *Hands Behind Your Back, Snot Rag*

As we drove back to the Children's Cottage Homes, Mr Maynard attempted as usual to engage me in conversation. I didn't try very hard to be sociable. Everything I had ever confided in him in the past had been ignored. As a nine-year-old the situation was very straightforward for me. For the last two and a half years Mr Maynard had kept me at 258 Queen's Road. I didn't know or care about a committee or the City Council or anyone else who may have been involved. He was the man I knew. He was the man I blamed.

Eventually he gave up trying to get me to speak. 'I don't know what we're going to do with you,' he said ruefully, and we continued the journey in silence.

I couldn't believe how excited I was to be heading for the Cottages. It was such a contrast from the last two occasions I had been driven there. I was so relieved to have escaped the clutches of the Bakers that I ignored all those memories from my first earlier stays. I had to believe the Homes had changed – because I certainly had.

It was a different Leslie Cummings being driven back

that day. There was nothing intentional about it, no master plan to alter myself and return. But I knew that while the last few years had weakened my body through virtual starvation, they had made me stronger psychologically. Although I hated confined spaces and I could never really relax when there was an adult near me, I wasn't the timid, nervous push-over that was shipped out in 1951.

Luckily for me I was thrown straight back into East 3 Cottage under the firm but fair leadership of Mrs Ingram. To my eyes she hadn't changed a bit. Grey hair always up in a bun, thick glasses hanging from her nose. The personification of a colonial Victorian lady in many ways. I think that was a throwback from the years she had once spent living in India.

I could see immediately that she ran her Cottage with the same friendliness as ever, if not more so. I realized I had missed her stories of living among tigers and taking high tea. As soon as the warm weather arrived she would produce a flimsy hand fan made of bright Indian silk and when I was in her good books she might sometimes let me fan her while she told us stories. As she spoke she closed her eyes and I could tell she was thousands of miles away in Calcutta, reliving so many wonderful adventures for us. If I made a noise she would snap out of her trance and remember a chore that needed doing. 'Come on, duckies, we can't be sitting around here all day.'

I don't know if it was because I was older but there seemed to be a better atmosphere in East 3. I didn't feel intimidated every day as soon as I woke up. I think I was just grateful to have a bed to sleep in – or try to sleep in. Years of being kept awake by force by Peter Baker had taken their toll on me. I thought I would sleep for a week once my body found a proper mattress to lie on. But I would stare at the ceiling in the dormitory for hours after everyone else had gone to bed, just tapping on the chair next to my bed the same rhythm I had made endlessly in my cupboard in Queen's Road.

But at least I was no longer wetting the bed. It took me a while to notice because it had now become such a habit, but I never did again after leaving Queen's Road.

One of the reasons for the better mood was the absence of Aunt Ross. She was still in the Homes but running her own Cottage now. In her place we had a lady called Aunt Round. She was exactly the shape her name suggests, short and powerful-looking. She didn't hit us for fun but she certainly never held back when she thought I had stepped out of line. I had been back in the Cottage for a week when I first felt her thick hand on the back of my head.

'Here we go again,' I thought. But at least I was eating.

The thrill of being away from the Bakers carried me through the first few months but I was definitely helped by making some good new friends. I had always felt a bit of a loner there before and the Bakers had trained me to look out for myself. I realized now, though, that I wasn't the only boy stuck in the Children's Home. There were other boys forced to be there who hated it as much as me.

As soon as I saw a boy making fun of a member of staff or doing something naughty I decided, 'I want to be his friend.'

Ralph Mitchell, Edward Harckham and Colin Foley were the boys I connected with immediately. I had known Ralph from my earlier stay but the others were new. Unlike me, they had stayed with their parents until they were ten.

Ralph was a livewire, always on the go and the only person never to be told to 'chop chop' by Mrs Ingram. Edward, or 'Teddy' as we called him, was a lot more studious. He earned the nickname of 'Professor' because he was always experimenting with whatever technology he could lay his hands on. He was the first person I knew to have a camera and he took lots of pictures of us. I don't know how exactly he did it, but I also remember him once stripping back some wires from an old radio amplifier and attaching them to the hot water pipes that ran throughout the dormitories. The next thing we heard was a mass of noises that sounded like talking and music all at once. Somehow Teddy knew that each Cottage had a radio relay box which emitted the signal throughout the building, so by listening through the pipes we could hear it. Unfortunately, as there were three radio stations at the time, without a tuner you'd hear them all at once. If you dared to stay up late enough and risk being caught, though, you could wait for the last station that was broadcasting and hear it perfectly without the interference of all the others.

Colin was always the quiet one, a thinker who was easygoing and even easier to like. The four of us got on very well together but we were never closer than when we were united against the staff. We did our best to make the days pass as enjoyably as possible but we never forgot that we were being held against our will. Our resentment towards the Homes was the thing that held us all together.

The older we got, the more daring we became. There was a boy in our dormitory who was born with a serious mental condition. He was very friendly although he couldn't communicate well. He'd mainly jump up and down while singing. He had a fantastic voice but he'd skip from one song to another and get them all mixed up. I'm proud to recall that no kid ever bullied him or took the mickey any more than we did to one another. He was one of us and, as we all knew, it was us against 'them' – the adults.

Even the houseparents and the other staff let John get on with his own life as far as possible, but one Saturday I witnessed Aunt Round holding a struggling boy's head under the bathwater. Normally I would have barely registered it because scenes like that were such a common occurrence. It wasn't the first time I'd seen a boy flailing for a grip on the edge of the bath, kicking desperately with his legs. Other boys told me it had happened to them as well. On this occasion I noticed the boy spluttering for breath was this boy from our dormitory – and he was being punished for wetting the bed.

I knew exactly how that felt. I also knew he couldn't be expected to help it if I hadn't been able to. I was fuming when I found the others and told them what I'd seen.

A plan was hatched and the four of us picked blades of grass to decide who was actually going to carry out the operation. Ralph got the short straw which I think he was pleased about. I volunteered to go along and keep guard.

Aunt Round always had a nap in the afternoons in an armchair in the dining room. She snored so loudly we knew she was asleep as soon as we entered the room. While I watched nervously for signs of Mrs Ingram, Ralph crawled quickly over to Aunt Round's feet and tied her shoelaces together. Then we ran down to the orchard and laughed in anticipation.

At teatime Aunt Round entered the dining room sporting a big bruise on her head. Our plan had worked!

She wasn't happy at all.

'There'll be no cakes today unless I find out who committed this wicked act,' she yelled.

No one moved. A lot of the other boys had heard it was us but they kept silent as well, even as we watched Aunt Round dump all our cakes into the dustbin. It was us against them and we felt on that occasion that we had won.

There was one figure at the Children's Cottage Homes who struck fear into even us. Assisting Mr Otterbourne now was a new Deputy Superintendent, an ugly, short, fat man with thin greasy hair, called Mr Bott. I quickly learned that he was one to avoid. He had the temper of Aunt Ross and the viciousness of Mrs Baker but double or triple their strength. The first time I set eyes on him I thought he looked like a villain from a silent film. Everything about him was unpleasant, from his dark suit to his toothless smile to his bad breath.

The first story I heard about Mr Bott quickly reminded me that the Cottages were not nice places.

Lots of kids used to pass the time at the Homes by climbing the trees in the orchards and the woods and raiding nests for eggs. We never realized it was cruel to the birds. Two of the best collectors were caught by Mr Bott climbing down a tree. At the foot of a nearby oak lay the bodies of two dead birds.

'You killed them,' he shouted into their faces.

'They were already there,' the boys said. 'We haven't been in that tree.'

Mr Bott didn't listen. He picked up the dead creatures and forced them into the boys' mouths.

'You killed it!' he screamed. 'You eat it!'

We always knew when Mr Bott – or 'Botty' as we dubbed him – was approaching because of the noise from the studs in his shoes. Wherever you were in the grounds, if you heard that distinctive 'clip clip' it was like a fire drill going off. Dozens of boys would dive for cover behind a wall or a bush or even another member of staff.

Sometimes for a joke I would sidle up to another boy and say, 'Botty wants to see you in his office' and watch him go pale. When the same trick was played on me, I never laughed.

Being summoned to Mr Bott's office was the worst thing that could happen. My knees would go weak, I would sweat. Mrs Baker, like Aunt Ross, had been violent but usually only if I wandered too near her. As a rule, if these women couldn't reach you they rarely went out of their way to hit out.

Mr Bott was different. He liked to make appointments for punishment. He knew the effect it had on us. He could see it in our terrified faces when we entered his room.

I remember my first time in that office although I can't recall what I had done to be sent there. Usually I was punished for being cheeky to him. My sense of humour was the only weapon I had but it got me into a lot of trouble. I cursed my stupid mouth as I walked towards his room. 'Please don't put me in the cellar,' I thought. 'I can handle anything apart from that.'

At least, I thought I could.

'Hands behind your back, Snot Rag.' He always called me that.

I tensed. I prepared myself as best I could. I could smell his stale, smoky breath as he stood in front of me, breathing heavily. It was as though he was waiting for me to relax. Then he struck. A savage punch in my stomach that knocked me straight to the ground. Before I could recover he appeared behind me and delivered a fast kick into the small of my back, right above the tailbone. All the fight disappeared from me there and then.

I really wanted to cry but I wasn't going to give him the satisfaction of seeing me do that. Not if I could possibly help it. I began to crawl towards the door, anxiously listening out for the sound of him following me. As soon as it was in sight I leapt to my feet, flung the door open and ran.

I tore out of the office, then out of the building, burning tears welling in my eyes. I didn't stop running for some minutes. I think I was trying to push the experience out of my body and make myself sweat. That way I could pretend the tears were sweat. I was in so much pain but I was angry as well. How could he do that to me? What could make a person so angry that he would treat me like that?

You didn't recover easily from Mr Bott's assaults. If anyone else hit me I was fine as soon as they left the room. But these punches always took longer to heal. I would be numb for days, unable to eat.

Office punishments were for special occasions but whenever you were within reach of him it was dangerous. Mr Bott delighted in twisting a boy's ear until he heard sobbing. More than once he twisted my ear so roughly that it tore. Only the sight of blood trickling over his hands made him let me go.

By the time I had been in the Homes a year Mr Bott had singled me out for special treatment. He obviously thought I was bad news. He would demand I appear in his office, then make me read out long passages from a copy of the Bible he kept in his desk drawer.

'I'm going to drive the devil out of you, Snot Rag Cummings,' he would say. All the while I read I tried not to inhale. The stench from his breath was worse in an enclosed space.

If I stopped reading or stumbled over a word he would twist my ear or whack the side of my head. He knew most of the words off by heart. I remember him walking around the room reciting, 'Damn the Devil and praise the Lord' and 'Seek the Lord and repent'. They were his favourite quotes.

I think Mr Bott was disappointed if I read too well because he didn't have an excuse to punch me. He was never far from hurting someone, though. As I read to him one day he spotted from his window a boy straying on to forbidden territory within the grounds. As I continued with the Bible lesson, the terrified youngster – he looked about five or six – was dragged into the room and attacked. He was punched and kicked so hard he couldn't walk out of the room unaided. I was told to finish reading and get him out of Mr Bott's sight.

Mr Bott often said, 'When I'm Superintendent there will be changes around this place.' As far as he was concerned, he planned to spend the rest of his life working at the Homes. That was bad news for every child there. We all breathed a sigh of relief when shortly afterwards Superintendent Otterbourne was replaced by a Mr Isacke instead.

Mr Isacke was a lot older than his predecessor but otherwise they could have been related. He was just as thin and tall as Beanpole Otterbourne and quickly established himself at the daily inspections. I don't know if he had been in the war, because he was probably too old, but he spoke as if he were running a squadron of soldiers rather than a children's home and we quickly gave him the nickname 'Kommandant'. He didn't set out to make himself popular and he succeeded in that. The only good thing about him was the fact that he didn't take pleasure in hurting us like Mr Bott.

Even though he knew we all realized he had failed in being promoted, Mr Bott still enjoyed showing off. I remember watching him poke the fire once when he said, 'Do you think I can put this red-hot poker on my tongue?'

We all murmured, 'No.'

I thought all my dreams were going to come true as I watched Mr Bott bring the glowing metal to his face – then suddenly he swung it down and touched the tongue of his shoe instead.

He was so amused by this that I could see he wanted more fun. His eyes fell on Ralph.

'You, boy – come here and let me burn those nasty warts from your knees.'

Ralf was horrified. It wasn't a joke. Before he could move, Mr Bott had pinned him to the floor and was waving the poker near his leg. Struggling desperately, Ralph couldn't stop the red-hot metal making contact. But as soon as it did, it was a different story. Even as he screamed in agony, Ralph somehow found the energy to shift his weight and Mr Bott fell to the floor, the poker burning his hand.

He gave Ralph four cuts of the cane for that. We all thought it was worth it to see Botty in pain.

Even though he was the most dangerous person I had

ever met, I spent hours dreaming of ways to get back at Mr Bott without being found out. It was the biggest challenge I'd ever had. And the riskiest.

I was often told to fetch his cup of tea and I never once did this without spitting in it first. I walked past his office once and saw him asleep at his desk. I don't know how I found the courage, but I tiptoed over and planted half a dozen drawing pins in his shoes. If he'd woken up I could have been killed. I didn't see him for a few days after that.

As the months passed I got braver. On more than one occasion I noticed him in the food store and so I crept over and slammed the door shut. The bolt was slid across and I'd left the room before he even noticed. Another time I noticed Mr Bott's fountain pen fall out of his breast pocket on to the kitchen floor and I quickly picked it up.

'Sir, you dropped this,' I said, and as I handed the pen back, I twisted its column a little way.

Mr Bott just grunted at me and put it back in his pocket. Half an hour later he came into the dining room and his wife asked him what the black inky stain was on his shirt. I don't think he put two and two together or I would have been in serious trouble.

My friends also began to fight back against him in the only way we knew how.

Ralph and I followed him out to the grounds and watched from a safe distance as he began to build a bench by the workshop. It was obviously thirsty work because he returned to his office for a cup of tea several times. Each time he went away he would chain his saw against a tree. We couldn't resist doing something. Somehow we managed to use the saw to cut through the branch that was keeping it chained, then we were able to slide it off the tree and hide it. It made my day to watch Mr Bott waddle back and then turn in a dozen circles like a dog chasing its tail. 'Where's it gone? I put it there.'

He realized he'd been the victim of a prank and exploded in rage. 'I know who did this! I'm going to make you pay for this. I know who you are!' he shouted, but he didn't move. He had no idea where we were. Or who we were. The next time he went back to the Cottage we replaced the saw on the tree as though it had never gone.

Playing tricks on one another was another way of escaping from the problems we all faced. Sometimes, though, the intended recipient was not the person who suffered.

One of our favourite pranks was balancing a bucket of water over a door, then waiting for someone to come in. I remember a few of us in our Cottage doing this to Colin one night. We'd all seen him go out of the dormitory to use the toilet, which gave us plenty of time to get the stunt prepared. The only buckets we had in those days were heavy metal pails, and looking back they could have seriously injured your head if they landed in the right place. That never concerned us then.

We all got into our positions facing the door and waited for Colin to return. We heard footsteps across the hall and tensed. But something was wrong. Colin was quite a tubby lad but these steps were too heavy even for him. And what was that noise?

Clip. Clip. Clip.

I froze. Part of me wanted to do nothing but another part knew we could all be thrashed for hours if Mr Bott was injured. The decision was taken out of my hands. The door burst open to reveal an already shouting Mr Bott. A second later he was drenched from head to foot.

I don't remember what was louder – the sound of him swearing at us or the cacophony of our laughter. The things we heard that day! For a religious man Mr Bott had very colourful language. Shaking with rage, he started to run into the room. Suddenly we were scared. He was going to wring our necks, he said, tear us limb from limb and wipe those stupid smiles from our faces.

Before he could touch anyone Mrs Ingram appeared at the door behind him. If it had been anyone else we would have been in worse trouble. She quickly took charge and told Mr Bott to go and dry himself. He wasn't happy. I think he wanted his revenge.

'Leave this to me,' she insisted to the blustering Deputy. 'I'll take care of it.'

What would she do? We'd made a mess all over the floor. Even Mrs Ingram must have wanted to throttle us.

But while Mr Bott was still in the room she fetched a mop to clear the mess, then as he walked away, she turned to us all, put her finger to her lips and said, 'Shhh – go to sleep.'

And that was it. No punches, no smacks, no bloodshed. I slept soundly that night and I'm sure it was thanks to her.

Mrs Ingram was a wonderful person in a terrible place. I remember her telling me, 'Leslie, you have a choice. You can either be very good or very bad.' I think she saw the potential in me to achieve anything. This made me feel so proud and there was nothing I would have liked more than to make her happy but I knew I couldn't control the future.

I wasn't even in control of myself.

TWELVE: *Ham and Eggs We Never See*

By eleven years of age I was quite a handful. The older I got, the more unforgiving I became of my surroundings. At the Bakers' I had three obvious enemies but it was innocent people whom I railed against: the shopkeepers I stole from, the kids I swindled out of food, the passers-by or authority figures who felt my fists or antagonistic attitude just because they were in the wrong place at the wrong time. Even the Bakers' dog suffered.

Back at the Children's Cottage Homes my anger didn't have the same focus. In Mr Bott, Aunt Ross, Aunt Round and Superintendents Otterbourne and then Isacke I had sworn enemies against whom I would do anything I could to score points. But there was a more general target for my anger – the Homes themselves. It was here that I was placed after my mother had disappeared twice. And it was here that she had arrived twice to rescue me. Everywhere I looked in the entire compound reminded me of the same thing:

This place is keeping me from my mother.

During my years at Queen's Road I had thought of her

less and less. Partly because I was too distracted just by trying to survive. Partly because there was nothing associated with her at that house. Even the arrival of Richard and later my other siblings up the road hadn't made that much impression. I still felt alone. Yet being back at the place where I had last seen my mummy had a powerful effect on me. Everyone at the Homes was my enemy now. They were all responsible for keeping the Cummings family apart.

I think that explains my behaviour as I neared my teens. I was angry at the whole institution.

I began to spend more time looking for ways of causing trouble. Once I was on my way to the dining hall for tea when an idea occurred to me. I sprinted into the bathroom, put all the plugs in the sinks and baths, then turned the taps on full power. Then I went to eat with everyone else.

I didn't know what to expect but I couldn't have asked for a better reaction. The thick stone floors in the bathroom didn't soak up a drop of water, so once the basins and baths began to overflow the water just had to spread. I forget who discovered the mess, but within seconds all the staff from the Cottage were in there, turning taps off and cursing. Some of the braver boys crept out of their seats and went to investigate the commotion. When they reported back no one could believe it. Laughter filled the room.

The appearance of a furious Aunt Round in the doorway ended the celebration.

'Well? Who did it?'

Everyone looked at their plates. She moved inside the room. Then suddenly a boy pointed at one of his friends and said, 'He did it, Miss.'

The accused looked shocked but he just pointed at someone else. 'No, it wasn't me, it was him.'

Soon we were all accusing one another. I could have stood on a table and shouted, 'It was me!' and no one would have noticed.

Some of the staff never hit out unless they were confident of the guilty party. Others, like Aunt Round, preferred to make an example. She reached for the nearest boy and *wallop* – he was knocked sideways. The boy knew he was innocent but he didn't complain. It wasn't the first time he'd have been punished unfairly. It happened to us all.

A few weeks later the bathroom flooded again and I was hit this time – even though I was actually innocent. Another boy had done it. I had started a craze and it felt very satisfying. The thrill of lashing out against the Children's Cottage Homes in whatever small way I could think of was irresistible.

Blaming one another for crimes was a daily occurrence. Once or twice I found it funny when someone I didn't like took a whack for something I'd done, but generally we were all just being childish. Trying to get one another into trouble was more of a challenge for our ingenuity than a genuine attempt to see another boy hurt. One boy would tell Mrs Ingram that I'd spilled something on the floor, then someone else would accuse him of stealing a cake, then that person would pretend he'd been punched by his friend. We were all so accustomed to being hit that it didn't worry us. When push came to shove, we all knew it was us against them.

Pain was such a normal part of our lives that eventually even punishments at school had little impact. I remember being given 100 lines by Mr Gardener, our form master, and told to complete them by the end of the day. When the final bell rang he walked over to my desk.

'Well, Cummings, have you done your lines?'

'No.'

'If you haven't done them by tomorrow morning, you'll get the cane. Is that clear?'

'Yes.'

The next morning I hadn't done the lines. Exasperated, he extended my deadline until the end of the day. Again I ignored it. This carried on for a week. In the end he just gave up.

He was never going to win that particular fight because I wasn't scared by his threat. When you spent afternoons and weekends dodging punches from Mr Bott and Aunt Round, a couple of lashes from a cane held no power.

I remember being summoned to the kitchen by the Deputy Superintendent one Saturday. A ball had smashed through a window, sending glass everywhere. I was innocent – but that didn't matter to him.

'Put your hands on your head, Snot Rag.'

I did as I was told. There was no point arguing with Mr Bott. This was the only man who scared me. Being within touching distance was never a good thing.

'Did you break that window?'

'No, sir.'

'If you confess I won't hit you.'

'You *won't* hit me if I say I did it?'

He nodded.

'I'll ask you again,' he said. 'Did you break that window?'

'Yes.'

Thump!

His fist knocked me directly to the floor. He stood over me, rubbing his knuckles.

'I won't tolerate liars, Snot Rag.'

When I stood up he hit me again.

A cane isn't much threat after that.

A few months after I arrived back in the Homes I finally managed to bump into my brother Richard. I'd already made a few half-hearted attempts at strolling towards his school after my class finished, but on this occasion I got lucky. He must have been held in detention because he was just leaving as I walked past.

It seems incredible to me now that no one had given me news about him, or my other brothers and sisters for that matter. He admitted he was still with the Bakers and in fact things had been nicer since I left. We decided that Mr Maynard might finally have taken all the complaints I made seriously although we both knew it was possible

Mrs Baker had decided I was more trouble than I'd been worth.

'What about the others?' I asked him.

'Still at the same place.'

I couldn't work out how they were all coping with these terrible foster parents but I was glad they were all near one another and in communication.

'How are they?' I asked.

Richard changed the subject at this point but he told me Philip was suffering most because he wet the bed. Both he and Janet were also raiding dustbins for food, just as I'd done. It was terrible to hear.

We agreed to try harder to stay in touch, then parted. I didn't see him again for almost another year.

But I did see Janet and Philip. As usual, nobody warned me. I was in the orchard one day and there was Philip, just playing with some other kids as though he didn't have a care in the world. I could tell he was relieved to be back at the Homes. He wouldn't tell me much about what had gone on while he was fostered because it made him too upset. I didn't share my experiences for the same reason.

I saw Janet a few days later. She looked healthier than Philip but no one in the Homes ever looked well. Sometimes I wished she'd never been brought back, though. When she was away, I could imagine she was being treated well. When she was at the Cottages I saw with my own eyes that she was as unlucky as the rest of us. Even after all the violence I'd endured and witnessed, watching your own kid sister suffer is the hardest of all.

And on one occasion I was partly to blame.

I was walking through the grounds when I heard Mr Bott shouting. Normally that was my cue to run the other way – but I saw he was angry with Janet and I couldn't help getting closer. I wish I hadn't. There was nothing I could do. As soon as Botty saw me, his face lit up.

'Well, look, it's your big brother come to protect you,' he sneered.

Then he turned to me and said, 'Hold her arms.'

I didn't move. I wasn't sure what he meant.

Suddenly he grabbed Janet's wrist and dragged her towards me. He pinned both arms behind her back and said, 'Hold her still. Or else it will be worse for both of you.'

I knew then what he wanted to do but I couldn't believe he would go through with it. Not with a girl. Not with my sister.

But he did. As I restrained Janet's small hands, he took a short swing with his right hand and punched her in the stomach. I felt her skinny body fall back into mine. She burst into tears and I felt sick. I couldn't believe he'd made me do that. Even though I knew he would have done something worse if I'd disobeyed, I was so ashamed of myself. To this day I don't know how she ever forgave me.

I tried to avoid Botty more than usual after that, but it was difficult because as an older boy my chores became harder and took up more time. There were windows to be cleaned and grounds to be swept but the worst job of all was delivering coal to the various Cottages. A delivery lorry poured the week's supply into a coal shed and then there was a rota for lads to shovel it into wheelbarrows and distribute it around the grounds. For smaller boys like me, the wheelbarrows were just too big to push. By the time I had loaded the barrow, it had become almost totally unwieldy. It would take two of us, lifting a handle each, to get the barrow anywhere near its destination. We never made a single trip without losing control and spilling the entire load. I spent many hours between Cottages desperately shovelling coal back into the barrow before Botty spotted us.

Just as I'd observed on my last stay at the Homes, boys like Teddy who had regular visitors rarely suffered the level of physical assault that people like me were subjected to. On my darker days I struggled to shake off the feeling that my mother was responsible for my suffering. 'If she just came by once a month, they wouldn't hit me so hard,' I thought. 'Can't she even do that for me?'

These mixed feelings didn't stop me waiting by the gate again most Saturdays, though. My own pattern was starting again.

If Mr Bott really wanted to get at people like Teddy, he would have to find another way. It didn't take him long to work out how.

One Saturday after the coal episode Teddy went to meet his mother as usual and was told there were no visitors that day.

'Why not?' he asked.

'It's once a month now.'

No warning, no indication of how long this new rule would stay in place.

'First Saturday of the month only,' he was told.

Teddy was devastated. We all had our private thoughts, which kept us going. Seeing his relatives so regularly was his. But it got worse. When his mother was allowed in, Teddy was sometimes informed they would have to confine their visit to the grounds only. No leaving the Homes for Teddy. He was so upset and I could see his mother was not happy either. She didn't look as though she enjoyed being in the Homes any more than we did.

Children weren't allowed to take visitors into the Cottages, which posed another problem. In bad weather the assembly hall in the Seamstress's building was made available, but I noticed a lot of visitors didn't bother coming rather than be made to sit for a few hours in that room.

A month in a child's mind is for ever and at the Homes we had no concept of time. We all lived day to day, hand to mouth. I knew from experience that it was dangerous to get comfortable. The only way to avoid disappointment was to avoid expectation.

Visiting adults seemed to be treated with the same disdain as us children. It was no good a visitor coming outside visiting hours – they would not be allowed access to their sons and daughters. During his four years at the Homes, Teddy's mother called many times outside regulation hours – it was such a long journey for her that she came whenever she could and hoped for the best. But they never let her in and if she left anything for her son they would not alert Teddy until she was well clear of the grounds.

What made it worse was the fact that Teddy's Cottage, for most of his stay, housed the Superintendent's office where all visitors had to report. Teddy and his mother would be just feet from each other and powerless to do anything about it.

This treatment affected Teddy very badly and he would go for days after another near miss barely uttering a word. His mother was his Achilles heel and Mr Bott knew it.

The behaviour of some of the staff seems to me now reminiscent of the Senators of ancient Rome. They did whatever they felt like, confident that no one had the authority to prevent them. Occasionally, however, even they were reminded that they were not above the law. I remember hearing emergency vehicle sirens one day and the whole Cottage piling outside to see what was going on. Gossip whipped round the area and for ages there was no activity near the police car and ambulance parked nearby. Suddenly Aunt Round was led out of the building in handcuffs. A few minutes later a bandaged boy was carried out and lifted into the ambulance.

Aunt Round was arrested for having sex with a thirteen-year-old minor. Judging from his injuries, he had obviously tried to resist. I never saw him again. If he was lucky, his parents would have had him removed.

I had heard rumours of staff being 'too friendly' with children when I was at the Homes the first time. Back then, I didn't know what the phrase meant. Having met the Bakers, I could see the signs for myself. I didn't really know whether or not something could be called 'sex', but I did know whether it was right or wrong.

One of our gardeners, Mr Bone, appeared in court in 1956 accused of exposing himself to some of the girls. Another housefather, Mr Prosser, actually assaulted a girl called Sheila. He made her sleep in her own room for a few nights and she woke up to find him touching her breasts.

Sex was often spoken about among us boys, and as I got older I noticed signs of it elsewhere. One of the Aunts, Aunt Jean, often seemed to have men visiting her at night. I saw her inviting a sailor in once and she said, 'This is my brother. He's come to stay.'

A few weeks later Teddy saw her with a soldier on the stairs and he was told the same thing.

Not everyone at the Homes was a bad person. I have spoken to some people whose years spent there were relatively painless because they rarely came into contact with the staff members who terrorized me. There was one couple we called Mum Cook and Dad Can who were from Scotland and were very friendly towards everyone in their Cottage. I'm sure they were strict when they needed to be, but no more. Mr and Mrs Peters were another good pair.

There were attempts made at providing treats for all of us. Apart from the Christmas parties hosted by local clubs, we were also given chocolate eggs by Woolworth's at Easter. Occasionally we were visited by these lovely old ladies who would arrive in a chauffeur-driven Rolls-Royce, always dressed immaculately in 1920s-style frilly dresses that smelled like a mixture of mothballs and sweet perfume. We never knew when they were coming, but as soon as we heard that distinctive engine sweeping down the driveway we'd all rush round to the Super's building because they never arrived empty-handed. They'd always have a piece of fruit for every single one of us but that wasn't the reason we were desperate to see them. The ladies were obviously very wealthy and were also kind and the rumour in the Homes was that they were trying to choose a child to adopt. Even as we dashed over to meet them we'd be licking our fingers to flatten unruly hair, tucking in shirts, wiping noses. Then we'd all line up excitedly, everyone thinking the same thing:

'Please choose me!'

There was one activity that I genuinely did enjoy. The 24th Portsmouth Scouts had its base within the grounds of the Homes and as soon as we were eleven or older, we could join. It was open to everyone, so plenty of lads from the village attended as well. The Scout leaders were completely separate from the staff so it was a breath of fresh air disappearing into that hut for an evening of games and projects once a week.

I really enjoyed being a Scout and especially liked the fact that every summer we were taken to a field a few miles away and allowed to camp out. It was such a relief being away from the Homes. Unfortunately my membership of the association didn't last long.

I remember walking home from school one day and

noticing an old bicycle abandoned near a river. I could see why nobody wanted it. It had no tyres and no brakes. Even so, I had never owned my own bike. Some of the richer pupils in my class even used to cycle to school on their shiny bicycles, which always made me jealous. Now was my chance to ride my own.

I dragged the thing up and straightened its handlebars, then climbed carefully on to the saddle. On the grass it was okay and slow but as soon as I reached the pavement the noise from the exposed rims was incredible. It was also ridiculously uncomfortable the faster I went, but it was too exhilarating to stop.

I nearly hit several pedestrians as I whizzed down the cobbled stones of Cosham High Street because without brakes I had little control. But I was whooping so loudly they should have heard me a mile away and ducked out of the way. It was great fun, and completely out of the blue, but eventually it became too painful and I threw the bike into a hedge near the Homes.

When I turned up at the Scout hut the following week I was as excited as ever. I hadn't been there long when the Scout Master told me to stand up.

'Did you come by bike, Leslie?'

I looked at him blankly. Riding that old boneshaker had completely slipped my memory. He could tell I was confused and began to get angry.

'Don't tell me you've forgotten careering down the High Street on that death-trap machine? Does that mean you don't remember hitting me as well?'

If I had collided with the Scout Master I didn't recognize him. He obviously recognized me.

'I'm afraid I don't accept behaviour like that from any of my boys, Leslie. You can leave now – and don't come back.'

My mouth fell open. Was he serious? How could he be? I had ridden the bike in the town; it had nothing to do with the Scouts. But he was deadly serious and refused to continue the evening until I'd left.

Being dismissed from the only thing I enjoyed was a hard pill to swallow. It was devastating in so many ways. It meant another evening in the Cottage, no more feeling normal by mingling with the town kids, and no more camping trips.

I honestly didn't even think I'd done anything wrong. 'What's the point of trying to behave?' I thought.

The camping trips may have been taken away from me, but I soon had the chance of another break to replace it. We were told by Mrs Ingram that we were going to stay at a holiday camp in Kent. I think the long school summer holidays were very difficult for the Homes to cope with, so this was an experiment to ease the burden for a few weeks. At the time places like Butlins were very popular and we all got excited talking about the fairground rides we would go on and the fun we would have in the swimming pool.

We set out in an old bus but the exhaust leaked so many fumes into it that that the driver had to stop every few miles so we could get a breath of fresh air. It was a long journey but we passed the time singing one of our favourite songs:

> *We are the kids of the Cottage Homes far, far away*
> *All we get is bread and scraps three times a day*
> *Ham and eggs we never see*
> *Super gets them for his tea*
> *Mums and Dads take us home*
> *'cos we're sad and all alone.*

I don't think the adults on the bus were very comfortable hearing it, but it kept us all distracted for a few miles.

When we pulled into the camp we were stunned. It wasn't a Butlins at all. It was an old wartime air base with block after block of Nissen huts with tin roofs. There were no roller coasters or Redcoats to entertain us, there wasn't even a single swing. Just shacks with cement floors and beds that had springs sticking out. We were all so disappointed.

'They've done it to us again,' I thought as two weeks of misery lay ahead.

By the next morning I'd changed my mind. Just being away from most of the staff was a holiday in itself. By breakfast we'd also discovered 1,001 things you could do on a deserted air base. By lunch we'd found a beach nearby, and suddenly a fortnight there didn't seem like long enough at all. Every day was an adventure of chasing, swimming and building sandcastles, and the weather was fantastic. Even when there were thunderstorms we all ran into the sea and pretended we were ships being attacked. Without doubt that was the happiest I ever was in the care of the Children's Cottage Homes – and we were more than 100 miles away.

I was always at my most relaxed when there were other kids around and we were away from adults. Even the most annoying boy was better than the staff. I remember playing Cowboys and Indians with Ralph Mitchell and he refused to fall down when I shot him.

'You're dead!' I said.

'No I'm not – I'm wearing my protective space suit. Your bullets can't hurt me.'

'But we're playing Cowboys and Indians.'

'Not now we're not.'

He always cheated, even when we played Snap. But I could never get angry at him. Kids looked out for kids. That was our rule.

As I reached my teens and became interested in girls, Ralph found a new way to torment me. There was a lass in the Homes called Tilly Smith who I thought was beautiful. Ralph told me I had a chance with her – but it came at a price.

'If you give me a gobstopper she'll give you a kiss.'

'Really?'

'Definitely. She told me.'

I don't know how many times I fell for that one although I did get my kiss eventually.

Girls became an obsession for all of us. Looking back, I was somehow able to disassociate the sexual demands of Mr Baker from my own instincts. If there was a danger that I'd assume all sexual activity took place between men and involved violence then I luckily escaped it. Girls were my only interest. Ralph and I were always hanging around them but at first we were more interested in cadging sweets than anything else. Once we invited a girl called Stephanie to climb our favourite tree with us. It was an ugly, barkless oak that was easy to get up and down and everyone called it the 'monkey tree' – I guess because that's what we looked like climbing it. We both liked Stephanie a lot but the real reason we'd let her play with us was so that we could see her up her skirt while she was climbing. As soon as she got a few feet up we both ran away yelling, 'Stephanie's got no knickers on, Stephanie's got no knickers on.'

It's amazing the risks boys will take to get near girls. In case of fire there were wrought-iron staircases that led down from the outside walls of the dormitories. These were never to be used except in emergencies – but they had another function for us. Not only could we escape from our dormitory using these stairs, but if we ran across to another Cottage we could get up into the girls' room. We called those steps the 'stairway to heaven' because you could creep over at night and chat to someone you liked or even get a kiss or two if you were lucky.

I remember standing down below, a trembling thirteen-year-old, and looking up at these beautiful girls who were hanging out of their window and encouraging a couple of us to venture up. This was fraught with danger. For a start, I had to take my shoes off or the vibrations from the metal could wake the houseparents, whose window I had to pass on the way up. And I had to remember to take some sweets with me to bribe the younger girls into not calling an adult. It was always worth it, though at that age I was still only interested in kisses. Just the warmth and friendliness of another person was so special to me.

I had a few close shaves when I was shinning past a window and I heard a houseparent walking around inside but none of my escapes was as close as one by a boy called Davy Knight. Davy – who suffered from asthma – was older and more sexually advanced than some of us. He had climbed up to visit a girl who had a false leg when they were suddenly disturbed by one of the staff. Panicking, he scooped up his bundle of clothes, threw himself down the stairs and fled back to our dormitory still half naked. He tipped the clothes down on to his bed and another boy screamed.

Sticking out from the bundle was the girl's false leg.

'Is that what you get when you kiss a girl?' one of the younger kids asked.

He was immediately hit by a rain of pillows.

'We'll be for it if the houseparents discover that's missing,' Ralph said. 'You've got to take it back.'

'It's too dangerous,' someone else chipped in.

'Don't worry,' Ralph said, 'I've got a plan.'

He disappeared out of the room, ran downstairs and returned with shoe polish all over his face. We all laughed but he was serious. 'We can't afford to get caught – get this on.'

Blacked up and giggling our heads off, Ralph, Teddy, Davy and I all set off down the fire escape, but as soon as we reached the bottom I tripped over Mrs Ingram's washing basket and cut my lip. While I sat nursing my injury Ralph and I started to argue over who was going to be squadron leader. Teddy, always the sensible one, said, 'Look, let's just get the leg back.'

We had to get it over with as soon as possible. If Botty or Mr Isacke found out what we were up to we'd all be for it.

It was a brightly moonlit night, which wasn't great for our clandestine mission, and Davy's asthmatic wheezing in the silence sounded like a train coming through. When we reached the other Cottage we spotted a housemother smoking a cigarette outside.

'Now what?' I asked Ralph.

'I don't know,' he said. 'You're the squadron leader.'

Just as we start arguing again, Davy grabbed the leg off Teddy and ran full speed up the stairs, past the house-mother and into the dormitory.

It was obvious, we all agreed – he was mad.

We waited and waited. Five minutes became ten and we didn't know what to do.

'I can't stand here like this, I'm going to go in and rescue him,' Ralph said.

No sooner had he reached the bottom of the stairs than Davy came charging out through the main door, closely followed by the irate housemother. We all span round, knocking into each other, and shot off. Behind us I could hear that angry voice shouting, 'I know it's you, Jimmy!'

'See, the polish worked,' a beaming Ralph said when we were all cleaned up and safely back in our beds.

'Yes, but when Jimmy says it wasn't him they'll track us down,' Teddy said.

'Not if we keep quiet.'

I don't know if Jimmy was punished instead of us but we were never rumbled for that particular adventure.

There was a great deal of camaraderie between us as we got older. We were more like brothers because we leaned on one another for support. Not openly, but just because we were all in the same position, all rooting for one another against the staff. I knew that I had a real family outside the grounds but Teddy, Ralph and the others were closer to me than Robert, Richard and Philip had ever been. I wished I could be as close to my siblings as I was to my friends but we just didn't know one another any more. We never even saw one another. In fact, Philip went on to be fostered by the Taylors and was lucky to have been placed with decent people.

'I should be with my family but these people won't let me,' I thought.

Very soon I would get the opportunity to put things right.

THIRTEEN: *You'll Go to Hell*

In summer 1957, when I was thirteen years old, I was playing in the grounds when I saw my brother Richard. He'd broken in and hadn't had trouble tracking me down. He told me he had cycled down from London.

'Why are you in London?' I asked him.

'I'm living with Mum.'

I was gobsmacked.

'You're living with Mum?'

Why was he living there if I wasn't? How had he even found her? He told me that she'd made contact and invited him up to live with her now that he was old enough, at fifteen, to leave school and support himself with work. He said he was also helping her out financially.

It hit me hard. I hadn't seen her for a decade yet here she was cherry-picking one of her children to live with her. I didn't know what to think. When Richard left I was still confused. A few weeks later, however, I had made my mind up.

'I'm going to live with my mother.'

Most of my friends thought I was mad, but one of them, Frank Goodman, said he would come with me. That was brilliant news. The idea of going to London was daunting for a boy on his own. But with two of us it would become an adventure.

The next day we walked out of the Homes, ostensibly to go to school, but we didn't and just kept travelling till we reached Frank's aunt's house. She was a lovely lady and made us welcome and even let us stay the night. Best of all, she gave Frank a £5 note and with that we bought two train tickets to London. I had never been on a train before. I couldn't decide if I was more excited about that or the fact I was going to see my mother again.

On the journey I began to plan how it would be with her. What would I say when she said she was sorry she hadn't come to collect us all those years ago? How would I react when she put her arms around me and said she was so sorry for leaving me?

The train from Portsmouth took us to Waterloo Station in London. From the address Richard had given me I knew that they lived in Acre Lane, Brixton. We asked a railway guard and he told us that at least we were on the right side of the river. We had about a three-mile walk ahead of us.

If anyone had told me to walk that far I probably would have found a reason to go in the opposite direction. It's different when you're on an adventure with your mate, though. We got there in no time. And then all I had to do was knock on the door.

I stood there for about five minutes, not doing anything. Frank got bored of waiting and started walking away. Then I composed myself and rapped on the door.

A lady answered. She looked tired and surprised to be greeting visitors, especially two such young ones. She clearly had no idea who I was. But I recognized her.

'Hello, Mum. It's me, Leslie. I'm your son.'

I had dreamed of her throwing her arms around me and hugging me to death as soon as she saw me. But that didn't happen. She just stood there, shocked, staring at me without blinking.

For a moment I worried she was going to shut the door again.

'Mum?' I said.

Finally she spoke. 'You'd better come in.'

Frank and I followed her into a small flat and she gestured to us to sit at the table while she made tea. I watched as she switched the gas on, boiled the water, prepared the cups and spooned the tea into a pot. All the while she didn't say a word.

I hadn't seen her since I was four but I would never have forgotten that face. There had been so much I'd wanted to say to it over the years. At that moment I couldn't think of a single thing.

Eventually Mum asked how school was but I could tell she wasn't really interested. It was just something to say. Frank started talking about London and that broke the ice.

After about an hour of torturous half-silence, Richard arrived home from work. He was just as shocked to see us as my mother had been, but at least he wasn't lost for words. We spoke for a while but then he told me we couldn't stay.

'Mum'll get into trouble if you stay,' he said.

'But you're staying.'

'That's different. I'm paying my way.'

I said goodbye to Mum and we left. I don't recall if she kissed or hugged me. I think I would have remembered if she did.

Richard walked out with us and we found some food and talked for ages. Eventually Richard said he had to go. It was an awkward moment for us brothers, but off he went. Frank and I spent that night underneath a railway bridge. Frank had no problem sleeping. I was too upset to relax.

Why hadn't she wanted to see me? Why didn't she even want to talk to me?

The answers were too hurtful to contemplate so I didn't. Not then. They would keep until after our adventure.

The next day Frank and I made our way back towards Waterloo and ended up by the river. We spent some money on food and drink but we didn't have enough to stay anywhere. We began hunting around for a spot that might tide us over that night when a man who'd been watching us for a while came over.

'You looking for somewhere to stay?' he called out.

We couldn't believe our luck.

'We don't have much money,' Frank said.

The guy shrugged. 'That's all right. Come on, it's this way.'

Frank and I followed him for a few minutes, happy at the prospect of getting a decent night's sleep. The man's house was quite big but pretty sparse. I couldn't imagine it being a very popular hotel.

'You'll probably be needing a bath, won't you, lads?' the man said when we were inside.

I looked at Frank. Was he thinking what I was thinking? Alarm bells suddenly began to ring in my head as we were led to the bathroom. We went in together and locked the door.

'We need to get out of here,' I said. There was one small window but it was jammed shut. I stood on the rim of the bath and pushed with all my strength.

'Hurry up in there!' the man called out.

I began to sweat as I shoved harder. 'It's stuck,' I said.

'Come on, lads, open this door!' He started to bang on it with his hand.

Panicking I made a fist and punched the glass. Seconds later I was through the hole with Frank close behind. We jumped to the ground and ran and ran.

It was still light and I could see I was bleeding quite badly from glass cuts in my arm. I took my jumper off and wrapped it around my elbow. A passing couple looked concerned and said I should go to hospital. I knew I couldn't do that so we took off again. I think the couple must have called the police because two cars suddenly screamed to a halt nearby. We hid behind some bins and waited till the policemen had passed.

Eventually we fell asleep. The next thing I remember is waking up in hospital. A nurse was standing next to me.

'Where am I?' I asked.

'You're in trouble,' she said, but she was smiling. Apparently a policeman had found me covered in blood in the early hours of the morning and rushed me into Casualty. Any later, she explained, and I would have bled to death.

I asked her where Frank was.

'Your friend's been sent back to the Homes. I know you're runaways.'

'I'm not going back to that place. My mum is going to collect me.'

The nurse took my mother's name and address and walked away. A few days later I was discharged and sent back to the Homes in a taxi. My mother had refused to collect me, as I knew she would, and that was the end of the Great Escape.

For some reason we weren't punished for running away. Other boys who'd escaped for a day or two were usually thrashed by Mr Bott. In fact we earned a little bit of fame for a few weeks among the other kids. Boys planning to do a runner would ask us for advice and girls would offer sweets in exchange for hearing about how brave we'd been. And that was how I got my kiss from Tilly Smith, so my journey wasn't a complete disappointment.

A few months later, following an argument with Mr Bott in the morning, I decided to run away again. I don't remember what the punishment was for but I do remember that he told me to report to his office after school and something in me snapped. I wasn't being a coward by not going into his room. I was just fed up with giving him the satisfaction of seeing me hurt. That's why I decided I needed to get away – again.

This time Ralph Mitchell decided to come with me. He had been impressed by the hero's reception I had received last time and wanted to join in.

We went to school as normal and promptly stole two bikes from the racks there. There was only one place I wanted to go: to London. To my mother.

I knew she didn't want me there but all my life I'd wanted to run to her. When it came down to it, I had nowhere else to go.

We set off up the A3 on our bikes in the pouring rain, past Petersfield, past Liss, totally drenched but singing as we cycled. When we got hungry we stole bread and milk from the doorstep of a house and rested under some trees to eat it. Then, fully energized, we leapt back on our bikes and set off on the next stage of our journey.

Half an hour later a police car drove up alongside us and made us pull over. Mr Lawrence, our headmaster, had reported to the Homes that we'd absconded and Mr Isacke had called the police.

'You picked bad weather to run away,' one constable said. 'You look like drowned rats.'

He asked us why we'd run and we both told him that we were sick of being used as punchbags by Mr Bott. He didn't say anything to that but took us to the station where we were given towels and blankets. I took my top off to get dry and showed the police a large bruise that Mr Bott had given me the week before. I was sure they believed me now.

Unfortunately within an hour the police had issued us with criminal convictions for stealing the milk and bread and we were driven back to the Homes and, I discovered a few years later, a new line was added to my file by Mr Maynard: 'Although there were allegations of being hit frequently, it does not appear there was any truth in this apart from one or possibly two occasions. However, it probably arises from Mr Bott's "rough-and-tumble attitude" to the boys.'

Having concluded that we were under no physical threat, Mr Maynard was charged with returning us to the Homes. For having the temerity to run away and for telling 'lies' to the police, we were both given six strokes of the cane – a permitted form of punishment at the Homes in those days. As we had brought shame on his operation, Mr Isacke took it upon himself to dish out the punishment. The Kommandant lined us up in his office at the same time and told us to pull down our shorts and bend over.

Ralph was struck first and I heard him wince. Five strokes later I could tell he had had enough. The sound of my friend's suffering was worse than the fear of being next in line myself.

I knew exactly what to expect when my turn came. The first lash of the cane made me want to scream, but I bit my tongue. 'It's just shock,' I told myself. 'It doesn't hurt.'

But it did. With the second stroke the Kommandant hit the same spot as his first shot. It was always worse when that happened – and I'm sure he knew it.

After the third lash I forced myself to relax. It wasn't easy but I knew from experience that being tense just made the pain seem worse. The fourth one still hurt like hell, but I didn't feel I was going to faint any more. I took deep breaths and tried to hum silently in my head.

I just would not give that man – or any man – the satisfaction of knowing he had beaten me into submission.

Painful as the Kommandant's caning was, the pair of us knew that we'd got off lightly. If Botty had been the one in charge of the punishment, we could have died. As it was, as soon as he saw me after my complaint to the police, he didn't even check who was watching. He just walked up behind me and thumped me squarely in the side.

'There's another one for you to report,' he growled, then walked away laughing.

Many of my friends suffered just as badly as me at the hands of Mr Bott. It didn't reduce my pain watching them being punished as well, but at least I felt I wasn't alone in my agony.

I always liked the fact that my friends were all so different. They all brought out a different side of my personality. Ralph and I were highly competitive and were always on the lookout for adventure, as running away proved.

Then there was my relationship with Teddy. Where he was concerned I was more like a pupil at the feet of a master. He was always fixing some old radio or electrical appliance, and I was completely baffled as he'd explain to me what this valve did or what was wrong with that and it would all go over my head. He was tall and had uncontrollable hair that would never lay down. He was always showing me some new invention and I was fascinated by him. Teddy was very hard not to like.

Mr Bott wouldn't allow Teddy to have a radio in the Cottage, but he did give permission for it to be used in the workshop, a place that was normally out of bounds. While he was in the workshop Teddy built a machine called an epidiascope, which was a gadget for projecting enlarged images of photos, postcards or objects on to a screen. I'd never seen anything like it.

One day he hung a white sheet in the darkened playroom and put on a show of pictures cut from magazines. When that was over we started putting our faces in the back of the epidiascope and watched them beam across the room. The only problem with this was the image on screen was upside down. With photos you just placed them in the machine the wrong way up, but it was not so easy to correct a human being.

Not easy – but not impossible, as I learned when I put my face inside it.

'Grab him!' Ralph yelled, and before I knew it I was hoisted aloft with one leg over his shoulder and another over Teddy's. My head was shoved into the back of the epidiascope and the room erupted into laughter as my face appeared on screen in full colour and with perfect sound. What nobody realized was that my deepening shade of crimson wasn't embarrassment – it was because I was upside down and only a few inches away from a very hot light bulb.

I loved being part of anything like this because it gave me a sense of belonging. But there was another side of my personality which never came out around these friends.

Every laugh I shared with Ralph, Teddy, Colin, Davy, Ronnie Mitchell and the others was only a distraction for me. I had a great time with these lads but the fun I had with them was only a temporary sensation. For a few hours it masked the burning rage that I struggled to keep in check the older I got. The transformation from me as a ten-year-old to four years later was stark. I only had to look at Mr Bott and my blood would feel as though it was boiling. The others hated him but in the same way some of them hated cheese. I despised him because of the punches and kicks and threats and torture he had subjected me to over the last three years. Everything about the Cottages made me furious. They kept me from my mother, they split up my siblings – and they had sent me to the Bakers'.

I got into a lot of trouble with a new friend called Charlie Barker. He was a year or two older than me and he was big for his age and tough. I never had any trouble from bullies at school when people found out I was a friend of his. Although most kids gave those of us wearing hand-me-down shoes and tatty flecked jumpers a wide berth, even so, it was good to have protection.

We did loads of things together but the episode which caused the most problems took place one summer. We sneaked out of the grounds and wandered over to the school which was obviously empty. It was quite an impressive building with lots of glass panels forming a wall which could be slid open during warm weather. That school had been a refuge to me so many times but I had also had my share of unhappiness there. That's why I threw my first stone through one of the windows. That's why I threw my second. And my third and all the others.

I remember getting a buzz as the first panel of glass shattered. As I watched Charlie destroy another one it just made me want to do it again. I felt genuine pleasure as each new stone found its target but that pleasure changed. I threw so many rocks that in the end I couldn't even hear the windows explode. By then I was just in a rhythm of destruction. Pick up, launch, pick up, launch. I wasn't throwing stones at windows any more, I was hitting back at all the people who'd hurt me over the years. That's what it felt like to me.

Hundreds of window panes shattering must have caused quite a racket because suddenly we heard a police siren and had to run. I wasn't quick enough, however, and I got put in a police car for the fourth time in my life.

I was sentenced to a fortnight in an 'attendance centre', which basically meant I had to report to Cosham Police Station and clean their windows. Each day I would return and repeat the same process again. It was tedious and tiring and I felt humiliated to have been caught by the police.

But nobody hit me.

Even after Mr Bott banned Charlie and me from spending time together and split us up into separate Cottages we still managed to find time for mischief, but I was capable of doing enough damage on my own.

That stint cleaning windows confirmed my hatred of the police. They were the ones who always took my mother away. They brought me to the Homes. And they believed the Bakers' lies instead of my truth. Any chance I saw of attacking them I now took.

I remember walking along Cosham High Street when I saw one of the inspectors from the station. He had been rude to me while I was attending there and as soon as I set eyes on him I wanted to get some sort of revenge. 'What can a kid do against the police?' I wondered. I ran up some steps on a bridge and waited for him to get near. Then I spat. It wasn't a great shot but made enough contact to send the inspector into a rage. He chased me the entire length of Cosham High Street before I shook him off. I could have run all night but I didn't even care if he caught me. The police never hit me. I could take their kind of punishment every day of the week.

Another hobby was throwing stones at police cars. If I stood behind a tree on a bend I would catch them as they had to slow down. That gave me plenty of time to take aim and fire. They never knew where the shower of rocks was coming from.

As my life at the Homes dragged on, it wasn't just the police who earned my ire. Anyone who annoyed me was likely to suffer a violent response from me. I once pushed a boy out of one of the bedroom windows because he accused me of something I hadn't done. For that split second I saw him not as one of 'us' but as part of the Children's Cottage Homes, my sworn enemy. At that moment I didn't care if he smashed his head on the pavement below. I was lucky that he landed on the fire escape which led down from the dorm. I could have been in serious trouble if that hadn't been there. When I thought about it afterwards I felt my breathing get shorter and my chest tighter. *What had I been thinking?* I was genuinely sorry – but I still didn't change my ways.

I remember throwing a chair at one schoolteacher and kicking another. There was no deterrent the headmaster could employ that would keep me in check. If he caned me, the Homes repeated the process, but I didn't care.

There was nothing they could do.

As a fourteen-year-old at the Children's Cottage Homes I didn't have any great ambitions. For as long as I could remember I wanted to be reunited with my family but I had seen my mother once in a decade and I barely knew my siblings. Each day I hoped for the best and expected the worst. I was rarely disappointed.

Even though I remained small for my age, I began to fill out. I think the sight of me in a fury could have been intimidating even as a young teen. And in those days I was in a fury more often than not. Woe betide anyone who crossed me – even if they were staff.

243

One of my most vivid memories is of lying in bed and talking with the others about the Superintendent.

'Mr Isacke's too old to be looking after young kids,' I said.

The others agreed, and encouraged, I went further in my criticism of him. All of a sudden the bedroom door flew open and standing there was Mr Isacke. He took a couple of seconds to get his bearings, then marched over to my bed and punched me in the face. My head was the perfect height for his fist.

My nose exploded in blood and I ran screaming to the bathroom. Pain gripped my body and I was so angry that he'd dared to touch me like that. As I ran across the hall I passed an open window and was so distraught that I just put my fist through the glass. It disintegrated into a thousand pieces but miraculously I didn't cut myself.

I reached the toilet and locked myself inside while I put tissue on my bloody nose. All the while I screamed profanities at Mr Isacke.

'You're going to pay for this, old man! When I'm an adult I'm going to come back here and break your stupid old face. I'm going to stamp on your head till your eyes pop out.' I didn't know what I was saying. The pain in my nose was so great I was delirious. But I went on, 'I'm going to kill you, then I'm going to kill your ugly wife and your stupid children. You're dead. You're dead!'

A strange thing happened next. Isacke must have heard the window smash and come down to investigate. Once he heard my threats he actually banged on the door and tried to apologize.

'Look, Cummings, let's not be too hasty. Come on out and we'll have a talk.'

I didn't listen. The verbal onslaught continued and eventually he retreated. He didn't look at me at the next inspection and he never touched me again.

That night in the bathroom I realized I was capable of anything. So did Mr Isacke. Very soon afterwards I was sent to see the priest at St Coleman's to try to get to the root of my anger. That building only reminded me of the Bakers and I hated every minute I was there – both of them. He told me, 'God loves you, Leslie.'

'There is no God,' I said.

'You'll go to hell for saying that.'

'I'm already there. Hadn't you noticed?'

I was then taken to see Archbishop King. I don't know why everyone kept thinking Catholicism was the cure for my problems. He was just as infuriated with me and my refusal to believe in God. After the meeting it was recommended I be admitted to a mental institution.

Fortunately this didn't happen and instead I was despatched to a church in Winchester where the priest promised to get results. That was before he had met me.

He told me that he was going to sort me out. I told him to 'fuck off'. He then grabbed hold of me and physically washed my mouth out with soap. Every time I could speak I told him I would kill him if he didn't let me go. When he finally released me I ran out of the room and hid. Before anyone found me I stole some matches, returned to the vestry and set light to a pair of giant velvet curtains. I stood there transfixed by the flames for what seemed like hours before I turned and ran.

Mrs Ingram's prophecy that I 'could be very good or very bad' came back to me. I could see which way I was going. I was fourteen, spiralling out of control, and there was nothing anyone could do to stop me.

FOURTEEN: *Do You Remember Me?*

I don't know if it had anything to do with the fright I gave Mr Isacke but a few weeks later I was given some very welcome news. After four years of being trapped at the Children's Cottage Homes I was offered the chance to escape. This time it wasn't another half-baked scheme to cycle to my mother or a few nights spent hiding in the woods. It came through official channels, which meant another visit from Mr Maynard.

As soon as he arrived at the Homes my instinct was to clam up. I had nothing to say to that man. Then I noticed he wasn't alone. A short and slightly overweight man, of about fifty years of age, stood nervously behind him.

'Leslie, this is Mr Goodchild. He and his sister are looking for a nice boy to come and live with them.'

A nice boy? For a second my heart sank. After my recent behaviour I was the first to admit that I didn't qualify as 'nice'. Why was Maynard telling me this? Then I realized he really was talking about me and I sensed an opportunity that I wanted to grasp with both hands. Despite my previous experience of fostering, I was desperate to place my trust in someone new. I just wanted to be cared for.

'Do you think you would like to visit Mr Goodchild's house and meet his sister?' Mr Maynard said.

'Yes, I would,' I said.

'Well then, hurry up and get changed. We can't have you turning up like that.'

I tore out of the room and charged through the Cottage yelling, 'Someone wants to take me away from here!' As I ran I started stripping off my work clothes so I was ready to jump into my slightly neater school outfit as soon as I reached my bed. Moments later I presented myself to the two waiting men.

'My God, I've never seen anyone change so fast,' Mr Maynard said.

He'd never met anyone who wanted to escape so desperately.

We drove to Mr Goodchild's house in the Copnor district, which worryingly I recognized as being just a couple of streets away from the Bakers' house. I didn't let it affect me and on the journey I tried to be as positive and friendly as I could manage. Looking on the bright side didn't come naturally to me, especially when it involved adults, but it hadn't escaped my attention that Mr Maynard had actually asked me if I'd wanted to go. At fourteen, that was the first time I recall ever being given a choice in my own life. It meant a lot to me at the time and encouraged me to think that things were going to improve for me now.

When we pulled up at the house on New Road East I was even more confident. Mr Goodchild's sister, Winifred

West, was a short, round lady with grey hair tied up above her head, glasses and a bottom that stuck out like a window ledge behind her. I could tell instantly from her warm smile and twinkling eyes that this woman had a good heart. I got an immediately warm feeling as soon as I met her.

We had a chat about all sorts of things and then Mr Maynard drove me back to the Home. For the whole journey I was bubbling with enthusiasm.

'When can I go back?' I asked him.

'All in good time. We can't rush these things.'

That annoyed me but I let it pass. I didn't want to ruin my chance of freedom by annoying Mr Maynard now. Over the next couple of weeks I visited New Road East twice more and on the second occasion Mrs West said, 'Leslie, would you like to come and live here?'

Would I? I jumped down from my kitchen chair and ran round to give her a hug.

'We'll take that as a yes then,' Mr Maynard said.

That day I left the Children's Cottage Homes for the last time. As Mr Maynard's car swept up the long driveway and out on to the road I didn't look back once. I didn't know at the time that I would never go back there again but I promised myself I would do everything within my power to make my new family want to keep me. Anything to keep out of reach of Mr Bott's fists.

During the journey Mr Maynard also revealed that my young brother and sister were now living with the Taylor family and seemed happy. I knew they had left the Homes and I had even managed to say goodbye, for once. But I hadn't heard from them since and I was grateful for the news – although I didn't trust Mr Maynard's opinion one bit. Since Robert had moved to live in London as well, I was the last one to leave the Homes.

Mrs West showed me my room, which was a nice size with just one single bed in it. I realized I had never had my own room before. I'd never really had anything to call my own. Now I had my own little slice of freedom. My own space in which to do whatever I wanted. Things couldn't be better.

A few moments later I was reminded that I could never relax. Not really.

We were downstairs and I had just thanked Mrs West for offering me lunch.

'Now, Leslie, we don't want you calling me Mrs West all the time. Why don't you call me Aunt Wynn?'

'Okay,' I nodded. 'I'd like that. What should I call Mr Goodchild?'

'You can call him Uncle Peter.'

I froze. It was that name again. My own cursed middle name and the first name of my sworn enemies in Queen's Road. Aunt Wynn sensed something was wrong but I told her I was fine. I couldn't tell her the associations the word 'Peter' had for me. But I felt sick even accidentally being forced to remember the Bakers. I thought I'd escaped them but here was their memory, invading my new home. I promised myself I wouldn't let them ruin my new life.

The first few months with my new foster parents were

very good. As well as having the luxury of my own room I remember eating real food for the first time in my life. Even if Aunt Wynn had been the worst cook in the world, the fact that she had made it herself would still have been an improvement on the tasteless meals of institution food. But she was a good cook and she took real pleasure in seeing my happiness when I ate. At first I didn't understand what was going on but then I realized. Aunt Wynn cared for me.

I had never known that feeling before.

As time went by I began to enjoy this new attention and realized that Aunt Wynn was a woman with a golden heart. There was nothing she wouldn't do to make my stay with them as pleasant as possible. She never got physically close or held me particularly, but I wasn't comfortable with that sort of behaviour anyway. Perhaps she sensed this. But coming home to her house was always a pleasure and I couldn't wait to leave school to get back. Whenever I walked in I would find her dressed in one of those flowery housecoats because she was constantly dusting, and she'd always be singing to herself as she went about her daily chores. I don't think she'd have won a place on any choir but it was a real pleasure to hear her skipping from one song she didn't know the words to to another and back again. 'La la la,' she'd sing, even to the Archers' theme tune when it came on the radio.

Then one day I arrived home and discovered she'd got a television. I'd never seen one before and neither, clearly, had Aunt Wynn.

In those days during the times when it was out of broadcasting hours, the BBC would put a test-card on the screen. Aunt Wynn would sit there for ages just watching the still image. After a few days I asked her why she did this.

'The man said I had to see if the picture stayed sharp and to let him know if it changed,' she said.

'What man?' I asked.

'The man who put the aerial on the roof.'

This man had disappeared ages ago and I think he only wanted her to check the picture while he was actually on the roof. Aunt Wynn wouldn't believe this was true, however. First thing in the morning she would switch the TV on and then if she saw that I was going into the living room she'd shout, 'Is the picture still sharp?'

Of course it always was. Sometimes if she was busy in the kitchen I'd call out, 'Picture's still sharp, Aunt Wynn,' even if I hadn't set foot near the room.

That television gave us a lot of pleasure as a little family. If I walked into the room and Aunt Wynn was watching a film she'd ask, 'What did he do that for?'

How did I know? I didn't even recognize the programme half the time. A few minutes later she'd ask another question and so it would go on. I could tell her anything in my answers and she'd nod as though they made sense.

I have many fond memories from those hours with her. I couldn't help being cheeky though, even when she'd allowed me to stay up late. At the end of the evening's broadcasting the BBC would always play the National Anthem and Aunt Wynn would always insist we stood while we sang along. 'Everyone stands for this,' she said.

My natural suspicion of being told any adult deserved special treatment – even the young Queen – meant I was instinctively uncomfortable about standing up. So even if I was up long after my bedtime, I'd still dart out of the room before the opening bars of 'God Save the Queen' could strike up. Aunt Wynn always tried to drag me back in but my excuses became more and more inventive. I remember one conversation to this day.

'Leslie, come back here. Whatever it is you're going to do can't be important enough not to stay and respect Her Majesty.'

'I'm going to the toilet, Aunt Wynn.'

'That can wait two minutes.'

'I won't stop the Queen from sitting on her throne, if she won't stop me from sitting on mine,' I said, and she collapsed in laughter, calling me 'cheeky monkey' as I disappeared.

Where Aunt Wynn was loud and warm though not particularly physically expressive, Uncle Peter was quiet and comparatively touchy-feely. He had the most obvious flat feet I'd ever seen and apparently was rejected for military service because of it. He also had a slight lisp which became more prominent when he was nervous. He had been a bus conductor in the past but worked long hours now for the Lord Mayor's office in the Guildhall, so he left most of my care to his sister.

He tried to involve himself when he was around and was very friendly to me, always patting me on the back after a day at school. When we all watched television he encouraged me to sit with him on the sofa. I hadn't been there very long when he asked if I'd like to learn to play the piano. Of course, I said. If nothing else I thought that girls might be impressed if I could play an instrument.

Uncle Peter had quite fat hands, which I don't think were the ideal shape for stretching across the keys, but he could play well enough from sheet music. For my lessons we would both sit on a stool in front of his upright piano in the living room and he would show me a chord and I would copy. If I didn't get it right first time he would stand behind me and put his hands over mine till I got it right.

I didn't enjoy being in such close proximity, especially with him behind my back. I was nervous about physical contact with anyone, and Aunt Wynn's standoffishness in that respect suited me. But that was my only grumble. We settled into a wonderful routine as a three-person family and I think we were all happy.

Mr Maynard visited about once a month and even he reported that he was pleased with what he found.

'You seem very happy, Leslie,' he said one day.

'That's because I am.' And I really was.

Because I was happier to be at home I no longer went out of my way to earn detentions at school. In fact, in order not to accidentally pick up a punishment, I found myself applying my brain to schoolwork for the first time in years. My grades improved and I was rewarded by regular compliments from the teachers. It was such an odd feeling to hear these people being nice to me.

'Maybe they're not all bad,' I thought. But the memories of being treated differently to the other children and all those canings still lingered.

Things got even better after that and I was made Head Boy. I don't know to this day how my name was even entered into consideration, but Mr Lawrence told me he'd been impressed by my recent behaviour and he always wanted to reward hard work.

I couldn't believe it. I'd never won anything before. I'd spent so many years being told I was second best – and believing it – that this felt wrong at first.

Later that year I also signed up for the Navy Cadets and I determined to make it work. I had a home life I enjoyed, I lived with people who cared for me, I was advancing at school and in Aunt Wynn I had the closest thing to a mother I could wish for. I had even experienced my first Christmas as part of a proper family. We had turkey, we had cranberry sauce, we had roast potatoes and we even pulled crackers. After lunch Aunt Wynn gave me my first Christmas present – a nice jumper – and then we sat down for her treat: the Queen's Speech. This was only the second year it had been televised. 'I bet this is why she wanted a TV,' I thought as we snuggled down together in the front room. I couldn't believe how happy I was. It was a strange feeling, one that was alien to me. I knew, though, that I liked the sensation and I wasn't going to risk ruining this idyllic life for anything.

Unfortunately someone else ruined it for me.

One of the reasons I was so comfortable at the house in New Road East was because I had my own space. Even after a blissful evening in front of the television with Aunt Wynn it still felt good to retreat to my own room. I could shut my bedroom door and keep the world outside. It meant so much to me after a lifetime of having no personal space at all.

Then one night all that changed. I remember vividly going to bed as normal with the strains of 'God Save the Queen' still ringing out downstairs. I changed into my pyjamas and had a quick wash. Then I switched off my light and climbed into bed.

Even though my insomnia was not as bad as it used to be and the sleeping tablets were a distant memory, I still occasionally took a while to drop off to sleep. Out of habit I still sometimes found myself tapping that same rhythm I'd started in the Bakers' cupboard. That night I heard Aunt Wynn trot through her usual bedtime ablutions before retiring. Next I heard Uncle Peter shuffling around as he too came upstairs. I wasn't intentionally listening to their movements. Their daily patterns were as familiar to me as my own.

This time something different happened. I didn't hear Uncle Peter's bedroom door open. In fact he walked straight past. The next thing I heard was my own door moving.

'Uncle Peter?' I said.

'Shh, lad,' he replied as he walked over. 'It's a cold night. You'll give your uncle a cuddle, won't you?'

As he spoke he pulled back my blanket and sat on the bed. Instinctively I moved away. I didn't enjoy physical contact. Lying down I felt extremely vulnerable.

I grabbed the blanket back and pulled it fast round me.

'I don't want a cuddle, Uncle Peter. I want to go to sleep.'

I watched him think about this and then he sighed and stood up.

'Okay, Leslie. Maybe tomorrow night.'

And then he left the room as quietly as he'd entered. I had my first restless night for ages after that. I don't recall sleeping a wink although I must have dropped off eventually. I was at a loss to explain what had happened. Worst of all, I couldn't get his words out of my head. 'Maybe tomorrow night.'

I should have told Aunt Wynn. But what would I say? 'Uncle Peter asked to cuddle me last night.' After all the stories I had told Mr Maynard and the police and various teachers in the past, I knew that this sounded very weak. I also knew that nobody ever believed me and that was another reason for my silence.

It would break my heart if Aunt Wynn didn't believe me. I didn't want to give her that chance.

I was so anxious the following night that I even joined Aunt Wynn and sang the National Anthem with gusto in the hope that she would decide to stay up for a few more hours. Uncle Peter mumbled his way through the words as usual. When Aunt Wynn couldn't be persuaded to remain up, even when I said we should check the picture every hour, I quickly ran upstairs and jumped into bed.

'It won't happen again,' I told myself. 'He knows I don't like it.' But just in case, I resolved to stay awake all night to make sure.

That was the plan, anyway. After such a poor night previously, I soon fell asleep. I was suddenly awoken by the realization that someone else was in my bed with me. It was Uncle Peter.

And he was masturbating himself under the covers.

I couldn't bear to breathe. I didn't want to disclose that I was awake but something tipped him off.

'Give your uncle a cuddle, Leslie. There's a good boy.'

'I don't want to,' I said. I was cold with fear. Memories of Mr Baker flooded my head. But I was older now. I was stronger. I wouldn't do that again. I wouldn't.

Uncle Peter didn't know that. He grabbed hold of my wrist and pulled it beneath the covers. I resisted on instinct at first – after a lifetime of rules and authority figures I wasn't at all comfortable fighting my foster father and he quickly overpowered my half-hearted efforts. When I felt my hand brush his penis, however, I fought him off in earnest. Authority figure or not, no man was going to touch me like that again.

He dropped my hand quickly but his other arm continued to masturbate. I didn't say another word. Eyes screwed shut, whole body tense, I lay as still as I could and wished I was dead.

We stayed like that until Uncle Peter climaxed. I felt sick listening as his breathing changed just like Mr Baker's always did. I wanted to scream the house down but I couldn't move. If I shifted an inch I would touch him. My only option was to wait.

A few minutes later he climbed out of bed and said, 'Goodnight.' I didn't reply.

Two nights later the same thing happened again. I was woken by the jogging of the bed. This time I told him to leave.

'If you don't like my cuddles you can go back to the Home,' he said. 'Do you want that?'

He knew I didn't.

Uncle Peter's night-time cuddles became a regular occurrence. In hindsight it was nowhere near as terrifying as the ordeals I was subjected to by Mr Baker. I was never hurt and apart from occasionally being asked to touch him – which I always refused – Uncle Peter limited his pleasures just to being near me.

But even though he drew no blood and left no bruises, he scarred me as much as any of the men or women who had physically assaulted my body. The sanctuary of my bedroom had been destroyed. The wonderful feeling of 'belonging' somewhere at last was taken away from me. Most damaging of all, the genuine love I felt for his sister was compromised. If I thought of her I naturally thought of him.

I felt cut adrift again. All my efforts at building a life with Aunt Wynn seemed a waste of time. I felt myself slipping back into my old way of thinking. 'What's the point?' I asked myself. 'What's the point of doing my best? What's the point of being nice?'

I didn't set out to revert to my old ways. It just happened and I didn't fight it.

I don't know if I was an explosion waiting to happen or whether Uncle Peter was the cause. I do know that from the moment he ripped up my domestic bliss I started slipping back into my old behavioural patterns, which wasn't good news for anyone. Not for me, not for my teachers, but most of all not for poor innocent Aunt Wynn.

The only one who escaped was Uncle Peter. With those words 'If you don't like my cuddles you can go back to the Home', he had me in his pocket.

Mr Maynard was one of the first to suffer my return to form. I hadn't exactly been happy to see him on his monthly visits but I always told him how content I was, which in turn satisfied him. Once Uncle Peter had started creeping into my bed, my original opinion of the man who had placed me in this house returned. Mr Maynard was the one who selected the Bakers and then ensured I stayed there despite my complaints. He was the same man who had selected Mr Goodchild. Was it a coincidence that I'd been farmed out to two men with similar goals? I wasn't prepared to give him the benefit of the doubt. As each visit drew nearer I became uptight and surly around the house. Worried that I might say something he'd regret, Uncle Peter began to send me out of the house before Mr Maynard's visits. He would report how comfortable I was and Mr Maynard was more than happy to write that down.

But I wasn't happy and I was looking for ways to prove it. I was fifteen when I realized I'd become an habitual thief. If it wasn't nailed down I considered anything mine. Bikes, bread, penknives, money – if it caught my eye and I thought I could get away with it, I was off. In the past I'd stolen food to survive and I took a bike to try to reach my mother. Theft had always had a purpose before. But now it was recreational. I stole apples I didn't want to eat and toothbrushes I had no need for just because the opportunities presented themselves. I once even stole a wheelbarrow. I'd always hated shipping coal around at the Cottages. But I'd spotted it unguarded in a neighbour's front garden and I could think of nothing else till I'd hidden it from its owner.

Aunt Wynn wasn't oblivious to my change of ways. She couldn't be. I'm ashamed to say that various odds and ends belonging to her ended up in my pocket. Of course I denied knowledge when she asked me whether I'd seen such and such. I'm sure she occasionally discovered entire drawers of swag in my room when I was at school but she never mentioned it.

Uncle Peter tried his best to stop me seeing my friends. If I asked permission for visitors to call he always said no.

If I said I planned to go out of an evening he tried to impose unreasonable curfews. Aunt Wynn always overrode him if she found out but it seemed important to him to keep me where he could see me. I began to wonder if he was jealous of time I spent with other people.

Friendships with some of my older pals became tested during this period. Whichever crowd I was out with always seemed to have a laugh. Even if we were all ex-Cottage Homes kids we didn't dwell on what we'd gone through with one another. It was probably because of the hard times that we were so upbeat. While I could be the life and soul of the group one minute, I was also the one most likely to flare up without notice.

Anything that reminded me of the Bakers was guaranteed to send me into a tailspin of rage. Sometimes it was a phrase I overheard that might make me think of Mrs Baker. The older I got, the more I grew to detest the entire Catholic Church because of what it stood for in my past.

I remember walking with mates past a church in Portsmouth. One look at its sign told me it was Catholic. I thought of all those recitals of 'Give us this day our daily bread' and the threats I'd had from various priests. Without a word I broke away from my gang and ran into the vestry. I didn't have a clue what to do when I got in, so I just ran up to the font and spat in the holy water. Not so long ago I'd been spitting in Mr Bott's tea. Sometimes it was the only thing I could think of doing out of frustration.

Like a lot of things, this became another habit. We'd be out, I'd see a church and go tearing in.

'There goes Crazy Cummings,' I'd hear behind me but I couldn't help myself. I had a point to prove. If I saw a priest in the street he always received a volley of abuse. I remember stealing another's bike. I didn't want it – I just didn't want him to have it. I rode it for a few miles, then dumped it on the local bowling green. Not only did I ruin the priest's day but I ensured a lot of old people couldn't play on their damaged grass for some time.

But I was happy. At least at the moment I committed these acts – an hour later and I'd even forgotten what I'd done. None of it gave me lasting pleasure. It was all just a show of rage, a fist shaken at the sky. I needed to show how angry I was and this was how it came out.

Once again it seemed to me that my control over my life was disappearing. I had been living at New East Road for about eighteen months when I received further proof. During Mr Maynard's monthly visit he made a point of waiting for me to return – much to Uncle Peter's discomfort – in order to tell me that Colin Foley, my old friend from the Cottages, would be coming for a visit.

I knew what that meant. I had visited and then moved in permanently. Without being asked, I was having my independence and, I worried, my own room taken away from me. Much as I liked Colin, I would have chosen to stay on my own if anyone had consulted me.

It was Aunt Wynn who was pushing for another foster

lad. Uncle Peter was vehemently against it, I learned later. At the time I was surprised that my deteriorating behaviour hadn't put her off. Then another possibility occurred to me: what if she wants a boy who's nicer than me? What if she keeps Colin and sends me back?

I could only reach negative conclusions when I thought of my friend's arrival. My treatment hadn't improved before, once my brother Richard was placed at the Bakers' house. Aunt Wynn was all I had in the world. I was going to be forced to share her now. I began to sulk in her presence although I saved most of my resentment for Uncle Peter.

Colin's visit duly took place and a few weeks later, as feared, he was sharing my small bedroom. It was good to see him but I couldn't hide how unhappy I was to lose my space.

I regret now being so hasty. I didn't notice at the time but Colin's arrival actually brought one very positive result that I hadn't considered.

From the moment he moved into my room Uncle Peter stopped climbing into my bed.

No wonder he hadn't wanted another boy in his house.

It took me a few weeks to conclude that my 'uncle' had stopped using me for his own sexual gratification. He didn't announce it and I assumed he was taking a break for some reason. When you live day to day for so many years, long-term patterns become invisible.

In truth, he didn't dare enter my bed with Colin in the room. One boy he could cope with. Two seemed a problem. A further thought occurred to me, though. Would he have climbed into Colin's bed if he'd arrived first? Or was there something about me that made him confident trying? Had the Bakers done something to me to make me vulnerable?

From then on Uncle Peter tried to keep close to me in other ways. He was very uncomfortable with the thought of me going out with friends – especially females. He put as many obstacles as possible in my way, from saying I would upset Aunt Wynn if I went out, to inventing chores that needed to be done immediately, to the ultimate threat: 'Do you want to go back to the Homes?' He was always safe knowing my answer.

At the age of sixteen I left school with no qualifications and got a job at the Co-operative Bakery. I thought nothing could be worse than boring lessons but on my first day I was taken into the flourmill and told to load the heavy bags of flour into the hop. Once I got the hang of it the foreman left and I was on my own. I didn't mind spending the hours in solitary silence as I threw down bag after bag, but it was really hard work. It reminded me of having to deliver coal in the wheelbarrow at the Homes and after a few weeks I asked for another task. I didn't expect the foreman to listen to me but he did. I must have been pretty persuasive.

I was moved on to the doughnut assembly line, which was a lot more fun. These days I imagine it's all done by machines, but back then it was my job to squeeze a couple of pumps of jam into the doughnuts. It didn't take me long to realize the potential for fun here, and if I packed too much jam into the bun I could imagine it exploding as soon as someone's teeth sank into it.

Although the work was monotonous there were occasional perks. Obviously nobody complained if a dozen or so doughnuts went missing in my direction, although after a couple of days I began to detest their sugary smell and never wanted to eat another one again. I also got on well with the other workers. They were mostly older than me but they didn't treat me like a kid. The best perk, however, presented itself when I was told I had to go to London to see a training film. I couldn't wait to tell my foster parents.

Aunt Wynn trusted me fully to get there and back unharmed. Uncle Peter was set against me leaving Portsmouth. When he realized I was going anyway he said, 'Well, I forbid you from going to see your mother while you're there.'

Of course, that just guaranteed I would do it. I knew before I set off that I had nothing to say to her – nothing that I dared to say, anyway. I was equally confident that it would be an uneasy visit, but if Uncle Peter was against it then I was definitely going to do it.

As it transpired, I had a good time with my brother Richard just talking about stunts we'd pulled at the Homes, and my mother looked less uneasy in my company. Much as I wanted a strong rapport with her, every time I looked into her eyes I saw the woman who had sent me away all those years ago and set in motion everything that had happened to me since.

When I got home I couldn't wait to tell Aunt Wynn about my London adventure. She was as kind as usual but Uncle Peter contacted Mr Maynard and lodged his displeasure that I'd disobeyed him. I was amused years later to learn of the response reported in my files.

'I think you only have yourself to blame for that, Mr Goodchild,' Mr Maynard said. 'You warning Leslie not to visit his mother probably gave him the idea.'

He was right about that.

Uncle Peter's determination to stop me seeing friends was eerie, especially his hatred of any communication I had with girls. He complained to Mr Maynard regularly that I wanted to bring girls to the house. Aunt Wynn was happy about this and she offered to make tea for any visitors, but he always intervened. I slowly realized he wanted to spend as much time as possible alone with me, even if he wasn't invading my bed any more. He became very possessive and couldn't abide me even talking to anyone else. Only his sister escaped his jealousy.

The closer he wanted me, of course, the further away I needed to be. When I was sixteen I hit upon a new way of causing mischief that satisfied my joint needs to meet girls and to escape Uncle Peter's clutches. I began to steal motorbikes.

The first time was the hardest. I was walking near the railway station when I looked at this old Norton 500cc and thought, 'I've never stolen one of those.'

In those days there was no security for bikes. You just hopped on, kicked the starter and leaned forwards. And that's exactly what I did. For a few minutes I looked like Bambi on ice. I was as dangerous as when I rode a tyreless bike down the cobbles of Cosham High Street, but then I got the hang of it and a feeling of raw satisfaction surged through me. I could feel the wind in my face, and a world of possibilities opened up before me. 'I can go anywhere on this,' I thought.

I realized soon enough that I didn't actually have anywhere to go, so I just rode it and rode it until eventually it ran out of petrol. Then I abandoned it by the side of the road and made my way home, my life transformed. I had only taken the bike out of boredom in the first place. I never imagined it could make me feel like this. The buzz of riding a stolen machine was unimaginable. I knew I would have to do it again soon.

Even though I never really did much more than cruise round the local area, every ride I took on a motorbike made me feel untouchable. In that saddle I was invulnerable from Uncle Peter, Mr Maynard, Mr Baker, Mr Bott. Even from my mother. I was in control of the machine and it made me feel in control of my life.

I noticed my whole personality change. After weeks of running bikes dry I spotted a girl waiting at a bus stop. I turned round and pulled up alongside her.

'Do you fancy a lift somewhere?' I asked.

She was shy at first but I could tell the bike excited her. Ten minutes later she was gripping my waist as she rode behind me and I was taking us both to a coffee shop. I knew she wouldn't have looked at me twice without the bike, but then without the bike I wouldn't have dared even to look at her. Without it I was the boy who was bullied into silence by Uncle Peter. With it I was a man.

Much as I enjoyed the sensation of riding, the sheer naughtiness of stealing the bike was still a big thrill. Occasionally I would admit to a girl how I had come by it. Nine times out of ten they were even more impressed with me.

Every opportunity I got, I used my thieving to show off to as many girls as possible. Looking back, my hunger for different faces – and bodies – seemed greater than my friends'. My earliest sexual experiences were with men. Was I trying to prove to myself – and them – that I only liked women? Even if I didn't like any of them for very long? Sometimes I asked myself what was wrong with me – why did I get bored of girls so quickly? Back then I didn't dwell on the problem and it's only now that I see the answer. I didn't want to get too attached. That was a weakness as far as I was concerned. I needed to be in control of the relationships.

I didn't want any woman to leave me again.

I loved those times. I was popular. I was admired, even. And, yes, I was in control.

Only once did I let the outside world encroach upon my thoughts while I was driving. I remember riding alone and building up speed as I came along the road that runs down Portsmouth Hill. I looked at the speedometer: 30

mph, 40 mph, then 50 mph. I was flying past other vehicles and heading straight for the T-junction at the bottom of the hill.

'What if I don't stop?' I thought. 'What if I keep going?'

I seriously considered it. No more Leslie, no more Mr Goodchild, no more Mr Baker. I could have ended it all there and then.

It was the sheer exhilaration of the speed that made me brake and carry out a dangerous high-speed turn. That was the day I realized the bike was the answer to my problems in another way. The angrier I was in my life, the more risks I took.

My luck had to end one day, of course.

My friend Frank Goodman was always game for a laugh with me and I often used to grab a bike, then pick him up. We'd ride around town until we found some girls to talk to or sometimes we'd just bomb along the main roads scaring other traffic. I forget how many pubs I got us barred from because I always seemed to get into fights. But we could always jump on a bike and disappear.

One day we were careering all over one of the coastal routes, showing off to a group of girls standing outside some shops, when the unmistakable sound and light of a police siren lit up the night. Inspired, I gunned the Triumph that I'd stolen and headed out of town. Ronnie and I were whooping with ecstasy as we felt the speed pick up and the volume of the siren dropping further and further back.

Then we got cocky. Once we were sure the cop car had

lost the trail, I turned the bike round and headed back. A few minutes later, there was the police car again, shocked to see us tearing back towards it. Once again they gave chase and once more I gradually put distance between us. I was worried about Ronnie, though. I pulled over as soon as I dared and said, 'You'd better get off. I don't want you getting into trouble if I get collared.'

In the end it was bad luck that caught me out. I was so intent on the chasing car that I didn't notice another vehicle swing out of a side turning. I saw it too late, braked and slid along the ground, still on the bike. I was all right although the bike was badly damaged.

By coincidence the car I'd nearly hit was driven by a police inspector who hadn't even been trying to find me. He was very excited to discover I had a fake gun with me. I'd won it in a bet from a man in a pub and I didn't have a clue what to do with it – although carrying it in my pocket reminded me of those games of Cowboys and Spacemen with Ralph back at the Homes. The inspector wasn't interested in this, though. He promised me a long spell in prison as a consequence.

'Or we can come to an arrangement,' he said.

Keen to keep out of prison, I agreed to his plan. The police would overlook the gun and I agreed to take the blame for numerous petty crimes that had been clogging up their books for too long. I told my foster parents this and Mr Maynard got the same story as well when he came for an emergency visit. But I could tell in their eyes they didn't believe this version of events. Not even Aunt Wynn.

That hurt me more than anything the police could do to me.

When I appeared before Portsmouth Magistrate Courts a few weeks later, I pleaded guilty to, among other things, stealing not only that motorbike but also eleven others, dangerous driving while uninsured and unlicensed, and, most interestingly, stealing the spectacles and shaving kit belonging to Mr Archibald Henderson. At seventeen I wasn't shaving enough to warrant such a theft for myself, but the magistrates ignored this and I was found guilty.

I was disqualified from driving for three years and sentenced to three months at HM Detention Centre in Cranbrook, Kent, starting in November 1961. The magistrate referred to it as 'the short, sharp, shock treatment' which sent a shiver through me.

From the moment I arrived, however, I realized I had nothing to worry about. The other 'minors' were terrified by the strict regime and the fierce warders. Compared to the likes of Mr Bott, Mr Isacke and Aunt Ross, these were amateurs. I knew they weren't allowed to touch their inmates, so the only deterrents left to them were their loud voices and solitary confinement.

I fitted in instantly and took up the various team sports on offer to drum some community spirit into the boys. Basketball and football were always fun and I enjoyed the respect the other inmates gave me once they saw that the place held no fear for me.

Unfortunately the warders there thought they were our worst nightmares and liked to try to prove it. I remember waking up on Christmas morning to the sound of one of the warders' voices. He was yelling at some of the others, 'I know it's Christmas but I don't want to see people moping about. I don't want you missing your family, being miserable – you all chose to come here.'

By the time I was eating breakfast he was still shouting the same hollow threats to 'cheer up or else'. It never occurred to him that for some of us just being safe from sexual abuse or not being forced to sleep in a cupboard on Christmas Day was a bonus. He was convinced we were all going through the worst time of our life and he wanted to make it worse still.

In the end I had enough. I stood up and said, 'I don't know what you're talking about. Why don't you just put me in chokey?' That was our name for solitary confinement.

'What do you want to go there for?' Obviously no one had ever requested this before.

'So I don't have to listen to your fucking voice going on and on all Christmas Day. You have no idea what it's like in the real world, so just shut up.'

That was the only time I ever knew of one of the staff manhandling an inmate. He flew at me, grabbed me in a headlock and dragged me to a cell. He was berserk with humiliation but I didn't care. I got my way and spent the rest of the holiday in peace and quiet.

I had my own room once more and that was fine by me.

I don't know how the detention centre affected other

boys, but it was so successful at reforming me that within two months of being released I'd graduated to stealing cars. I don't think I went out looking for a gang of friends who could teach me how to break into any vehicle and start it up without keys, but I certainly found one at a local pub. I'd only been out for a day and I didn't look back. I can't remember how many cars I hotwired and dumped before I was caught, but the police report was more than forty pages long.

When I appeared in front of the magistrates this time they decided to take a different approach to punishing me. They said if I pledged to make an effort to stay on the straight and narrow I could escape with probation. I made the promise and they let me go. Once more, I responded to being given a chance. They trusted me to change my ways and I respected them for it. I think it was all I needed. As a result, my behaviour improved almost overnight.

However, before I turned over a new leaf completely, there was still a piece of business which I felt only the 'old' Les could conclude.

I was walking back from work one day when I found myself at the top of Queen's Road. I thought about continuing past but stopped. No, I realized, I had unfinished business on that street. I walked along to number 258 and knocked on the door. Mr Baker himself opened it.

I stared at him for a few seconds, then said, 'Do you remember me?'

His eyes narrowed to a squint. I had filled out a lot in the seven years since he'd last seen me and I could see him trying to place my face. Then Peter Baker wandered over, asking, 'Who is it, Dad?' and that's when I snapped.

I launched myself at Mr Baker with a single punch to his face and down he went. As I climbed over his body to get to his cowering son, Mr Baker kicked at the door to keep me out. But he couldn't. I looked at him jerking around on the floor and I kicked him. Then I kicked him again and again, harder and harder. I did it for so long I felt like I was watching a film. I wasn't in control, I couldn't help myself. I could hear Peter Baker and his mother screaming and I could see the blood appearing on the wall and the floor and I noticed it was on my shoe as well. That's when I decided to stop.

How had I let this snivelling coward bully me for so long, I wondered. 'Look at you, you're pathetic,' I said. Then I spat on his face and walked away.

As I left Queen's Road I was aware of a barrage of new sensations in my body. The adrenalin was coursing through me and I felt almost dangerous. But I also felt sad, and scared, and disgusted, and angry. I was incensed that I had let the Bakers make me resort to violence in the same way that they lived their lives.

And then I felt relief.

Relief that it was over. Relief that I would never see the Bakers again. Relief that their nightmarish grip over me had been broken. Relief that I would never act this way again.

I could easily have walked down to the Children's Cottage Homes and done the same to Mr Bott, Mr Isacke,

Aunt Ross and so many others. But I wasn't like that any more. I swore to myself that I would never punch anyone again unless in self-defence and I have maintained that promise to this day. The era of Crazy Cummings was over.

I walked home and had a cup of tea with Aunt Wynn. I spent the entire evening expecting a knock on the door from the police but it never came.

The Bakers wouldn't bother me any more. Now I had to see if it was too late to save the rest of my life.

FIFTEEN: *Mum, I'm Scared*

One of my greatest regrets is the way I treated Aunt Wynn. I wish I could hug her just once more, to say sorry and that I loved her. She was such a wonderful person and she always looked for the best in me. I admit that once I started to go downhill, she had to look very hard, but she never stopped trying. Aunt Wynn was the one person in my entire childhood who showed any care for me. It wasn't her fault that I was too wrapped up in other problems to reward her in the way she deserved. We had some marvellous times but I know I offset them with the worry I caused her.

To this day I wish she had been my real mother.

I was three months short of my eighteenth birthday when I met another woman who would change my life. Her name was Bonnie, she was a few years older than me, and she was beautiful, fun and saw in me something more than the outward signs of 'danger' which kept other people at bay.

I remember the day we met. It was New Year's Eve and as I walked past what turned out to be her house, it was blowing a blizzard. Her sister, dear Dot, was waiting outside for a chap called Terry whom she would eventually marry. The snow was drifting and in the morning it would be eight feet high in some places. And that's the night I saw Bonnie struggling through the snow and decided I would talk to her.

I know now that the age difference probably helped my attraction to her but then I could only see that at twenty-four she was beautiful and caring – in fact my complete opposite. She had a clear grasp on morality, she wasn't afraid of hard work and she was the most honest person I ever met.

Somehow we clicked. Bonnie was fascinated by me but wary as well. She knew I was 'dangerous'. Where she was reliable, I was unpredictable and prone to excessive mood swings and overreactions. But she also knew I loved her. Whatever other baggage I was carrying, that was the most important thing. Our relationship quickly became intense and serious.

After a few months of seeing Bonnie every day I announced to Aunt Wynn and Uncle Peter that I would be leaving them.

'Where will you go?' Aunt Wynn asked.

'I'm going to live with Bonnie,' I said.

'Are you sure?' she said.

'More sure than I've ever been about anything. I love her.'

That was good enough for Aunt Wynn and we began to reminisce about the good times we'd shared, while she also tried to uncover as much about my future plans as possible. She seemed so happy for me that I knew then I could never tell her about her brother's behaviour towards me.

Uncle Peter remained silent through the entire conversation, but as soon as Aunt Wynn was out of earshot, he said, 'You're not going anywhere.'

I had been expecting something like this.

'You can't stop me,' I said.

'I'll tell Mr Maynard. He can stop you. You're still under his authority.'

I stared straight into Uncle Peter's eyes and said calmly, 'If you try to ruin this for me I'll tell him about all those times you climbed into my bed and tried to make me masturbate you.'

There was a definite crackle of energy in the room when I mentioned that taboo subject. Neither of us had ever referred to it before. It was one of those many unspoken things in my life. I hated talking about bad things because it made them seem more real.

Uncle Peter looked at me for a few more seconds, then left the room. That was the last time I ever saw him. I packed my bags and left the next day.

Moving out of New East Road was about more than me moving in with Bonnie. I was making a decision about my own life for once. I remember the day Mr Maynard had asked if I'd like to live with Aunt Wynn. That had felt good but it was a yes or no answer. Now I had made a decision all on my own and I'd followed it through.

I walked out of their house on 16 March 1962, the year the sea froze over it was so cold. It was also my eighteenth birthday, the day I became an adult and the day I made myself a promise: 'I will never be a victim again.'

I should have added, 'Look out, world.' Because if I wasn't going to be a victim then the chances were that someone else would be, even if it was accidental.

To my regret, that next victim was Bonnie.

She was the best thing that had happened to me although it was always going to be a bumpy ride for her. After so many years of being told what to do I immersed myself in the extremes of freedom. I know I was selfish and unreasonable and I know I hurt her. I was totally in love but I had no idea how to behave. Bonnie always looked for something good in me, however, almost as if she was attempting to justify her decision to stay. Sometimes she clung to the smallest of hopes.

I said one day that I didn't like those thugs who hurt old people.

'Hah, so you do have some principles then?' she laughed.

I had no idea what 'principle' meant but it gave her something to work with.

Over the next few years we married and I flitted from job to job, always manual labour with little responsibility, and we changed rented rooms in the Portsmouth area quite regularly. Somehow Bonnie found a way to cope with my self-destructive streak. When my anger threatened to boil over with other people, she was there to calm the situation and lead me away. I hadn't told her about my visit to the Bakers' house but she could tell that I had a fury in me that was more than skin deep. After my revenge on Mr Baker I had sworn never to let myself lose control like that again – because it made me like them. But it was hard. Without Bonnie, I would have broken that promise to myself.

She even tolerated a lot of my odder habits. After years of starvation at the Bakers', I could become very agitated during the preparation of a meal. If I saw food I wanted it then and there. It took me ages to shake off those fears that I'd miss out again.

Bonnie did so much for me, but without doubt her greatest gift to me was the birth of two wonderful children, Russell and Cilla. I was still in my mid-twenties and struggling to look after myself when they came along. I didn't have a clue at the time how to raise children but I knew how not to. I never laid a finger on either of my children and I would kill anyone who ever did.

I felt so honoured to be a father. How could anyone not want to be with their kids, I wondered. I realized it was still a very raw subject with me.

When I first met Bonnie I told her that I was an orphan – just as I'd told that psychiatrist years earlier. It seemed better than being 'abandoned'. When I was twenty-one we were driving to London for a day out when I announced, 'I'd like to visit my mother.'

Very little about me surprised Bonnie by then, but this knocked the wind from her sails. Typically, though, she took it in her stride and we finished the journey to Rita Road in Vauxhall, where Richard told me our mother now lived, talking about how it was going to be.

I needn't have worried. I don't know why, but Bonnie was the one who put my mother at her ease even though it should have been the other way round. She didn't know then what that woman had put me through but I bet she would have been just as friendly for my sake.

I began to visit my mother once or twice a year whenever I was in the area. I never had great expectations of the trip. It just seemed important to maintain some connection with my roots even though this was obviously never a priority for her. What made it harder for me was the fact that after she'd moved to London she'd begun a new relationship with a man called William Jamieson – and they'd had three children.

I don't suppose she stopped to think how this looked to Robert, Richard, Philip, Janet and me. From our point of view she had given one set of kids away and gone and replaced them with another. And these were allowed to live with her.

Out of the blue I now had a new family: Raymond, Mary and Bill Jamieson. But I'd never really known my real one.

I honestly don't know why I continued going to see Mum. I never left in a better mood than I'd arrived. I remember being there once and talking to Richard about the old days.

'Do you remember that time Otterbourne caught you in the coal shed?'

'He could pack a punch.'

'Not as bad as Botty. You were lucky you never met him.'

Suddenly we were interrupted. It was our half-brother Raymond.

'Hey, can you change the subject? You're upsetting Mother.'

I could have said a lot of things at that point but all that came out was, 'Oh, sorry.'

It was like that every time. We never spoke about the things that had happened to us because she didn't like it. Was it guilt or boredom? Was she annoyed every time she saw me or shamed because of the way she had treated me? I couldn't comment now because she never would then. I wasn't even allowed to ask about my father. Seeing my new family have a relationship with their dad tormented me every visit.

But as Richard said, 'You'd never get the truth from her anyway. She tells us what she feels like saying.'

Raymond went on to have his own children. He told me later that my mother would not tolerate any telling off or smacking of her grandchildren in front of her.

'She couldn't bear to see them cry, even if they were being naughty,' he said.

I was only openly angry with my mother once. She was talking to my daughter Cilla and asked when her birthday was. Ignoring the fact that she should have known, Cilla told her.

'Right, when it's your birthday I'm going to send you the loveliest card,' my mother said.

I couldn't help butting in when I heard that.

'Don't you ever tell my children you're going to do something that you know you won't do,' I said. 'I will not have them hurt by your broken promises.'

The whole room fell silent. Mum was obviously uncomfortable and Cilla didn't understand why I had shouted at her granny.

My years with Bonnie and our young family were amazingly happy but I know I never gave them the life they deserved. I wanted to, I really did, but every time I was faced with a choice between keeping on the straight and narrow and a new adventure, I chose the dangerous option. My hatred of being moved around like a chesspiece in a game I wasn't playing wouldn't leave me. If I sensed I was losing control in my job or my private life I did something to prove I was still the boss. Even if it had a terrible impact on my wife. At work I would suddenly resign or announce that I'd taken a new position miles away and just expect Bonnie to follow.

And I know now she was aware of my infidelity but she never said.

I rarely thought consciously about my childhood but it was always there in every action I took, every argument I picked, every decision I made. I never got over that need in my own mind to let women know I was in charge. That's why I had the affairs, to make them love me and want to be with me, but then they couldn't have me. I regretted it every time, for hurting them and of course for the damage it was doing to my wife. But I couldn't help it.

I wish now I'd had the confidence to share my past with Bonnie or anyone else, but if there was one thing I'd learned as a child it was that you were on your own. I'd told Mr Maynard, my teachers and several policemen that I was being abused by various guardians and they all ignored me. On a rational level I knew that my wife would believe everything I told her and she would try to help me. But I couldn't risk it. *What if she didn't?*

I couldn't face being alone again.

As much by accident as design, I discovered my calling in life. I realized that I could sell. One day I was working in an office, the next I'd had an argument with my boss and I was selling cars on a forecourt. All those years of concocting stories to try to avoid punishments were paying off. I could spin a yarn to make an Eskimo buy snow.

And I had another skill. I realized that I could read people. A dozen potential customers might stand in a room but I could sniff out the time-wasters in seconds. I think I developed this instinct in the Children's Cottage Homes. Everyone I met underwent the same assessment: is he or she a threat? Will they hurt me? I never realized I still weighed people up until my first sales job.

Bonnie and I eventually split up after fourteen years

although we remain friends to this day. She'll never fully appreciate how important she was in my life and not just because she is the mother of my children.

After our divorce I became even more selfish. My career in sales only fuelled it. I admit I was the master of short-term gratification and instant results. I would say or do anything to get what I wanted – whether that was a commission or a person. After a while I honestly couldn't tell the difference.

I married again in 1977 but the problems I had as twenty-year-old were still there and within ten years I was divorced again. I worked so hard to find happiness. I walked over so many people but nothing I did changed a thing. Every morning I woke up and the world made me angry. I couldn't put my finger on why, although it seems obvious to me now. I was always on the defensive and too easily reminded of the helplessness of my childhood.

I kept reminding myself, 'I am no longer a victim,' and I would go out and show how in control I was by closing another deal or seducing another woman. But the feeling was always there and I only had to see my mother or my sister or my brothers to be reminded.

At the age of forty-four I made a life-changing decision. I boarded a plane to California and waved goodbye to my past. When I stepped out of Los Angeles airport I was a different man – I just prayed my demons had not travelled with me.

For years I truly believed I'd changed. I married a

beautiful American artist and she helped me develop the creative side of my own personality. I began to write in my own unique fashion and even had several plays performed. I worked hard to repair the damage my education had suffered and with my new-found skills I quickly became a success in the field of sales and marketing. Radio jingles, newspaper promotions, advertising slogans – they all came easily to me. I sold cars to people who already had several, home improvement products to thousands who would never use them, and even cemetery plots to the live and kicking. Professionally and personally I was fulfilled. We lived in a wonderful beachside property and enjoyed round-the-year sunshine and a very nice standard of living.

The only downside to my new existence was the separation from my children. In making the journey to save myself I knew I was denying them access to their own father just as I had been denied to mine. But I made as many trips as I could, invited them over whenever they wanted, and we spoke on the phone several times a week.

After two years of living the American Dream I realized that I was actually happy. And that's when I received a reminder that my problems had been buried but had not gone away.

In August 1990 I got a call from my half-brother Raymond.

'It's Mother – she's dead.'

He was obviously upset so I assured him I would be

over for the funeral and booked a flight immediately. I was still trying to work out my own feelings when the phone rang again.

'I meant to tell you before,' Raymond said. 'I'm afraid she didn't leave any money, so I hope you weren't expecting anything.'

I knew what my feelings were then. I exploded down the phone line.

'You called me back to tell me that?' I shouted. 'I never got a penny from her when she was alive – why should I believe that I'd get any now she's dead? She was your mother, not mine. All she was to me was the name on my birth certificate.'

Raymond was shocked and said, 'So you won't be coming over after all, then?'

'I'll be there all right,' I said. 'But I'm coming for me, not for you or her.'

I brooded about that conversation for hours. Whenever anyone reported news of my mother back to me they always said, 'She tells everyone how successful you are over in America.' I hated the way she tried to take credit for my achievements but in a way she was responsible.

On the flight back to England I didn't shed a single tear. My main emotion was anger – with her and myself. 'How dare she leave me again?' I thought. But it wasn't because I was going to miss her. By her dying I knew I had lost the chance to tell her what she had done to me. Why didn't I ever tell her? Why had I always been so worried about hurting her feelings?

The church was very busy. Seven of her children were there – only Janet stayed away – and most of her grandchildren. As far as I could see, the only ones to shed any tears were Raymond and Mary.

I'd told Raymond that I would be attending for my own reasons, but sitting there I couldn't work out what they were. I knew I hadn't flown halfway round the world just to cry. All my tears for my mother had dried up when I was still a child.

The last time I'd been in a church I'd sworn at the priest and spat in his font. I really didn't know why I was putting myself through the turmoil again now. I wasn't the only one who was confused and the whole ceremony had a surreal edge. There was so much tension in the air that I sensed it would take only the slightest spark to set it off. I didn't have to wait long.

As soon as the priest said the words, 'We have come to lay our sister Jean Jamieson to rest,' Robert was on his feet immediately.

'Jean Cummings!' he said. 'Her name was Jean Cummings.'

'Our sister, Jean Cummings Jamieson,' the priest quickly corrected himself.

I realized my brothers were just as angry as me. Robert expressed it most. He followed the hearse to within a foot as it left the chapel and didn't let it out of his reach until the coffin was lowered into the ground. Our London siblings gave us space but I envied them their bereavement. They were only suffering the pain of loss – the loss of what they'd once had. We were suffering the loss of something we'd never had.

Suppressed emotions came to a head that day and there were a lot of things said between Robert, Richard, Philip and me that we all regret. We took our anger out on one another because we were the only ones left. The real targets were out of our reach. My mother had just been buried and Portsmouth City Council, who were responsible for our care in her absence, would always be untouchable.

Or at least that's what we thought at the time.

In our own way I knew we were all going through the same emotions. We'd all tried to forget the pain she'd caused us over the last thirty years but it was only ever buried just beneath the surface. It was always going to come out one day. We didn't discuss it but I know they must have been asking the same questions as me. Did she ever love us? Why did she leave us in Portsmouth? Did she ever think of us? If she could have turned the clock back would she still leave us?

There was one more: why didn't one of us ask her all these questions when she was alive?

I spent a few days with my children after the ceremony, then returned to America. I prayed the physical distance would help my mental anguish. In its way it did. I threw myself back into my work and before I knew it, that Pandora's Box of emotions at the funeral was a distant memory. I'd buried them again, in another shallow grave.

Financially I enjoyed even greater success as I learned new ways to exploit my talent for creative selling. The work was hard and the hours long, which put huge pressure on my marriage, but I instinctively avoided having lengthy periods of downtime. The busier I became, the less chance there was that I would be tempted to dig up my demons.

The only time I paused for breath in my life was when I knew I would be seeing Cilla and Russell. A healthier bank balance meant I was able to afford regular transatlantic visits to see them but I eventually realized that no amount of dollars could protect me when I most needed it. In 1995 my son Russell was diagnosed as being in an advanced stage of AIDS. I packed a bag and got on the first plane. I didn't know if he had a year or a week to live but I did know I was going to be there with him for all of it.

I'd only known for six years that my son was gay. I suppose the thousands of miles between us made it easier for him to hide, and for me not to notice. In 1989, on one of my trips back to the UK, I met Cilla and Russell for dinner as usual. Russell was by now twenty-one years old. As we chatted, the town of Bognor came up a few times in the conversation and I asked innocently if he had a girlfriend there.

'You mean boyfriend,' Cilla laughed.

They both collapsed at that like it was the funniest joke in the world.

'Are you serious?' I asked, but that just made them collapse even more.

'Look,' I said, completely confused. 'It's okay – but I need to know if you're being serious or not.'

By now they were just laughing at me. I must have looked so funny to them as I tried to work out what they were up to. There's nothing nicer for a father than seeing his kids get on well together – although I didn't feel like it at that moment as they both took the mickey out of their old man.

The more earnest I was, the harder they laughed. Eventually they felt sorry for me and Russell said, 'It's true, Dad. I'm gay.'

I had to hide my disappointment – not because he was gay, but because I knew the sort of life he could expect. I have many close friends in California who are gay and over the years they've told me that being gay is a hard life – there are some people who will never accept it and consider it their right to abuse complete strangers. After my own childhood I'd always dreamed that my children would 'fit in'.

But I told him it was fine. If anything, I told him off for not confiding in me earlier. Then I said, 'I love you. In fact I love you both very much and you being gay isn't a problem as long as you are safe. There's a big bad bug out there and you will break our hearts if you are careless.'

How those words came back to me six years later. He cried as he told me, 'Dad, you did tell me to be careful and I'm sorry I've hurt you.'

But it wasn't my pain that I was worried about.

It was an honour for me to be with Russell in those last few weeks of his life. He was getting weaker by the day but

Bonnie, Cilla and I tried to help him live as normal an existence as possible. This was what he wanted.

Russell was so much more comfortable with his illness than the rest of us. That was him all over. If anything, I was the one who struggled to cope.

I remember the pair of us going to his local Waitrose to buy a little food. As usual Russell was dressed quite flamboyantly and as we walked down an aisle a group of teens began saying loudly, 'We've got to get some faggots!'

My blood boiled instantly but I looked at Russell and even though he'd obviously heard, he didn't flinch. I guess he was used to it. But that didn't make it right. Holding back at that moment was very hard for me, and I finished our shopping in a bit of a daze.

When we got to the checkout the teens were at the next till. I prayed that they wouldn't notice us but a second later I heard that word 'faggot' again. That was it. I flipped.

I'm not going to repeat here exactly what I said. I used every profanity I could think of and squared right up to them and shouted, 'I could kill you right now and if you had any idea what we're going through I'd get away with it as well.'

I could tell they were terrified but I didn't stop. I couldn't. I hadn't felt a rage like this for forty years.

One of the kids was black. I took one look at him and shouted, 'You're a minority. You know how it feels.' I looked at all of them. I was shaking. They had no idea what I was going to do next.

I admit – neither did I. And that scared me.

We left the shop and went home. Russell needed to get some rest, so I sat down in the lounge – and cried my heart out. For weeks I hadn't allowed myself a single tear because I was determined to stay strong for my son. But that encounter in the supermarket had affected me. I hadn't wanted to think about it before but I knew that day that Russell had been abused like this all his short life. The way he was so non-confrontational told me he was resigned to it. He was bigger than I was.

I was so angry with myself for not being there to protect him over the last few years. My life in America was everything I needed – but it had come at a terrible cost. That day I truly realized what it was.

The next few weeks were hard to take but I held the tears back again. I suffered so much in my childhood but nothing compares to the trauma of watching my son waste away. Right up to the end he was so brave and his sardonic wit didn't falter for a day even when I knew he was in pain. I remember watching a documentary with him about children starving in Africa and he said, 'See, Dad, there are millions worse off than me.'

We were very well attended by medics and health workers during this time. I remember being asked by one of them what my greatest fear was.

'I'm petrified that Russell will die alone,' I said.

One sunny morning, three days after Russell's twenty-seventh birthday, I was alone with him when I sensed that something was wrong. To this day I don't know what it was; it must have been instinct. I picked up the phone and called Cilla and Bonnie.

'Get back to the house. Now.'

Watching my son's last hour of life is the single hardest thing I have ever had to do. Bonnie held one of his hands, I held the other, and we all told one another how much we loved one another. By now Russell was slipping in and out of consciousness. As he laboured to find each new breath we wondered which would be his last.

Suddenly his eyes opened.

'Mum, I'm scared,' he said.

And then he was gone.

My one consolation is that Russell died surrounded by the people he loved. His funeral was hard on every one of the crowded congregation, but where my mother's service had been the source of so much anger, this was a celebration of a wonderful life.

From the very first time I had held his tiny body in my arms twenty-seven years earlier and felt his breath on my cheeks, I fell madly in love with that boy. I'm so proud to have been his father and I would give my life for one more minute of his company.

SIXTEEN: *I Should Have Done This Years Ago*

I may have buried my son but I would never bury his memory in the way I tried for so many years to bury many others. I think of him every day and that is exactly how I want it.

Thoughts and emotions about my own childhood, on the other hand, I wilfully suppressed somewhere deep inside me. There is so much I never discussed with my siblings, and when in 1998 my brother Robert died, I realized that I would never have that chance with him again. But would I really want to? I was in the USA, Philip had moved to South Africa, and at the time Richard was living in Portugal. Looking back, we were trying to get away from the past by running away.

But as I found out in 1999 – I hadn't run far enough.

Seeing Peter Baker's face staring out at me from the *Portsmouth News* website instantly brought everything back to the surface. It triggered a rage in me that I didn't think I was capable of any more.

It also set in motion a chain of events that would change my life for ever.

After decades of attempting to ignore my past, I realized

that I needed to confront my demons. If Peter Baker could invade my San Diego sanctuary so easily and provoke such turmoil in my mind, I was in danger of letting him win again. And as I'd promised myself that day in 1961 when I last saw him cowering in his own doorway, I would not be a victim any more.

The National Health Service in the United Kingdom is respected around the world but the majority of people who use it are being treated for physical conditions. There is a reluctance in the country to ask for help with mental problems. In America this is not the case. Many of my adopted countrymen use analysts as a matter of course. I decided I would give it a try.

I didn't get very far. I made an appointment and set off nervously. I got as far as the building, I went inside and announced my arrival. I sat down to wait to be called. My turn came, I got up and went to the door I'd been assigned. The door had a plaque on it carrying the doctor's name and qualifications but I didn't take in any of this information. All I could see was his profession: 'therapist'. Except in my mind, it read like this:

The Rapist.

I ran out of the building and decided I would find another way to fight my battle. That is when I started writing this book.

When I was young I believed that talking about my problems gave them more reality. Now I was going to prove it. I thought, 'If I can write an account of my life then no one can ignore it again.'

Most of the words you have read tell stories I have never revealed to another living soul. Finding the strength to put pen to paper has not been easy. In order to write each line I have had to relive each memory – in many cases painstakingly. It has been long-winded, there have been many, many tears, and it has taken me almost as many years to compose as it did to live. By 2006 I had completed it but something was missing.

'This story doesn't have an ending,' I realized.

I decided that day that I would write the final chapter my life deserved and I knew exactly what it should say.

'I've suffered in silence long enough,' I told myself. 'My abusers have gone unpunished for too long. I'm going to have my justice.'

I realized that fifty years later many of the villains in my story would be dead. Police action has very strict time limits where accusations are concerned. For crimes that took place so long ago I would struggle to build a case. If I couldn't reach the abusers themselves, however, I could take my complaint to their bosses: Portsmouth City Council. But what did I want from them? I didn't need money and there would be no serving councillor who was directly responsible for my suffering. I considered my options for a long time and then I decided.

'I just want Portsmouth City Council to say sorry. I want them to admit what they did to me.'

Living in America, I realized that my options were limited. I visited a website called Friends Reunited and I put a call out for information on anyone who had been a child at the Children's Cottage Homes during my stay. Over the next few days and weeks the replies started to come in. Names I hadn't thought of for forty years were suddenly appearing in my inbox and everyone had their own stories. One had become a counsellor; another worked in the dockyard for years. Some had spent many years in prison, others had never got as much as a speeding ticket. Emails led to phone calls, which led to plans being made. For the next stage of my journey I would have to be on English soil.

While efforts to investigate my past were being prepared in California, developments in another direction were also being made back home.

After years of investigation, my brother Richard had managed to track down our mother's family in Ireland. What's more, he'd discovered that she had a sister – and she was still alive. I knew I had to see her – but I couldn't do it alone.

In June 2006 I set off for the UK for six weeks that would define the rest of my life. Normally when I fly out of Los Angeles, I have the meal, swig back a few gin and tonics, tune into the classical channel and nod off. This time I just could not sleep. I joined a group of other Brits in the 747's bar area and pretty much drank until dawn – which is usually somewhere between Iceland and Ireland. I was nervous about so many things but they were all forgotten as soon as I landed and I was greeted by the welcoming arms of my daughter Cilla.

A few days later Cilla, her children Macy, Hallie and

Brett and I flew out to Dublin to meet our new relative. Richard had warned me that I would be shocked when I saw her, and he was right. Aunt Nellie could have been my mother's twin. She had the same voice and the same mannerisms. It was as though the funeral sixteen years ago had never taken place.

But I knew it wasn't my mother. My mother would never have given me such a powerful hug as soon as I stepped through the door. My mother wouldn't have been so overcome with joy to set eyes on me.

I couldn't believe that this woman could physically be so similar but emotionally come from a different planet.

Whereas my mother could never relax while I was around, Aunt Nellie couldn't do enough for us. She could tell I felt awkward and she immediately tried to put me at ease.

'You'll have a drink with me now, won't you, Les?'

'No, I don't think I should. I feel emotional enough.'

'Ah, go on,' she said. 'Go on, go on, have a drink.'

Soon the wine was flowing and we chatted for hours as though we'd known each other a lifetime. Aunt Nellie showed me photos of my mother as a child, dressed in pretty dresses and looking well kept. She gave me one picture to keep but I later gave it to my daughter. It is of no use to me.

I could tell Aunt Nellie was at a loss over her sister's actions in Portsmouth. She swore the family had had no idea of what was going on. After my grandfather had come over and tried to save us, they'd lost contact. Nor could she tell me why my mother had left Ireland in the first place. Over the years I've come up with many theories that might explain everything – why she ran away, why she wouldn't let us live with our Irish family, why she treated us the way she did – but Aunt Nellie wouldn't be drawn on any of them. I admit I felt that she knew a lot more that she revealed but I couldn't push her to tell me. I was so grateful to her for even seeing us and being so welcoming.

I wasn't the only one she charmed. My grandchildren were immediately at ease with her and were quick to mimic her wonderful Irish accent. They all walked around the room saying, 'Ah, have a cuppa tea, go on, go on,' and Aunt Nellie laughed as hard as the rest of us.

As we came to leave I was struck once more by the likeness between my aunt and her sister. I couldn't waste a single chance to see her so I waved walking backwards for as long as I dared. As I saw her eyes fill with tears I was overcome by the strange urge to run back and say, 'I forgive you, Mummy. I love you so much, Mummy.' Ridiculous, I know, for a man of sixty-two. Then one final wave goodbye and I came crashing back to reality.

The visit to Dublin left me with more questions than answers, but I felt so much better for having met Aunt Nellie. It gave me the strength to tackle the next stage of my journey.

One of the conversations I'd had before I left America was with my own little sister, Janet. I told her that I was planning to seek an admission from the Council that the abuse really happened. If I was lucky I would even get an apology. She said that she'd like to tell me her story first.

I know this sounds strange, but none of us Cummings children had ever discussed in detail what had happened to us. I knew parts of all my siblings' lives because mine had occasionally overlapped with theirs, just as they knew parts of mine, and I'd witnessed certain things with my own eyes. Actual details, however, were scarce. Janet and I agreed to talk when I reached Portsmouth.

I was horrified by what I learned.

I had joined her scavenges around bins for food and I had seen the bruises left by physical attacks. But I never knew she was raped as an eleven-year-old. And I never knew that she gave birth to a son when she was eighteen but had had him taken away by the Council. She had never seen him since.

I could feel the hairs on my neck stand up as she took me down this long road from one disaster to another. It was hard to believe that so much horror could be packed into one childhood. For Janet, though, the effects lasted long after. Whereas I channelled my suffering into anger and determination to take on the world, she was not able to. She was broken. For as long as she has been my sister, other people have taken advantage of her. From my conversations via Friends Reunited with other Children's Cottage Homes survivors, I knew she wasn't alone in reacting that way. I was suddenly inspired.

'I'm not going to fight Portsmouth City Council just

for myself,' I decided. 'I'm doing this for my sister and everyone like her.'

The following day I put the next part of my strategy into action. I called into the offices of the *Portsmouth News*, and explained my intentions to their reporter Nick Brooks. It felt so good to tell a stranger my story and know that he believed every word. When I declared that I was seeking an apology from the Council, he promised further coverage. The first instalment of my fight ran that week.

From the newspaper offices I went to a restaurant in Portsmouth and waited for my fellow diners to arrive. A few minutes later in they came, forty years older but still the same in my eyes: Ralph Mitchell, Teddy Harckham and Colin Foley – three of the most important figures in my life.

We'd already done a lot of our catching up by email and phone, so within minutes of being together we reverted to being those four small boys from the 1950s. We were calling one another by old nicknames, reminiscing about people we'd all thought we'd forgotten, even recounting the pranks we'd played on one another.

'Do you remember when we put tadpoles in your sandwich?' Ralph, still a chatterbox, asked Colin.

'Of course I do, although I never understood why.'

'It was to improve your sperm count,' I said.

'Well, it worked – I had fifteen children!'

We laughed so hard during that meal that anyone watching would have thought we were talking about the happiest times of our lives. Reality kicked in, however, when Teddy said, 'Shall we visit the Cottages?'

I had planned to go to Cosham during this visit to the UK but not yet. As the moment approached I grew more apprehensive. I was just glad I had fellow survivors with me.

On the journey there our reminiscences grew darker. Once we arrived a cloud descended over us. Most of the buildings have long gone, replaced by a housing estate. One Cottage remains, used as an office for Social Services.

After so long with just my own memories it was moving to watch my three old friends working through their individual painful associations with each inch of the grounds.

'I kissed Tilly Smith under that tree,' I recalled.

'I got a punch from Mr Bott on those steps,' Ralph said.

We all nodded in recognition.

There were so many memories. Going apple scrumping, chasing one another around the air-raid shelter, playing Cowboys and Indians – or Cowboys and Spacemen in Ralph's case – and shinning up the fire escapes. Most importantly we remembered how it was always us against them. The kids against the adults.

Here we were, almost fifty years later, and the kids were taking on the adults again – only this time we weren't defenceless. I told the others of my plan to seek acknowledgement from the City of Portsmouth and they all wanted to join in.

'If you don't mind, I'm going to see how far I can get

on my own first,' I said. But I promised to keep everyone informed. Any progress I made would help them.

The next part of my fact-finding mission I had to do alone. I stood for half an hour at the top of Queen's Road before I plucked up the strength to knock on the door of number 258. I didn't for one moment expect Mr or Mrs Baker to answer, and I knew that Peter Baker had also died, but it was still a nerve-racking few moments waiting for a response.

A young lady answered and showed more kindness in those few minutes than I had ever experienced at that address before. She told me her family rented and no, she had never heard of the name 'Baker'. Her husband joined us at the door and, despite sensing my discomfort, invited me in. This young couple didn't know me from Adam and yet they wanted to help. I didn't have the heart to tell them of the horrors I had suffered in their home – they didn't deserve to have their happiness ruined as well.

As I sat down in their front room it took all my concentration to keep my surging emotions in check. To my right was where Mr Baker would sit in his chair. In front of me was where I would stand before being dragged over to him. On the floor, just a few feet from where I was sitting, was the spot where Mr Baker laid me on the floor and violated my body with unknown objects.

There was worse to come. I asked if I could see the cupboard under the stairs. Part of me hoped they would say, 'Enough is enough, old man, please leave our house.' I really didn't know if I could go through with it. But sensing it was obviously important to me, the man said, 'Of course,' and led the way.

Even as I approached I felt goose pimples run up my arms and back. The door had been painted over but I would still recognize it anywhere. And it was so tiny. The claustrophobia that I have suffered all my adult life began to kick in. Could I do it? Could I look into that space of a thousand nightmares?

I bent down and suddenly I was back in the 1950s looking down at that child. I could hear the crying, feel the pain, remember the fear every time that door was shut – fear that eventually turned to relief as I found sanctuary from the Baker family. Gulping a deep breath, I pulled the door open and waited for the memories to hit me.

There were the scratch marks on the door. There were the flakes of wood where I had gnawed the support beams with my own teeth. The blood had long vanished from the floor but the stench of my fear was still tangible to me.

I wanted to scream and run from the house but I had work to do.

'Do you mind if I take photographs?' I asked.

'Go ahead.'

Once more, part of me wished they'd said, 'No.'

There was only one way to get the pictures I needed. Holding a torch like a weapon in front of me, I crawled forward and stopped. 'Come on,' I thought, 'you have to do this.' Another few giant breaths and then I pushed myself through. The sweat was pouring down my face. I simply could not believe what I was doing. I was inside my torture chamber. I had chosen voluntarily to squeeze back inside it. No one had sent me there, no one had that power any more.

I snapped furiously with my camera. Each burst of the flash sent a new message.

I chose to come in here.

You can't hurt me any more.

I have come back to confront you.

And I have won.

I closed my eyes and ran my fingers over the walls on to the bricks and wooden beams just as I had done as a small boy. I could feel the indentations and torn slices of wood. I sat quietly for a few moments and then I did something I had never done before.

I climbed out when I wanted to.

I thanked the family profusely for putting up with my strange requests and then darted out of the house. As soon as I was back in my car I called Cilla. My hands quivered as I held the phone.

'You're so brave,' she said. From the way I was shaking I didn't feel it. But I knew she was right. I felt brilliant. The longer I sat in that car, the more elated I became. I could almost feel the bad memories lifting one by one from my body.

I cursed. 'I should have done this years ago.'

'You obviously weren't ready then,' Cilla said.

'I'm ready for anything now.'

I wasn't *quite* ready. Before I actually confronted the Council I needed to do one more thing. In many ways it was the toughest task yet – both practically and emotionally.

While still in America I had made enquiries of the Council about any personal files from my time at the Children's Cottage Homes. I didn't hold out much hope for their survival but it was worth a go. I was staggered to be told that Portsmouth Council did have extensive records from that period. It would take some digging, but in theory I could see them when I was next in the UK.

After numerous phone calls a social worker agreed to show me my personal files. I couldn't believe it when I was told the venue: a children's home. I knew I could not do this alone and so my brother Richard drove down from his home in Kent, where he'd moved after Portugal, to give me moral support. I know our brother Robert would have cheered to have found this resource during his lifetime.

As she handed over the file, the social worker said, 'I've had a look. You won't find anything to support your abuse claim in there.'

My hands trembled as I opened the old paper files. I had no idea what would be in the dusty folder or what it would say. I handed my brother some of the pages and we both read in silence.

Suddenly I saw Richard stiffen.

'Take a look at this,' he said, handing me a sheet of white paper.

'What is it?'

'Just read it.'

I couldn't believe what I saw. Very clearly, the document stated that my father was a man called Reg Scrimgeour. Not only was he *my* father, he was also the father of Robert, Richard, Janet and Philip. I looked at my brother. This single piece of information was worth more than gold to us.

'We've got a father,' I said slowly. 'We've got the *same* father.'

I couldn't wait to tell the others but first we had more to explore.

The names leapt off the page like fresh punches into my face: Mr Bott, Mr Maynard, Mr Baker, Peter Goodchild, Hilda Baker, Aunt Ross, Mr Otterbourne, Mr Isacke. Each person who had caused me physical harm and years of mental distress.

I couldn't wait to see what was said about them. Or what they said about me.

I finished reading the documents and stared at Richard. We were both having the same thoughts. According to the records in front of us, I was Satan's representative on Earth. I had bitten every hand that ever fed me – and I was fed very well, by the way, according to these statistics – I had stolen from everyone who tried to help me, and I had concocted wicked lies to get innocent parties into hot water. My educational ability was even described as 'backward'.

And the social worker was correct: there was no mention of sexual abuse.

I laughed. I couldn't help it. No, the files didn't say the

words 'sexual abuse' but they didn't need to. They very neatly gave a list of every recognized symptom instead. I was belligerent, I was erratic, I was attention-seeking, I stole food, I wet the bed, I screamed in the night, I ran away from home a dozen times and I voluntarily told lies to the police and my teachers. I felt the anger rising inside me as I watched the social worker carefully make copies of each page for me.

If she couldn't spot the signs now, what chance did today's victims have?

Armed with this evidence, I was able to complete my next task. On 5 July 2006 I went to the Council offices with a reporter and photographer and handed over my official claim for an apology from the City of Portsmouth.

They would not be able to ignore the forgotten victims any more.

SEVENTEEN: *I've Won*

Over the next few days the local newspaper published several stories and printed my phone number. I received dozens of calls from people who said the same thing: 'I used to be in the Children's Cottage Homes. Can you help me?'

Each person had his or her own story of neglect and abuse and I found myself listening to and consoling every one. I had come to England to find peace for myself and I had accidentally found a way of helping others. I just hoped I didn't burn myself out first. I only had a couple of weeks left in the country.

The complaint I delivered to Portsmouth Council was extremely detailed, including copies of my social services records, photographic evidence taken mostly by Teddy Harckham, and witness statements from other Homes kids as well as surviving staff members I had persuaded to talk. In essence it included three claims: that the City of Portsmouth was responsible for my sexual, physical and mental abuse and its ramifications; that I was seeking an apology. And that I did not want financial compensation.

This final point seemed important to me. In fifty years

money had done nothing to alleviate my suffering. This point was also likely to make the Council less reluctant to talk to me.

Two days later I received a letter from Stuart Gallimore, Director of Children's Services, who wrote that because these were serious allegations he wanted my permission to contact the police. I was expecting this. Of the thirty-eight former residents of the Homes who had contacted me in the last few weeks, several had said they had independently sought compensation in the past. They had all been met with this reply and given up, unable to cope with what would be a traumatic process. I couldn't help wondering if the council hoped this would stop me in my tracks as well. But unfortunately for them, I wasn't going away.

A few days later I was requested to attend Fratton police station in Portsmouth to make a statement. I was not looking forward to this. Not because I felt I was in the wrong – but because twice I had reported my assaults to the police, and twice they had been ignored. I really didn't know if I would be able to dredge up the details of my abuse for new sets of ears that did not want to hear.

In order to write my statement, DC Lorraine Bell and DI Linda Dawson asked me to go through the whole ordeal. I had a written account and gave them a copy but they asked lots of supplementary questions and wrote everything down. 'So far, so good,' I thought.

DC Bell expressed surprise that I had not contacted the police sooner.

'I did do – twice,' I said.

'Well, we have no records of it.'

I pulled out my social services files and referred them to the point where I approached the policeman on point duty when I was eight years old.

They both acceded that I was right.

'I have to ask,' I said, 'why has it taken fifty-four years for the police to believe me?'

They didn't have an official answer but they could confirm one very important thing: from what they'd heard and read, they believed me now. Only a victim can truly know how that feels. To have someone in authority say, 'Yes we believe you,' is tantamount to winning the lottery.

I left Fratton police station feeling ten stone lighter because I felt they had listened. I still had doubts that the investigation would be pursued with enough resources, given the date of the crimes, but it was a start. Now it was time to rally the troops.

If meeting up with Ralph, Teddy and Colin after all these years had been moving, seeing a couple of dozen other faces from the past enter a room for a mass reunion was mind-blowing. It was incredible how after so much time we all still recognized one another by sight. Still the same laughs, the same senses of humour, the same person-alities. For a couple of hours it was 1957 all over again and we were snatching cherries from the orchard, arguing over girls and trying to get one another into trouble with the houseparents. The only time we came back to the present day was to pass round photographs of our new families.

Towards the end of the meeting the mood in the room changed. One by one people had stopped reminiscing about the fun times and had begun to reveal tales from their darker pasts.

Within minutes the laughter was replaced by anger. Hostility filled the air and someone suggested marching to the city centre right then to demonstrate against our plight. The Council would be in session – we would be able to make our case directly.

I knew this was a bad idea. I wasn't the only one. My mobile rang and a policeman told me that he'd heard about a possible demonstration. One of our group had already spotted an off-duty officer in the bar and obviously he'd phoned his fears through to the station immediately. Given the potential of alcohol-related problems, the policeman recommended we desist. Although I agreed with him I didn't want to concede face now.

A few minutes later, DC Bell called me with news. If we could make our way peaceably to the Council offices, we would be met officially.

When they saw the size of our group a new room large enough was found in the Guildhall. It was also conveniently away from the Civic Centre where a number of university graduates were posing for photographs.

The meeting did not go well initially. Our group could not understand why Stuart Gallimore required DC Bell and DI Dawson to be there. The presence of a counsellor from a victims' support group proved equally contentious. He was subjected to a torrent of sarcasm from various angry survivors of the Children's Cottage Homes who wanted to know, 'Where were you fifty years ago?'

We didn't get anywhere with the Council's spokesman but DI Dawson had better news. There was going to be a complete investigation into our allegations and over the next few days full statements would be taken from everyone. This duly happened and the process began. When I heard from DI John Geden that he had been moved to tears by Janet's statement, I really believed we were getting somewhere.

I knew the police could only do so much. To get my admission from them I needed to speak to the Council members themselves. Call after call went unanswered or was put on hold. Only following a great deal of questioning from *Portsmouth News* reporters did Council leader Gerald Vernon-Jackson finally say in print, 'I would be happy to speak to Mr Cummings.'

The point of the meeting was not to win an apology there and then. I knew that wasn't how these things worked. If they admitted to something too hastily they would lay their organization wide open to potential litigation. I needed them to know that I was serious in my claim – and that I would not be swatted away like others before me.

On 27 July I was granted an audience with the Council leader and, once more, Stuart Gallimore. From my years in sales and marketing I had a few tricks up my sleeve. I'd gone in wearing an expensive suit and after introductions I invited them to sit down. They did. It was their own room, their own meeting, but I felt they were ready to listen to me.

Whether it was the intention of the two men or not, I found the meeting difficult and unhelpful and I did not think the council would be supportive of my complaint. I could have walked out any number of times but I was determined not to give in. I had come so far and, as I pointed out to them, I had thirty-eight other lives riding on this.

'I have to make you aware of how deadly serious I am in this claim,' I said. 'I will be resolute in demanding recognition that this abuse did occur.'

Half an hour later they were very aware. They had no idea how to react to me because I was a force that was completely alien to them. The irony is that my life in Portsmouth Council's care had taught me never to respect authority. I certainly would never respect these men.

Mr Vernon-Jackson asked me what I expected from them after all these years had passed.

'I've been reading that the City of Liverpool plans to apologize to the black community for the city's participation in the slave trade 200 years ago,' I said. I looked at both men, then continued, 'If that city can apologize to its citizens for something that occurred 200 years ago, why can't you apologize to the very people who suffered for something that happened a few decades ago?'

Neither man was prepared to comment on this and I left the offices disillusioned by my city's leaders. At least we all knew where we stood. I immediately contacted a solicitor and commenced legal proceedings. The wheels were turning.

At another Cottages reunion, this one even larger, I agreed to represent the entire group. In the end nineteen people filed independent claims. Once again, hostility towards the Council was in the air as talk turned to unhappier times. The last thing I wanted to do was lecture my fellow sufferers, but I did say a few words at the beginning: 'If we are attempting to get justice, we have to play this game by their rules.'

At the end I proposed a toast. 'Raise your glasses to remind all those who abused us, we are still here and you didn't win in the end.' The forgotten kids would yet be remembered.

One of the highlights of the reunion for me was seeing how happy it made my sister, Janet. It was lovely to see her laughing. Years on the breadline can take their toll on a person but she has never been anything but a good mother to her lovely children. I was still shaking from her revelation about her baby being taken by the Council. 'What a tragedy,' I thought, 'that another child out there will never get to know just how special he is.'

Soon after, I was with Teddy, Ralph and his wife, Liz, discussing our next move. Ralph said, 'Do you know what – we should try to track down Janet's son.'

I thought that was a tremendous idea but we already had so much going on. Where would we start?

Then a truly amazing thing occurred. At that precise moment my mobile phone rang. After all the publicity the

Portsmouth News had given my campaign I expected it to be another Homes victim.

'Are you Leslie Cummings?' the caller asked.

'Yes. Who's that?'

'Well, this is a little difficult, but it says in the paper your sister's name is Janet.'

'That's right. Why?'

'Well, I think my half-brother may be your sister's son.'

I couldn't believe it. The name 'Janet' appeared on the lad's birth certificate and he was still known by the name she'd chosen for him.

I took the woman's number and rang my sister, who didn't live far from where we were.

'Janet, can you get yourself down here? I've got a surprise for you.'

When she arrived I called the half-sister back and put Janet on the phone. They spoke for about twenty minutes like old friends. It reminded me of how easily I'd clicked with Aunt Nellie in Dublin.

The next stage was arranging a meeting between mother and son. On Sunday 6 August Janet and I waited anxiously outside a coffee shop in Port Solent. It took all my energy to keep her calm.

'What if he doesn't like me?' she fretted.

'Then he's normal – no one likes you,' I teased. She completely forgot her nerves after that.

Even I began to worry eventually, but suddenly her son, appeared. He rushed straight over to Janet and hugged her. As the tears flowed he introduced us to his two children, a girl and a boy. In a heartbeat, my sister had gained two new grandchildren.

A few minutes later a newspaper photographer and journalist arrived to cover the story. Janet, normally self-conscious and shy, was oblivious to the crowd now forming around us as the photographer snapped away. She was in the limelight for the first time in her life and she deserved it.

'If we never get anything else out of this campaign for justice,' I thought, 'we'll always have this.' But seeing my sister so happy inspired me to fight even harder.

After six harrowing and wonderful weeks, it was time to return to America. I'd really enjoyed spending so much time around my grandchildren and Cilla but I had to get back to my life in the States. I could also pick up the next phase of my campaign for justice from my Californian office.

Over the next eighteen months a lot of wheels were set in motion. I formed an organization called the Children's Cottage Homes Justice Project and created a website to support it (www.tcchjp.co.uk). Ralph is the Project Chairman and I am its spokesman. As well as following each phase of my campaign, visitors can find full details on how they can pursue a claim from their local council for either compensation or recognition or both. There is information on accessing your personal files, legal aid, utilizing the media and how to organize your group and get co-operation from the police.

I also stepped up my campaign against the councillors of Portsmouth City and even from San Diego I continued to plan. In spring 2007 I flew back to the UK and immediately contacted the BBC. I told them about my fight and they agreed to make a film about the Children's Cottage Homes. I returned to Cosham once again to be interviewed and the finished result was broadcast as part of their *Inside Out* series on 7 March 2008.

I believe that programme and its potential audience of millions was the single most powerful weapon our group had used. But we had employed plenty of other tactics to make the Council sit up and take notice of us.

We caused many Council meetings to be suspended through our loud demonstrations inside the building and I personally bombarded the members with petitions to speak at their meetings. At every chance I got, I stood up in front of those ladies and gentlemen and demanded justice. Every time I was told to stick to the meeting's agenda and every time I ignored it. I repeatedly told the Council, 'If it was good enough for you to break the rules when we were children, then it's good enough for us to break them in this council chamber today.' And I never obeyed their rules, not once.

I can't say it has been straightforward and there have been times when I've thought of quitting. In May 2007, when I learned that the police would not be bringing any charges based on our statements, due to lack of forensic evidence, I was low. They said all the houseparents who had been accused of abuse had died. I regret that we never had the chance to make them pay. But I only ever have to think of my sister's suffering and my big brother, Robert, who died aged fifty-eight without his day of justice and I'm fired up instantly. 'The Homes' survivors need me.'

Then on 28 May 2008 I received the word that I'd been waiting for.

I was told by our solicitor Alan Collins that the City Council was about to reach a settlement for the nineteen of us who had pressed ahead with claims. I couldn't believe it. The following week, on 2 June, a vote was passed and it became true. £92,000 was offered by the Council to be shared among the claimants.

Despite various pleas, not one Portsmouth City Councillor had been willing to help our cause. This settlement was won after a long and hard battle with the help of the media and many friends pulling together, which makes us all very proud indeed. But the very people citizens are supposed to go to failed at every level to assist us.

To many, this settlement will make a difference. One of our group told me, 'With that money I can afford to get a proper psychiatrist to help me with all the problems the Homes caused me.'

To me, though, money was never the goal. I just wanted the Council to believe me. I wanted them to admit that it had all happened. If they were decent enough, they would apologize.

By offering the money to us, the Council announced that I had achieved what I wanted. However they dressed it up, the fact that they had agreed to offer a settlement was tremendous vindication of our claims.

Of course, in his interview with the *News*, Council Leader Gerald Vernon-Jackson appeared to be the only person who could not see he had lost. 'We are not accepting liability. It was important to find a way for those people who feel they were badly treated to be recognized in some way and acknowledged. I have a great deal of sympathy for them, and if this provides the recognition they need, I fully support that.'

The man has not said 'sorry' but he has authorized a settlement and says he hopes this provides us with the recognition we crave. To me that means one thing. It means we are no longer forgotten.

I followed every step of the process as the Council moved towards the settlement. Only when I was sure the vote had been passed did I afford myself a smile.

The Council believed my story. After all these years I wasn't called a liar any more. I didn't have to run. And I had my justice.

'I've done it,' I thought. 'I've won.'